THIRD EDITION

Dance Technique &
Injury Prevention

Justin Howse

Routledge • New York

First published in North America in 2000 by
Routledge
29 West 35th Street
New York, NY 10001
www.routledge-ny.com
By arrangement with A&C Black

Third edition originally published in 2000 by
A & C Black (Publishers) Limited
35 Bedford Row, London WC1R 4JH

Second edition 1992
First published 1988

ISBN 0-87830-104-6

Cover photograph by Catherine Ashmore

Typeset in Baskerville

Printed and bound in Great Britain by The Bath Press

Contents

Section Two • *Injuries: Pathology, Causes, Treatment, Prevention, Nutrition* 61

Section Three • *Specific Injuries: their Cause and Treatment* 104

Section Four • *Strengthening Exercises* 145

Section Four contains a series of exercises, illustrated by 160 specially-modelled photographs.

Section Five • *Technical Faults and Anatomical Variations: their Causes, Consequences and Treatment* 178

Foreword

Dame Ninette de Valois

This book gives us the opportunity to indulge in some serious reflection. It is full of highly technical observations on movement as related to the world of ballet and is accompanied by helpful illustrations. A great deal of it should be rewarding to students, dancers, teachers, repetiteurs and ballet staff in general. I dare to add that, in my opinion, it is also food for thought for choreographers. Today it is not customary for choreographers to give either scientific or practical thought to their choreographic demands. Let us recall that a composer has to remember to keep within the range of a singer's voice. It therefore seems right for a choreographer to study more carefully not only the limitation of dancers' limbs but also the limitation of their general stamina.

Preface

We have written this book in response to various requests from many different quarters. The content and layout of the book reflect the whole variety of interests and requirements of these different people. We have tried as much as possible to cover the various aspects of knowledge which have been requested. We realise, therefore, that one or more sections of the book may be of no interest at all to some readers but of the utmost importance to others. We originally considered publishing it in more than one volume but found the financial saving would have been negligible and indeed, if someone wished to purchase the entire work it would have been considerably more expensive. The reader must therefore pick and choose those sections which are of interest.

When deciding on the content of the book we found that there was nothing available on the market to fill the needs of dancers, teachers or those treating dancers' injuries. Even in anatomy and physiology the available text books were either far too simple or too complicated. In particular there was nothing at all covering the consequences of technical faults in dance or the problems that can be associated with particular injuries in a dancer. Hence the final decision to try to incorporate all these various aspects of anatomy, technique and injury into one volume.

Section 1 has a twofold aim. Primarily it is directed at student teachers who are required to learn anatomy and physiology and have to take an examination in the subject as part of their teaching diploma. This section should cover everything that they will be required to know. Its secondary purpose is to provide a reference section for those who wish to check up on anatomical names used in the later sections.

Section 2 should be of some interest to the medical practitioner and physiotherapist but is particularly aimed at dancers and teachers in order to give them an insight into what actually happens as a result of an injury, the general cause of injuries and also some idea of the value or otherwise of the treatment which may be offered. There is such an abundance of advice available now for those who are suffering from any type of sports injury, which must include dance injuries, that it is difficult for the average person to evaluate the usefulness or otherwise of treatment that is proffered. Unfortunately, many aspects of treatment which are widely advertised and discussed are completely useless. We would particularly urge dancers to read and think carefully about the sub-section on nutrition and fluid intake.

Sections 3 and 5 are the most important of all. Section 3 is aimed at helping the injured dancer to recover as rapidly as possible from an injury and then take steps to prevent a recurrence. Section 5 is directed at the prevention of injury by discussing the important consequences of various technical faults in the hope that more effort and attention will be paid to the elimination of the faults once their consequences are understood.

Section 4 is included to aid those who wish to devise their own muscle strengthening programme, although text and photographs can never be an adequate substitute for a visit to an exercises orientated physiotherapist or a good body control teacher.

The illustrations, whether diagrams or photographs, have been intentionally somewhat exaggerated where it is necessary to emphasise or clarify a point. Particularly when looking at a dancer for a technical fault or anatomical problem the variations from the normal may be very slight, so a good eye and a great deal of practice may be required to sort out the true cause of a dancer's injury. So often the apparent reason for the injury is merely a culmination of far less obvious underlying causes which will each have to be dealt with or removed if recovery is going to be permanent.

In order to avoid the clumsiness of he/she we have referred throughout the text to 'he' but the statements made usually refer to both sexes, apart from the few occasions when a remark very obviously refers to one or other sex alone. Most of the photographs are of male dancers because it is usually easier to see their muscle outlines.

Acknowledgements

The authors wish to acknowledge their very great debt to all the people who have given so much assistance in enabling them to produce this book. It is impossible to mention everybody but they would particularly like to thank the following: first and foremost all the dancers and dance teachers and professional students without whose willing assistance they would have been unable to work out the various causes of the different problems and devise the most effective forms of treatment. Frequently, the injured dancer has allowed some new form of treatment or different approach to be tried thus enabling us to expand our knowledge.

Our grateful thanks for the actual production of the book must go to Joy Ball and Maureen Spencer for all the typing, word processing and alterations; to Irene Prentice for most of the line drawings and for some additional drawings to Sarah Howse; to Mike Ethrington for his tremendous help and advice with the photographs; to Machael de Souter for acting as a model for all the photographs of the exercises in Section 4; to Judith Roose for posing in the correct and incorrect postures; to Phil Harris for the proof reading, correction and help with the layout of the book; to Anne Watts of Messrs A. & C. Black for all her help, advice and particularly her patience; and, finally and most importantly, to Sherley, Tim and our children for all their forbearance and toleration when we were having to spend time on the book which should really have been spent with the family.

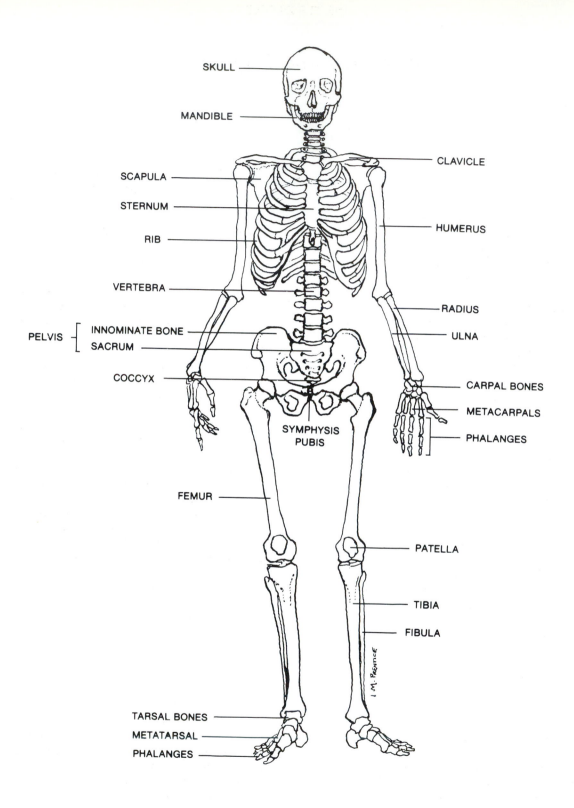

SKULL

MANDIBLE

CLAVICLE

SCAPULA

STERNUM

HUMERUS

RIB

VERTEBRA

RADIUS

PELVIS { INNOMINATE BONE

ULNA

SACRUM

COCCYX

CARPAL BONES

METACARPALS

PHALANGES

SYMPHYSIS
PUBIS

FEMUR

PATELLA

TIBIA

FIBULA

TARSAL BONES

METATARSAL

PHALANGES

1.1   The Skeleton.

Anatomy and Physiology

1.1 The Skeleton

The skeleton forms the scaffold upon which the other tissues are built and it forms the basis of the shape of the human body. Many lower animals have no skeleton at all; good examples of these are the jellyfish and worms. Ascending the animal scale the skeleton can be in two forms – there is the exo-skeleton or a skeleton that forms outside, as one sees in the lobster and other shellfish and insects where the hard covering of the body forms the scaffold and all the muscles and soft tissues are lying within this hollow scaffolding. Higher up the animal scale the endo-skeleton, or inside skeleton, has been developed and this is seen in fishes, birds and mammals. This endo-skeleton once again may be in two forms – cartilaginous as in most fishes or bony as in birds and mammals.

In human beings the skeleton is made up of two main tissues, namely cartilage and bone. Bone itself is very hard and can only sustain a relatively small amount of bending before it breaks. In children the amount of bend that can take place before fracturing is far greater than in a mature adult and this greater flexibility can result in partial or greenstick fractures in the child. Cartilage is less hard than bone and will permit a significant amount of bending and this allows some movement to take place. This is seen, for example, in the costal cartilages at the ends of ribs where these join onto the sternum, or breast bone. Where one bone meets another bone, a joint is formed. There are various types of joint and these are dealt with in **Section 1.2**.

The diagram (Fig. 1.1) shows the human skeleton and names the more important bones. The skull, which contains and protects the brain, is supported on the vertebral column; the vertebral column also contains and protects the spinal cord. Part way down the vertebral column lies the thoracic cage, within which are the heart and lungs. At the lower end of the vertebral column is the sacrum, a collection of bones which, as a result of evolution, have become fused or joined together to form one bone. At the tip of the sacrum there is the coccyx and this is usually movable, although only passively, and it represents a rudimentary tail.

The sacrum forms part of the pelvis, the sides of the pelvis being made up of two large bones called the innominate bones. These join at the back to the sacrum at the sacroiliac joints and at the front they form the symphysis pubis. Both of these joints allow a very small amount of movement. At the sides of the pelvis are the hip joints from which the legs extend downwards. As far as the upper limbs are concerned, the attachment of the shoulder girdle to the rest of the skeleton is far less secure and definite. At the inner end of the clavicles, or collar bones, there is a joint with the breast bone, but apart from this the sole connection with the rest of the body is by the various groups of muscles around the shoulder girdle.

The main functions of the skeleton are as follows.
a)   To act as a scaffold and provide a support for all soft parts of the body, thus giving the body its shape.
b)   The muscles are attached to the bones and it is the contraction of the muscles, combined with the rigidity of the bones of the skeleton, which allows accurate and precise movements of the various parts of the body to take place.
c)   It has a protective role where it encases the brain, spinal cord and the heart and lungs. However, the chest or thoracic cage has a secondary function which will be mentioned later in connection with respiration.
d)   Within certain bones there is red marrow which constitutes part of the blood-forming tissues of the body.

The Parts of the Skeleton

The skeleton can be considered in two parts:
a)   the Axial Skeleton which is composed of the skull, vertebral column, sacrum and rib cage;
b)   the Appendicular Skeleton which is composed of the shoulder girdle and upper limbs and the innominate bones and lower limbs.

THE AXIAL SKELETON

The skull, which encases the brain, together with the jaw bone or mandible forms the heaviest part

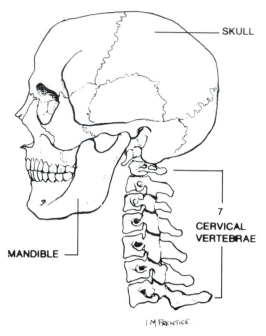

1.2   The Skull and Cervical Spine.

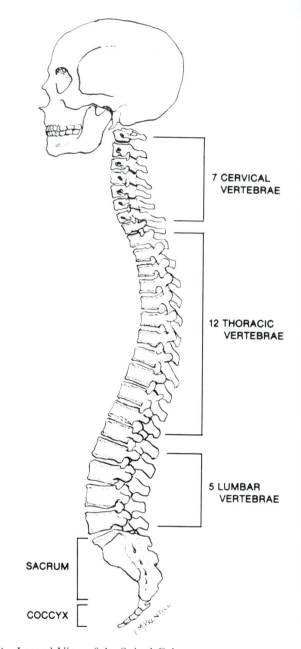

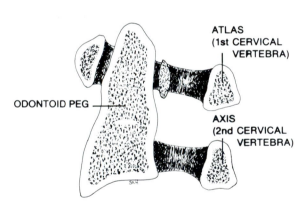

1.3   Sagittal Section through the Atlas and Axis (the First and Second Cervical Vertebrae).

1.4   Lateral View of the Spinal Column.

of the body (Fig. 1.2). It sits at the top of the cervical spine. The cervical spine comprises seven separate vertebrae. The first and second cervical vertebrae are highly specialised and totally different from all the others in the body (Fig. 1.3). The first cervical vertebra is also called the atlas, the name being derived from classical mythology concerning the hero who had to support the whole world upon his shoulders; the atlas takes the whole weight of the skull. It is very much the shape of a

ring and it is without the normal vertebral body. Only a nodding movement takes place between the skull and the atlas. The second cervical vertebra is known as the axis because it allows rotation to take place between the atlas and the axis. The movement is made possible because of a peg which extends upwards from the vertebral body of the axis. This goes up into the ring of the atlas and is kept in place by a very strong transverse ligament. It is known as the odontoid peg and developmentally represents the body of the atlas. The remaining five cervical vertebrae are similar to the others in the rest of the spinal column. As will be seen from the diagram of the spinal column (Fig. 1.4), the vertebrae tend to become gradually larger as they descend. There are slight variations in the shape and structure of the vertebrae in the cervical, thoracic and lumbar regions but these variations need not concern us. The diagrams (Figs. 1.5) show a typical lumbar vertebra from above and from the side and the various parts have been named. Some of these areas will be referred to in later sections of the book.

As will be seen from the drawing of two adjacent vertebrae from the back (Fig. 1.6), the articular processes or facet joints hook over each other. These are little synovial joints (vide-infra) which glide over each other, allowing some movement between each vertebra. Between the vertebral bodies are the intervertebral discs. These discs are made up of tough fibro-cartilage. They act between the vertebral bodies very much like a piece of india-rubber, permitting some compression and some stretching to take place as the vertebral bodies move, one in relation to the next. It is, however, important to remember that only a little movement takes place between each individual vertebra and its adjacent neighbour. It is these small amounts of movement which, when added together, produce the degree of flexibility which is obtainable in the spine as a whole. However, there are differences between the various areas of the spine. The cervical and lumbar regions are relatively mobile whereas the dorsal or thoracic region is relatively immobile.

As will be seen from the lateral diagram of the vertebral column (Fig. 1.7), this does not form a straight line. There are four distinct curves. In the thoracic and sacral regions this curve is convex towards the back or posteriorly, whereas in the lumbar and cervical regions the curve goes in the opposite direction with the convex of the curve directed anteriorly towards the front of the body. Initially, in foetal life, the whole spine is curved in the same direction, which is that retained by the thoracic and sacral areas. These two areas are known as primary curves; later, secondary curves in the opposite direction take place at the cervical and lumbar regions. The points of greatest stress are where the curves change direction and these areas are more liable to sustain injury. This is particularly so in the lower regions where the weight of the upper part of the body is being transmitted downwards, e.g. in fractures of the spine the most common area is in the lower dorsal/upper lumbar region, and for soft tissue and

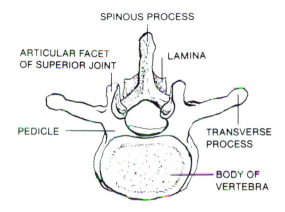

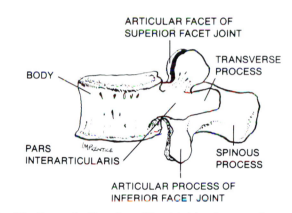

1.5   The Parts of a Vertebra. The third lumbar vertebra is typical but the shape differs slightly at various levels. The lumbar region is of greatest interest to the dancer.

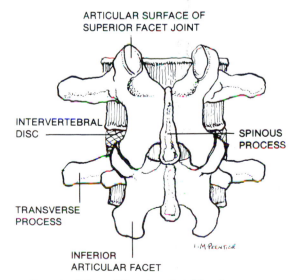

1.6   Posterior View of Two Lumbar Vertebrae.

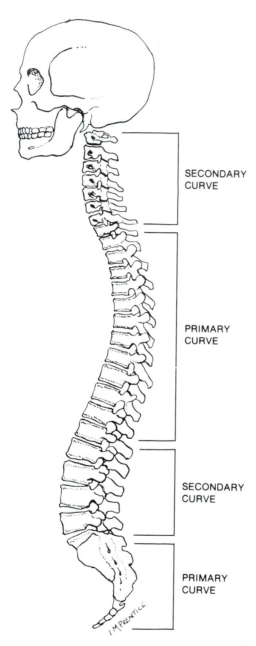

SECONDARY
CURVE

PRIMARY
CURVE

SECONDARY
CURVE

PRIMARY
CURVE

1.7   The Spinal Column showing the Primary and
Secondary Curves.

disc damage this occurs most commonly at the
lower lumbar area between the 4th/5th lumbar
vertebrae and the top of the sacrum.

The vertebral column ends with the sacrum. This
forms part of the pelvic girdle together with the
two innominate bones.

The thoracic cage, or rib cage (See Fig. 1.1 on
page xiv), is made up of twelve ribs on each side.
At the back there are joints between the ribs and
the thoracic vertebrae. At the front the lowest two
ribs, the 11th and the 12th, have no attachment to
the sternum or breast bone. The remaining ten ribs
are joined to the sternum with short lengths of hard
cartilage, known as the costal cartilages, the 8th,
9th and 10th ribs having long pieces of costal
cartilage which combine with that of the 7th rib
and then meet the sternum. This combination
produces the curve that one sees at the lower end of
the rib cage from the bottom of the breast bone
curving away and downwards towards the side,
where the rib cage at that point forms the upper
part of the abdomen.

THE APPENDICULAR SKELETON

The Upper Limbs (Fig. 1.8)
The upper limbs start at the shoulder girdle. The
collar bone, or clavicle, is the only bone which has
an actual joint with the central part of the skeleton.
This occurs at the inner end where it meets the
sternum. At the outer end of the clavicle there is a
joint between it and the acromion process of the
scapula or shoulder blade. These joints give little
strength to the attachment of the shoulder girdle to
the rest of the body and the shoulder girdle is in
reality suspended by powerful muscles which are
attached at one end to the spinal column and rib
cage and at the other to the clavicle and the
scapula. The bones of the upper limbs comprise the
clavicle and scapula which together form the
shoulder girdle, the humerus, radius and ulna,
carpal bones, metacarpals and phalanges. Of the
carpal bones the scaphoid is the only one deserving
special mention. It is a common site for a fracture
in adolescents and younger adults following a fall
on the outstretched hand. These fractures are
notoriously difficult to show on an X-ray taken
during the first two weeks following the injury.

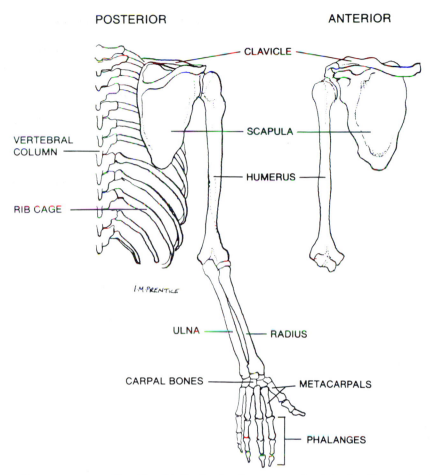

POSTERIOR ANTERIOR

CLAVICLE

VERTEBRAL
COLUMN

SCAPULA

HUMERUS

RIB CAGE

I.M. PRENTICE

ULNA RADIUS

CARPAL BONES METACARPALS

PHALANGES

1.8   The Right Upper Limb and Shoulder Girdle. In the diagram on the right the rib cage has been omitted as it would have obscured the front (anterior) surface of the scapula which lies against the back of the rib cage.

The Lower Limbs (Figs 1.9 and 1.10)
The pelvis is formed by the sacrum and coccyx, which is the lowest portion of the vertebral column, and the two innominate bones. These latter join anteriorly to form the symphysis pubis (a cartilaginous joint) and posteriorly to the sacrum at the two sacroiliac joints (very strong, of fibrous tissue and cartilage). The bones of the lower limbs comprise the innominate bone, the femur, the tibia and fibula, the tarsal bones, metatarsals and phalanges. The innominate bone is made up of three bones which have become joined together to form one bone – the ilium, the ischium and pubic bones. Two tarsal bones in particular need recognition – the talus, which forms part of the ankle joint and the calcaneum (or os calcis) which is the heel bone.

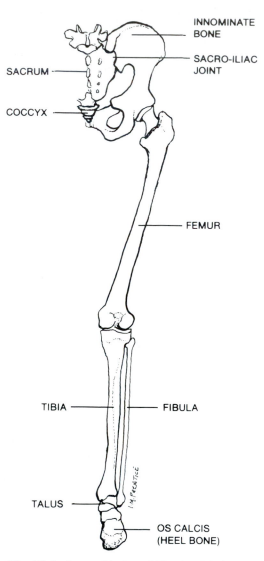

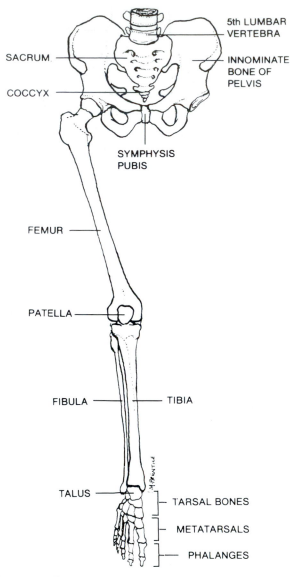

1.9   The Right Lower Limb and Hemi-pelvis from the back (posterior).

1.10   The Right Lower Limb and the Pelvis from the front (anterior).

1.2 The Joints

The function of a joint is to allow movement to take place between two bones and it is the presence of joints which allows the skeleton as a whole to be flexible. There are several types of joint and these various types possess different degrees of mobility, from the fully mobile joint to the joint which is fixed without an appreciable degree of movement.

Types of Joints

The first type of joint that we have to consider is the synovial joint (Fig. 1.11). This type allows a free movement range. The ends of the bone are covered with hyaline cartilage. This is extremely smooth and shiny and allows movements to occur with very little friction. The joint is lubricated by synovial fluid and is surrounded by a layer of tissue called synovial membrane. Synovial membrane

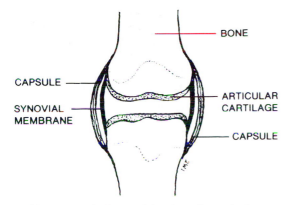

1.11   Diagrammatic Coronal Section of a typical Synovial Joint.

produces the joint fluid and also helps to absorb any debris that might form within the joint. Outside the synovial membrane is a strong capsule made up of fibrous tissue. In addition to the capsule which extends completely around the joint, there are various ligaments present. These may be a local thickening of the capsule to give a band of much thicker stronger tissue, or they may be separate from the capsule forming a very strong fibrous band. The ligaments are present to help limit the movement of a joint and to give stability to the joint. In limiting movement of the joint it prevents dislocation by stopping a movement going further than stability will allow.

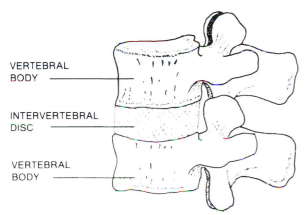

1.12   Intervertebral Disc.

   The other important type of joint is that which has cartilage or fibro-cartilage between the bones. The chief example of this is the intervertebral disc lying between the bodies of adjacent vertebrae (Fig. 1.12). This type of joint allows a little movement as the fibro-cartilage is elastic and can be slightly

stretched and slightly compressed. Additionally, as it has a certain amount of elasticity, it acts as a shock-absorber between the bones. Thus, in jumping, all the intervertebral discs help to absorb the shock of the landing which would otherwise be transmitted up to the skull and the brain with a very much more serious jarring effect.

   The final type of joint is the truly fibrous joint which allows little or no movement. An example of a fibrous joint which allows no movement is that between the flat bones forming the vault of the skull. An example of one which allows a little movement is that between the lower end of the tibia and fibula.

Joint Movements

Only the synovial joints have any significant degree of movement and this includes all those joints which the layman would look upon as being actual joints. In order to avoid misunderstandings, the proper term must be used for each plane of movement (Figs 1.13, 1.14, 1.15 and 1.16).

Extension is straightening out a joint so that the bones forming the joint will tend to come into a straight line with each other.
Flexion is bending a joint so that you produce an angle between the two bones forming the joint.
Abduction is a movement taking the limb, or part of the limb, away from the mid-line.
Adduction is bringing the part towards the mid-line.
Rotation is a movement at the joint where the part can rotate upon the axis going through the joint.
Circumduction is the ability to move the part around in a circle and is usually a combination of flexion, extension, abduction and adduction.

There are various types of synovial joint giving different possible ranges and planes of movement. The ball and socket allows a free range in all directions, e.g. the hip joint. The hinge joint allows only flexion and extension, e.g. the interphalangeal joints of the fingers and toes.

   It is very important that the correct terminology is used otherwise confusion will result and, when injuries are being considered, incorrect treatment or incorrect rehabilitation may be given. The difficulty applies very particularly in the case of dancers who refer to a good extension of the lower limb or hip as the ability to lift the leg up against the trunk. This movement is, in fact, flexion of the hip joint or if taken out sideways, a combination of abduction, external rotation and flexion. Although later in the book it will be seen that the authors have, whenever possible, tried to accept the

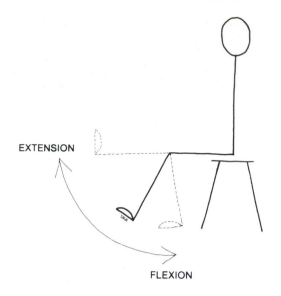

1.13   Flexion and Extension of the Knee Joint.

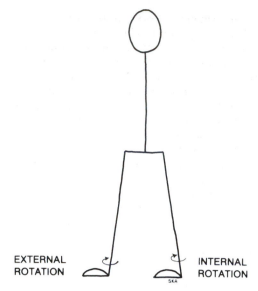

1.15   External and Internal Rotation of the Hip Joint.

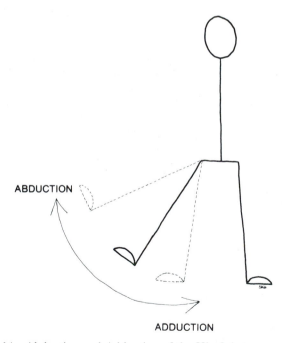

1.14   Abduction and Adduction of the Hip Joint.

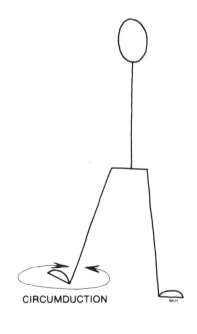

1.16   Circumduction of the Hip Joint.

terminology used by dancers, in an area such as this where infinite confusion could occur with possibly dangerous results, use of the correct anatomical terminology is mutually advantageous.

There are various limiting factors when considering the range of movement in any particular joint. Starting from within and working outwards, the first factor is when bone comes up against bone from the two sides of the joint when it is being moved in any one particular direction. However, in the majority of joints, before that takes place the capsule and ligaments will limit the range of movement. These give the second limiting factor. With early training ligaments can be stretched to a certain extent, thus increasing the range of movement above that normally expected from that particular joint. The next factor is tension in the muscles controlling the joint movement; these can be relatively easily stretched and the muscles can be actively lengthened. Finally, apposition of soft parts may prevent further movement taking place, e.g. someone with fat thighs and fat calves will be unable to flex the knee as fully as if they did not have this excess tissue. Activity at the limits of the range of movement of a joint will gradually stretch soft tissues, particularly before the age of puberty, thus increasing the range of available movement. There is, however, a considerable variation from one person to the next in their natural range of movement in any particular joint. This is in part due to a variation in actual anatomical shape of the joint but also some people have, as part of their congenital makeup, very lax ligaments and very stretchable soft tissues and it is these people who in lay terms are often referred to as being double-jointed and who, in extreme cases, can become contortionists.

Important Joints

THE UPPER LIMBS

The joint between the scapula and the humerus is a ball and socket joint (Fig. 1.17). The socket is very flattened and more like a saucer. It is known as the glenoid cavity. As a result of the shallowness of the joint a very wide range of movement is possible between the upper arm and the trunk. However, this range of movement does not take place entirely between the scapula and the humerus; much of it, particularly elevation of the arm, is made up by the scapula itself sliding over the chest wall. At the lower end of the humerus there is the elbow joint (Figs 1.18 and 1.19) which gives an articulation the upper ends of the radius and ulna. The joint between the ulna and the lower end of the humerus is a straightforward hinge joint but at the upper end of the radius the joint is rather more complex as it allows the radius to hinge up and down in relation to the humerus and also allows the radius to rotate in relation to the ulna and the humerus. A similar rotatory movement takes place at the lower end of the radius and ulna. This allows the movement of pronation and supination where the hand can be held either palm down or palm up with this rotation taking place entirely within the forearm. As will be seen from the skeletal diagram (Fig. 1.19) the bones of the wrist and hand are

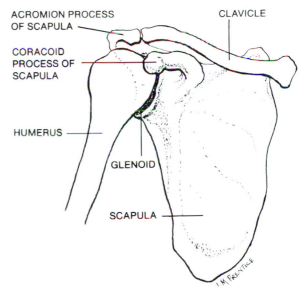

1.17   The Right Shoulder Joint.

complex. Most of the wrist movement is an up and down hinge action but there is a certain amount of sideways movement of abduction and adduction available (condyloid joint). The joints in the fingers between the metacarpals and the phalanges are also all of a condyloid type. Those between the phalanges themselves are purely hinge. However, at the base of the thumb the joint between the metacarpal and the carpal bones does allow some sliding and rotation so that the thumb can not only be flexed and extended but also abducted, adducted and circumducted to enable it to be brought across the hand in opposition to the various fingers. Without this movement the grip which we use in the hand would be non-existent and the extremely fine precision movements and uses of the hand would be impossible.

THE LOWER LIMBS

The pelvis is formed by the sacrum, which is part of the axial skeleton, and the two innominate bones at the front (Fig. 1.20). There is a joint between the sacrum and the innominate bones at each side. This joint is extremely strong with many ligaments crossing within the joint and also some fibro-cartilage. Very little movement takes place at the sacro-iliac joint. Anteriorly the innominate bones come together at the symphysis pubis, and once again very little movement takes place at this joint where there is fibro-cartilage between the bones. During pregnancy the fibro-cartilage and ligaments soften, giving far greater mobility and allowing delivery to take place. Delivery is also

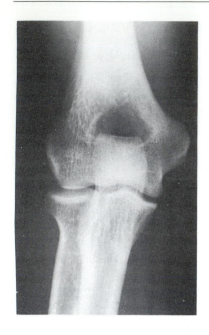

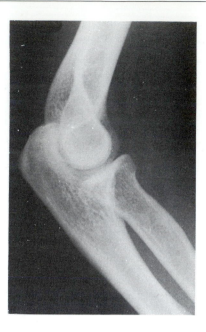

1.18A (left)   The Elbow Joint.
A.P. X-ray view.

1.18B (right)   The Elbow Joint.
Lateral X-ray view.

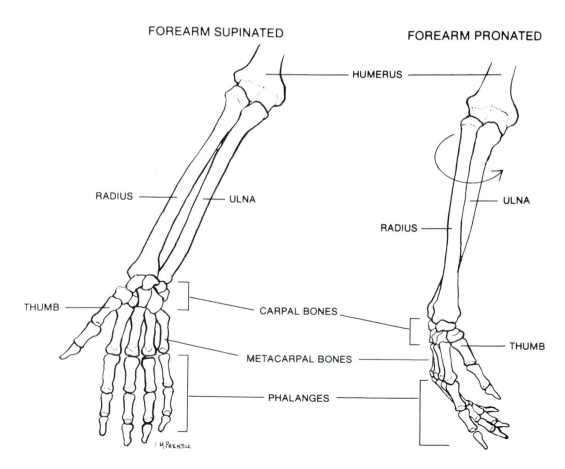

1.19   The Right Forearm and Hand.

made very much easier for the female by a difference in shape of her pelvis from that of the male.

At the sides of the innominate bones are the hip joints (Fig. 1.21). These are very large ball and socket joints but, unlike the shoulder joints, the acetabulum, which is the socket or cup part of the joint, is very deep. The head of the femur forms a ball which sits inside the acetabulum. As a result the joint is very strong and extremely stable. You will see from the diagram that the head of the femur is joined onto the shaft of the bone by a neck of bone called the femoral neck. As result of this the shaft of the femur stands out a little way from the pelvis, giving a far greater range of movement in all directions than would be possible if the ball was directly at the top of the shaft.

At the lower end of the femur is the knee joint. As far as its action is concerned this is mainly a hinge joint but as will be seen from the diagram (Fig. 1.22) it is potentially a very unstable joint because the upper end of the tibia, which forms the other side of the joint from the femur, is almost completely flat. Structurally it is a condyloid joint but functionally a hinge joint. If it were not for the ligaments the lower end of the femur would be able to slide around in all directions on the tibia. In

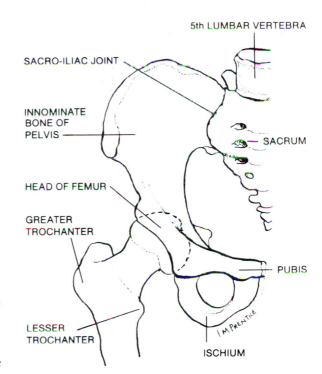

1.20   The Right Hemi-pelvis and Hip Joint.

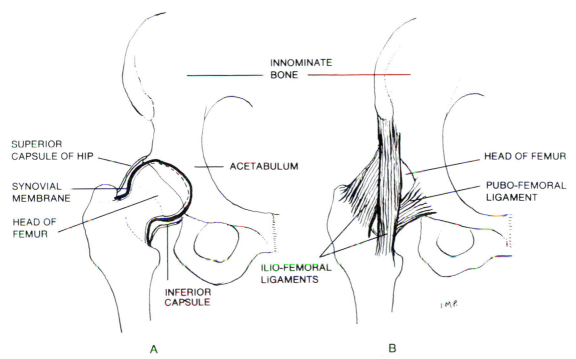

A   B

1.21   A. Section through the Right Hip Joint (Diagrammatic).   B. Ligaments at the front of the Right Hip Joint.

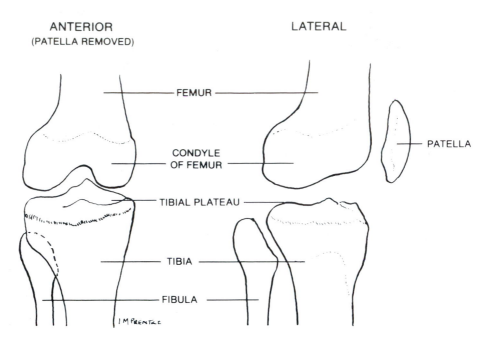

ANTERIOR
(PATELLA REMOVED)

LATERAL

FEMUR

CONDYLE
OF FEMUR

TIBIAL PLATEAU

TIBIA

FIBULA

PATELLA

1.22   The Bones of the Right Knee Joint from front and side.

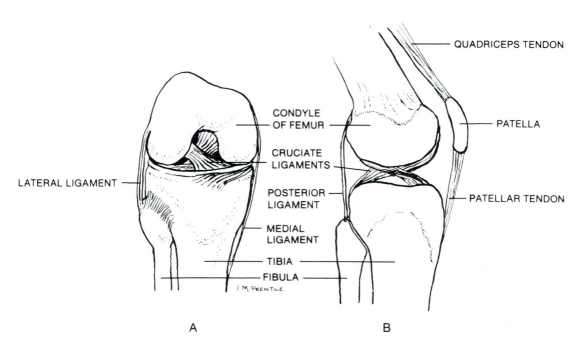

QUADRICEPS TENDON

CONDYLE
OF FEMUR

CRUCIATE
LIGAMENTS

LATERAL LIGAMENT

POSTERIOR
LIGAMENT

MEDIAL
LIGAMENT

TIBIA

FIBULA

PATELLA

PATELLAR TENDON

A

B

1.23   A. The Right Knee Joint. View from in front with the knee flexed, looking at the end of the femur and the upper end of the tibia.

B. Diagrammatic view of the Knee Joint from the side.

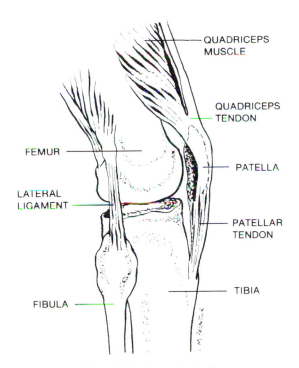

1.24   The Right Knee Joint (lateral view).

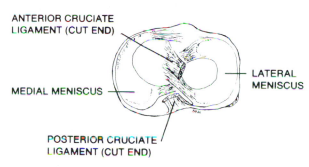

1.25   Upper end of the Right Tibia. Viewed from above to show the menisci (cartilages).

addition to the hinge movement there is a very small amount of rotation possible when the knee is partly flexed but not when it is fully extended.

The diagrams (Figs 1.23 and 24) show the ligaments which stabilise the knee. The lateral collateral ligament runs from the lower end of the femur laterally to the upper end of the fibula and is cord-like. The medial collateral ligament runs from the lower end of the femur medially to the upper end of the tibia and is strap-like. Within the joint are the cruciate ligaments, so-called because they cross over. They extend from the notch between the condyles of the lower end of the femur to the front and back of the plateau at the upper end of the tibia. They can be seen in the diagram. The knee is peculiar (but not unique) in possessing two menisci or semi-lunar cartilages as they are commonly called (Fig. 1.25). These are composed of fibro-cartilage and are attached at the outer edges to the capsule of the joint. The inner margins are free. They help to slightly deepen the joint at the upper end of the tibia producing two shallow saucers. In addition they move very slightly when the joint is bent and straightened during normal activities and as a result help to circulate the synovial fluid around the inside of the joint. The cartilages themselves take no weight in the normal function of the knee. However, if a partly flexed knee is twisted whilst weight-bearing, a cartilage

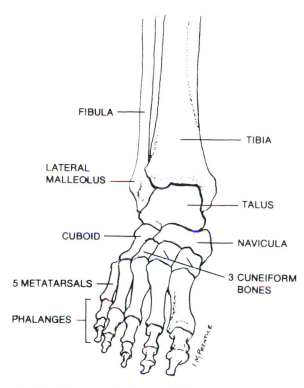

1.26   The Right Ankle Joint and Foot.

can be trapped between the femur and the tibia and the twist can produce a tear in the cartilage.

Anteriorly lies the quadriceps muscle which leads into the quadriceps tendon, the patella and the patellar tendon. These together help to give anterior stability. Posteriorly the posterior capsule, aided by the hamstrings, gives stability.

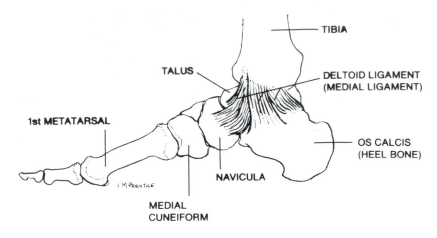

1.27   Ligaments of the Medial Side of the Right Ankle Joint.

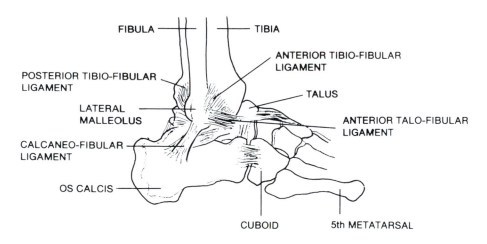

1.28   Ligaments of the Lateral Side of the Right Ankle Joint.

At the lower end of the tibia lies the ankle joint. This is a hinge joint where no other type of movement is available (Fig. 1.26). The joint is very stable. This stability is maintained on the lateral side by the lower end of the fibula which forms the side of the ankle joint. Medially there is a downward projection of bone from the lower end of the tibia forming the medial malleous and giving medial stability. The collateral ligaments of the ankle are extremely important in maintaining ankle stability and they are frequently the site of injury, particularly the lateral ligament. The medial ligament or deltoid ligament, so-called because of its shape, can be seen in the diagram (Fig. 1.27).

The lateral ligament is more complex (Fig. 1.28). The portion most commonly damaged is the anterior talo-fibular ligament.

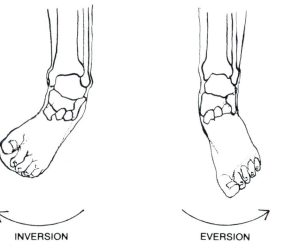

1.29   Inversion and Eversion.

Like the hand, the joints of the foot itself are complex. In the tarsal region rotatory movement is possible, allowing inversion and eversion. This largely takes place around the talus. The upper part of the talus forms the hinge of the ankle joint. The lower part of the talus articulates with the calcaneum and this bone, together with the other bones of the foot, can rotate around the talus. In the anterior part of the talus there is the head of the bone and this sits in the saucer-like socket of the navicular, forming the axis of rotation for inversion and eversion (Fig. 1.29). Some inversion and eversion also takes place in the anterior tarsal bones and between the tarsal bones and the proximal ends of the metatarsals. As in the fingers, the joints between the metatarsals and the phalanges are condyloid and between the phalanges themselves, simple hinge joints.

1.3 The Muscles

General Considerations

Muscles are the meaty parts of the body and are responsible for all movements that take place within the body.

TYPES OF MUSCLE FIBRES

There are three different types of muscle (Fig. 1.30) and they have very specific and different functions.

Striated or Skeletal Muscle
This muscle is also referred to as voluntary muscle because it can be controlled at will by the brain and nervous system. It includes the muscles controlling the limbs, muscles of facial expression and the muscles of respiration. It is known as striated muscle because when sections of the muscle are examined under a microscope the cells have the appearance of possessing striations or stripes. It may also be referred to as striped muscle (Fig. 1.30). The striated muscle fibres are gathered together in bundles and these bundles are surrounded by fibrous tissue, sometimes also called areola tissue or connective tissue. The various bundles of muscle fibres are themselves assembled and run longitudinally in the muscle as a whole. A large number of muscle bundles are bound together by areola tissue to form one anatomically named muscle.

At the ends of the muscles there are attachments to the bone. These may be in the form of a direct attachment where the fleshy part of the muscle is

STRIATED (SKELETAL)
Voluntary muscle

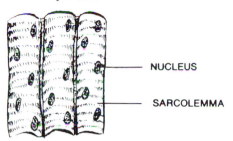

NUCLEUS

SARCOLEMMA

UNSTRIATED (BOWEL WALL, ETC.)
Involuntary muscle

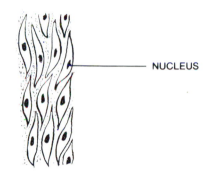

NUCLEUS

CARDIAC (HEART) muscle

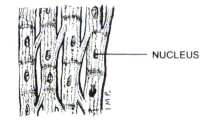

NUCLEUS

1.30   Diagram of the three types of Muscle Fibres.

attached to the bone. The fleshy muscle may come together to form a band or sheet of white fibrous tissue which may then be attached itself to the bone or, as is seen particularly in the extremities, this fibrous tissue may form a long tendon which is usually round or oval in cross-section. These tendons allow the pull of the muscle to be exerted some distance away without the presence of the muscle bulk producing an unwieldy organ. Hence the muscles which are largely responsible for flexion and extension of the fingers and toes end before they reach the wrist or ankle and the action of the muscle is then carried down via a tendon to the tips of the digits. This allows a very much more slender and functionally useful organ to be developed.

The groups of muscles themselves are in their turn surrounded by dense unstretchable fibrous tissue which is known as fascia. In the diagram of the cross-section of a limb (Fig. 1.31), in this case the leg, about a third of the way down from the knee, it is possible to see how these layers are made up. The skin surrounds the limb as a whole. Beneath this is a layer of fatty tissue which is called the superficial fascia. Then comes the deep fascia which is the dense fibrous tissue which is unstretchable. This envelope of deep fascia contains the various muscles themselves; there are often extensions of fibrous tissue from the deep fascia passing between the different muscles. These layers are usually less dense than the fascial layer itself. At this level there is also a very dense band of fibrous tissue connecting the two bones of the leg, the tibia and fibula; this is known as the interosseous membrane. Not only does it help to hold the two bones together, but it also gives an additional area for the attachment of the muscles.

The whole muscle is attached at each end, one called the origin and the other the insertion. The origin is that end which in general use of the part remains static and the insertion is at the end which is pulled and moves. Also the origin, as far as the limbs are concerned, is usually the proximal end, i.e. the end nearer to the trunk. However, their roles can be reversed; for example, if an object is grasped by the hand either the object can be pulled towards a stationary trunk, or the trunk can be pulled towards a stationary object.

The action of each muscle as a whole is controlled by one or more nerves. Many muscles have their nerve supply from several different nerves; when these nerves enter the muscle they gradually divide down until an individual nerve fibre reaches an individual muscle fibre. When the nerve fibre is stimulated it will in its turn stimulate the muscle fibre to contract completely. It cannot stimulate the muscle fibre to contract partially. This is known as the all-or-nothing law. This contraction shortens the muscle fibre. Depending upon the number of muscle fibres stimulated so will depend (a) the power or strength exerted and (b) the amount the whole muscle will shorten. By a very highly developed and sophisticated neuro-muscular control system the human being (or other animals,

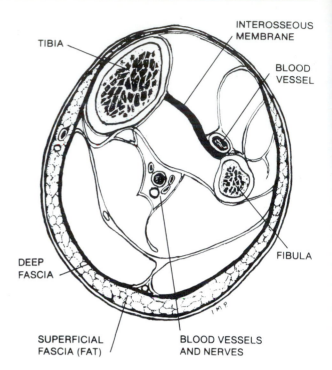

1.31   Cross-section of the Leg (upper third).

of course) can achieve amazingly delicate control of actual movements. In those areas of the body where very fine control is required the muscle fibres and nerve fibres are far more numerous (e.g. those concerned with the use of the hand) than in areas where less facility is required.

The stimulation down the nerve fibre is electrical but the stimulation between the nerve ending and the muscle fibre is chemical in nature. Even at rest a few fibres are being constantly stimulated in turn and this maintains what is known as muscle tone. There are two types of voluntary muscle fibre and these are referred to as fast and slow fibres. The proportion of different fibres in an individual muscle determines whether the muscle as a whole is more suited to a prolonged supporting role or to quick, rapid response action.

Unstriated or Involuntary Muscle
This is the name given to the muscle which controls various internal organs of the body (Fig. 1.30). This type of muscle is in the whole of the alimentary tract and also around much smaller structures such as glands and blood vessels. The conscious portion of the brain has no control at all over the action of these muscles, hence the name involuntary muscle. It is also known as unstriated muscle because on microscopic examination there are no striations or stripes as were found in the skeletal muscle.

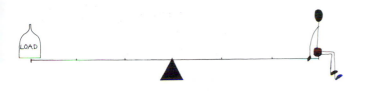

1.32   First Order Lever (balanced, with equal arms and equal weights).

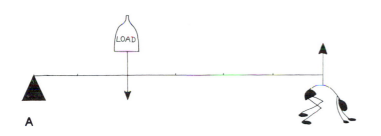

1.33   First Order Lever (balanced, with unequal arms and weights). Distance × load = distance × effort. In this case $2 \times 2 = 4 \times 1$.

   This may be found where the skull joins the cervical spine. The pull of the muscles in the back of the neck balances the weight of the front of the skull, the face and the mandible.

1.34   A. Second Order Lever. The load is nearer to the fulcrum than the effort. The force applied by the load will be greater than that required by the effort.

B. (below) Second Order Lever, as occurs at the foot and ankle with the dancer on demi-pointe.

Cardiac Muscle

This is the third type of muscle and is only found in the heart (Fig. 1.30).

   Cardiac muscle will contract without stimulation, but the rate and rhythm is under the control of nervous impulses. The control of cardiac muscle will be dealt with later.

ACTION OF MUSCLES

Before passing on to the individual muscles it is important to consider how muscles themselves produce movements.

Muscles and Levers

It must be emphasised that muscles can only contract and therefore pull, they can never at any time push. Movements are therefore brought about by using the bones as levers; there are three types of orders of levers, a first-order lever being like a see-saw (Fig. 1.32), with the balancing point referred to as the fulcrum. At one end of the lever is the 'load' and at the other end is the muscle action producing 'effort'. If no movement is taking place the part is in equilibrium and the force applied by the 'load' and the force applied by the

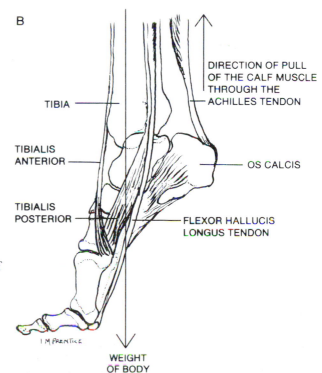

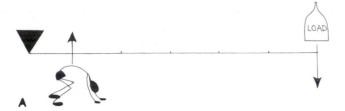

A

1.35   A. Third Order Lever. The
effort is nearer to the fulcrum than
the load. The force of the effort
therefore has to be greater than the
force of the load.

B. (below) Third Order Lever. In
this instance the force of the effort
has to be very much greater (about
seven times) than the force of the
load.

'effort' are balanced out, though this does not mean
that the actual number of kilograms being exerted
at these two points is necessarily the same. Anyone
using a lever in order to try to move something
heavy will realise that the longer the lever, the less
force needs to be applied to move the object. This
can be very simply worked out and expressed as an
equation: the 'effort' multiplied by the distance of
the 'effort' from the fulcrum equals the 'load'
multiplied by the distance of the 'load' from the
fulcrum. As the diagram shows (Fig. 1.33), if the
'load' is two units and the distance of the 'load' is
three units, these figures multiplied together give
the figure of six. On the other side of the fulcrum,
if the distance of the 'effort' is six units from the
fulcrum then the 'effort' required to move the
'load' will only be one unit because the 'effort' and
distance multiplied together will also produce a six.
An example of a first-order lever is the head, on the
spine, where the weight of the face is counteracted
by the muscles in the back of the neck.

In the limbs the other two types of lever are very
much more common. In a second-order lever (Fig.
1.34) the 'weight' or 'load' will lie nearer to the
fulcrum or point of movement than the 'effort' —
in this case the muscle contraction. This is well seen
in the foot when a dancer rises onto half pointe; the
fulcrum is at the ball of the foot, the weight of the
body is being transmitted down through the shin
bone and ankle and the lifting force is by means of
the calf muscle which is inserted through the
Achilles tendon into the back of the heel. Once
again, because of the levers the distance from the
fulcrum at the ball of the foot to the ankle joint is
less than the distance from the fulcrum to the back
of the heel, so the effort in the calf muscle is
slightly less than the actual weight of the body. It is
only slightly less because the differences in the two
distances from the fulcrum is only small.

Finally in the third-order lever (Fig. 1.35) the
'effort' or muscle contraction lies between the
fulcrum and the weight or 'load'. This is seen at the
elbow joint, where the biceps and brachialis muscles
are inserted just in front of the elbow but the

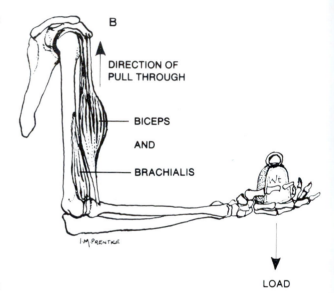

B

DIRECTION OF
PULL THROUGH

BICEPS

AND

BRACHIALIS

I M PRENTICE

LOAD

weight that is being lifted is situated further from
the elbow, usually in the region of the hand.
Because of the great difference in distances from
the fulcrum between the 'effort' and the 'load' the
actual force that is required to do the lifting is very
much greater than the actual weight of the 'load'.
This is because the distance between the fulcrum
and the insertion of the muscle is very short,
whereas the distance from the fulcrum to the hand,
which may be carrying the weight, is about seven
times greater; hence if the weight being lifted in the
hand is only one kilogram, the force of contraction
in the biceps muscle to lift this must be in the order
of seven kilograms. If measurements are done in
other areas of the body, particularly the lower
limbs, it will be seen that the actual force required
in the contracting muscle can be several times the
body weight and, when jumping, this may reach
between a half and three-quarters of a ton (500 –
700 kilograms).

A further important aspect of the use of levers is
the difference in distance moved by the 'effort' and
the 'load'. In first-order levers this can be either the
'effort' or the 'load' having to move further. In

second-order levers the 'effort' has to move further than the 'load', because the 'effort' is further from the fulcrum. Thus the muscles producing the movement have to shorten more than the distance the 'load' will move. In third-order levers, which are the commonest type in the body, the 'effort' moves a much shorter distance than the 'load'. This has the great advantage of allowing a large movement to be made with only very slight shortening of the muscles producing the movements.

Muscle Contraction

A muscle contracts as a whole by the separate contraction of its individual muscle fibres. At rest, a few nerve impulses are constantly being supplied to the muscles so that some fibres are always contracting and maintaining what is known as 'tone' in the muscle. In other words, the whole muscle never relaxes completely. During a voluntary movement, depending upon the power required, an increasing number of muscle fibres will contract at the same time, and then in succession, in order to maintain the muscle contraction and to control its speed.

The muscle groups do not act singly but always in concert with other muscle groups; if this were not to happen the movement would be largely uncontrolled. For example, when picking up a cup of tea to carry it to the mouth, if the muscle groups initiating the action contracted by themselves the tea would be thrown into the face of the drinker! All movements are carefully controlled. The most important initiating group is known as the 'prime mover'. The groups of muscles acting in the opposite direction are known as antagonists. During a movement the antagonist group will also be maintaining some contraction and will relax gradually in a compensatory manner. Gravity also plays an important part and will frequently act with either the prime mover or with the antagonist and may at times practically eliminate the action in the antagonist, especially when lifting.

Modern electrical tests on muscles (E.M.G. testing) have shown that, much of the time, the antagonist muscles are not actually being stimulated during a movement and that their antagonistic controlling action is taking place by means of elastic recoil. Whether this happens or whether there is actually some active contraction in the antagonist will depend upon the movement which is taking place: whether it is finely controlled, whether it is taking place with or without the assistance of gravity, etc. In addition, the prime mover or the antagonist may receive help from other groups of muscles which are known as synergists. These tend to act as co-ordinators of movements. They also help to counteract any unwanted directional force in the prime mover. As an example: the pectoralis major, when contracting to move the humerus in relation to the scapula, also exerts a dislocating force on the shoulder joint (the scapulo-humeral joint). The coraco-brachialis is a synergistic muscle for this movement and by contracting, not only aids the movement of the arm, but also by acting at a different angle to the pectoralis major counteracts the dislocating component of the force exerted by the latter.

During different movements, first one group and then another will be prime movers, antagonists or synergists. It is because of this combined action of the muscle groups that, during regimes of strengthening exercises, not only do the prime movers have to be exercised, but also the antagonistic and synergistic groups. It is the action of the various groups which produce a well balanced and controlled movement. Although the groups of muscles are all composed of voluntary muscles, the antagonistic and synergistic actions are controlled reflexly. So just as they can be made to contract reflexly they can also be inhibited reflexly, as may occur with injury or pain.

NEURO-MUSCULAR CO-ORDINATION AND ENGRAMS

Individual muscles can rarely act alone. There is a prime mover or agonist. There are synergistic groups which assist the prime mover. There are antagonist groups which oppose the prime mover. There are stabilisers which fix joints in order to allow the movement to take place. Co-ordination training develops pre-programmed automatic multi-muscular patterns. These are known as engrams. Constant, exact repetitions or practice will produce an engram, a condition where individual muscles or movements are not consciously considered. Proprioceptive feedback gives sub-conscious and conscious monitoring of the movement and shows whether it was successful or not. These automatic engrams can only be developed by voluntary repetition of the precise programme. This must be followed accurately otherwise the input of information will vary each time and the engram cannot be developed. It follows that initially the pattern must be slow enough to be accurate.

An engram allows a complicated movement to be performed far more rapidly than would be possible if conscious thought of each part of the pattern were required. At the same time as the movements are occurring, the engram will also produce

inhibition of unwanted movements. This inhibition
is an essential part of the regulation of
co-ordination. Inhibition cannot be produced
directly and consciously and is achieved by regular
and accurate repetition of the pattern of desired
movements. Co-ordination of the most rapid,
complex and skilful actions is automated by
engrams rather than by a voluntary controlled
series of movements. The activation of the
engram(s) is voluntary and under conscious control.
In learning exercise patterns and, of course, far
more importantly in learning dance technique, or
for that matter any other technique, accuracy is
absolutely vital in order to develop the correct
engram. If inaccuracies are allowed during the
development of a technique, this will produce 'bad
habits' and these very inaccuracies or bad habits
will themselves become an engram. Once this has
taken place, the modification of the faulty engram
will be extremely difficult and may call for that
portion of the technique to be learned again from
scratch. Hence the importance of learning any
complex series of movements accurately from the
start. As already stated, in order to achieve
accuracy the pattern will have to be learned slowly.
The number of repetitions required to produce a
really well-developed engram numbers in hundreds
of thousands or millions and not just hundreds or
thousands. However, this is not as bad as it sounds
because an action is usually made up of a series of
engrams. It is the sum of the engrams which
produces the final result. As already mentioned, the
initiation of an engram is under voluntary and
conscious control although the constituent parts of
the engram are themselves not by that stage under
voluntary control. What the mind does is to select
the stored engrams, put them together and produce
the desired result.

The use of engrams is probably seen and
appreciated best when one considers a musician
such as a pianist or organist. In this case, the
symbols on a page will initiate engrams which allow
the fingers, and in an organist the feet as well, to
perform the complex series of manoeuvres.

It has to be admitted that some old proverbs
certainly appear nowadays to have a scientific basis,
e.g. practice makes perfect (the formation of the
engram); you cannot teach an old dog new tricks
(the difficulty in trying to change an engram).

RED AND WHITE MUSCLE FIBRES

It might be felt that this subject is too abstruse to
be included in a book of this type at all. However,
the excuse for including a few sentences on the
subject is that dancers frequently ask about this as

they have either read about it or heard about it
and feel that they should be doing something about
red and white fibres in order to improve their own
performance.

Because of the presence of red meat and white
meat in fowls, it has long been thought that there
might be a difference between types of muscle
fibre. However, in mammals there is not this overall
appearance of red meat and white meat.
Nevertheless, within muscles themselves there have
been shown to be variations in the type of muscle
fibre, some being dark and some being light.

The 'red' fibres are also known as slow twitch
fibres and are also called Type 1 fibres. They tend
to proliferate in endurance training.

'White' fibres are also known as fast twitch fibres
or Type 2 fibres and they tend to proliferate in
sprint-type exercise.

Both fibre types are normally extremely stable
and do not change from one type to another.

Type 1 slow twitch fibres metabolise by oxidative
phosphorylation and thus are high in aerobic
capacity. They have a slow speed of contraction
(hence the name slow twitch) and they are also
slow to fatigue. These fibres are small in diameter.
They have a low threshold of recruitment (i.e. they
respond early to electrical stimulation from the
nerve fibres) and they generate low forces but
because of the low threshold and early recruitment
they contract more frequently than Type 2 fibres.

Type 2 fast twitch fibres metabolise by glycolysis.
They have a fast speed of contraction (hence fast
twitch) and are also fast to fatigue. These muscle
fibres are large in diameter. They have a high level
of recruitment (i.e. they need much more electrical
stimulation to make them contract) and they
generate high forces. However, they contract less
frequently than the Type 1 fibres.

To complicate matters a little further, there is
also an intermediate fibre which is a sub type of
Type 2. It is a fast oxidative glycolytic fibre
(F.O.G. fibre). These F.O.G. fibres have a fast
speed of contraction and an intermediate rate of
fatigue.

Having said all that, the best advice to the
dancer is that he forgets about his red and white
fibres and that he contents himself with carrying
out his proper exercise programmes, allowing his
various types of fibres to look after themselves.

Individual Muscles

TRUNK MUSCLES

As will be seen from the diagrams (Figs 1.36, 1.37
and 1.38) there are a large number of trunk

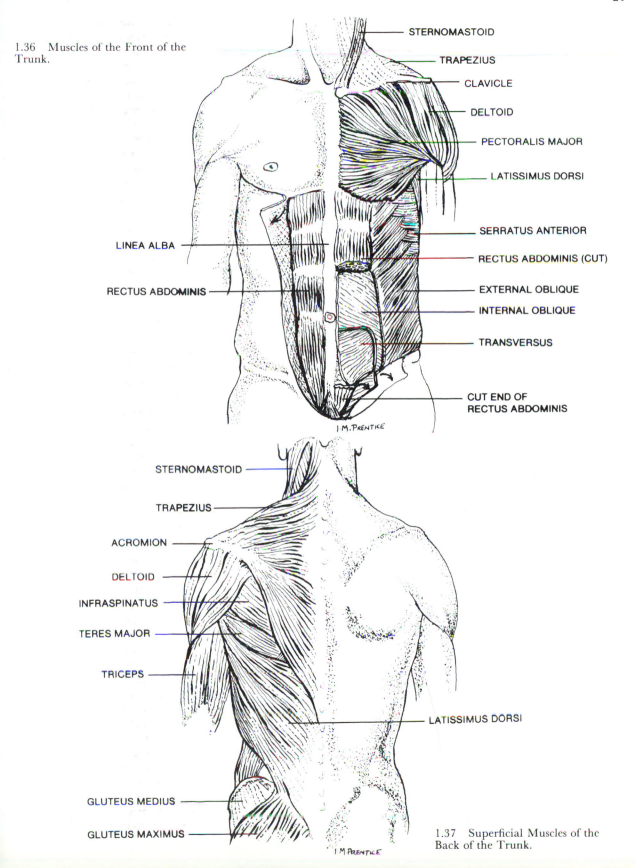

1.36   Muscles of the Front of the Trunk.

STERNOMASTOID

TRAPEZIUS

CLAVICLE

DELTOID

PECTORALIS MAJOR

LATISSIMUS DORSI

SERRATUS ANTERIOR

RECTUS ABDOMINIS (CUT)

EXTERNAL OBLIQUE

INTERNAL OBLIQUE

TRANSVERSUS

CUT END OF
RECTUS ABDOMINIS

LINEA ALBA

RECTUS ABDOMINIS

I.M. PRENTICE

STERNOMASTOID

TRAPEZIUS

ACROMION

DELTOID

INFRASPINATUS

TERES MAJOR

TRICEPS

LATISSIMUS DORSI

GLUTEUS MEDIUS

GLUTEUS MAXIMUS

I M. PRENTICE

1.37   Superficial Muscles of the Back of the Trunk.

muscles. The diagrams show the major muscles and name them. Detailed knowledge of the names of the individual muscles is unnecessary for dancers; it is usually more convenient to consider the muscles in groups and from the way they act rather than by their anatomical names. However, it is helpful to be familiar with the more important muscles and groups by name.

The trunk as a whole is supported and stabilised at the back by the long sacro-spinalis muscles which extend from the pelvis to the base of the skull and many other smaller muscles, and at the front by the anterior neck muscles, the intercostal muscles and other muscles attached to the rib cage and, from the dancer's point of view, possibly one of the most important groups in the body, the abdominal muscles. The muscles of the abdominal wall lie in several layers. Running down the centre of the abdomen are two stout muscles, one on each side of the mid-line, the right and left rectus abdominis. There are then two oblique layers, the external and internal obliques, the latter lying deep to the former, and then finally a transverse layer of muscles. A contraction of these various layers gives strength and support to the anterior part of the trunk and plays a very important part in maintaining the proper curves in the spinal column. At the sides of the trunk, the quadratus lumborum

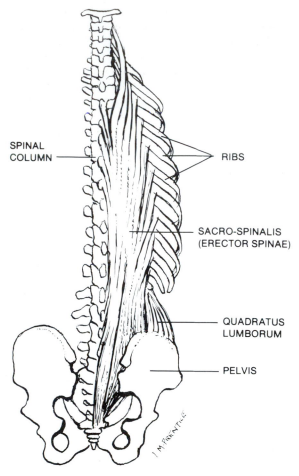

1.38   Deep Muscles of the Back of the Trunk.

1.39 (below)   Muscles of the Right Shoulder.

A. View from the front
   with the rib cage removed (vide Fig. 1.8).

B. View from the back.

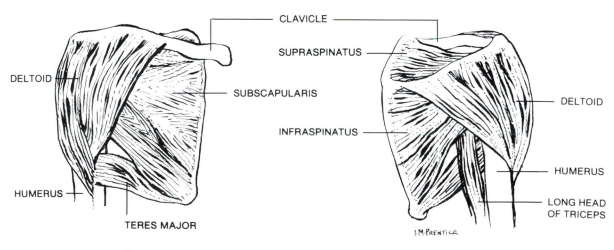

A

B

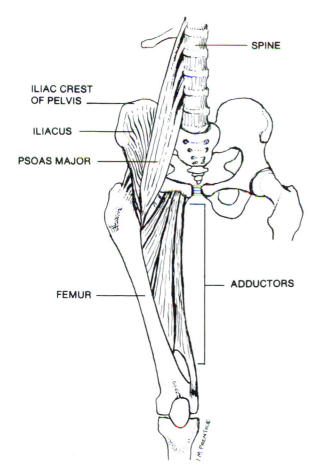

ILIAC CREST
OF PELVIS

ILIACUS

PSOAS MAJOR

SPINE

ADDUCTORS

FEMUR

1.40   Muscles of the Right Hip (view from the front).

the humerus are all responsible for the various movements between the humerus and the scapula. Shoulder movements take place at this joint between the humerus and the scapula and also at what has been termed the scapulo-thoracic joint. This is not a true joint in the proper meaning of the word but the scapula is only connected to the rest of the trunk by the joints between the two ends of the clavicle; otherwise it is held and suspended by all the muscles that run from the trunk into either the scapula or the upper part of the humerus. As a result, the scapula is free to move around the chest wall and elevation of the arm is a combination of movements at the joint between the humerus and the scapula and between the scapula and the chest wall.

Below the shoulder joint the muscles can be considered entirely as groups; in the arm there are the flexors and extensors of the elbow, in the forearm the flexors and extensors of the wrist and the muscles which rotate the hand and wrist in relation to the elbow and then flexors and extensors of the fingers. When strengthening muscles for use, such as lifting in the pas de deux work, consideration has only to be given to the strengthening of groups of muscles rather than individual muscles.

muscle helps the lateral portions of the abdominal muscles to give lateral strength. The large muscles of the shoulder girdle, namely latissimus dorsi, serratus anterior, trapezius and pectoralis major, play an extremely important part in the stabilisation of the upper part of the trunk, although as will be seen from the diagrams (Fig. 1.37) the latissimus dorsi takes origin from the mid-part of the back right down to the pelvis through the lumbo-dorsal fascia. Extremely importantly it also sends a slip of muscle to the lower angle of the scapula, thus helping considerably in the stabilisation of the scapula on the trunk.

UPPER LIMB MUSCLES

In addition to the shoulder girdle muscles shown in previous diagrams, Fig. 1.39 shows various other groups around the shoulder girdle. The deltoid muscle and the other short muscles arising from the scapula which are inserted into the upper end of

LOWER LIMB MUSCLES

Around the hip there are several small muscles which are responsible for rotation of the femur, but they are not very strong. Most of the them rotate the femur laterally or turn the leg out. Rather than acting as weak hip rotators their function is that of stabilisation of the hip joint. Their role can be considered as acting as adjustable ligaments. However, the turn out is carried out in the erect posture mainly by the adductor group of muscles (Fig. 1.40). The gluteus maximus (Fig. 1.41), which is a very large muscle, extends the hip (remember the true meaning of extension). Abduction of the hip is carried out largely by the tensor fasciae latae and the gluteus medius and gluteus minimus (Figs 1.42 and 1.43). Flexion of the hip joint is largely carried out by the psoas major and iliacus muscles, (Fig. 1.44), with some help from sartorius. In the thigh, additionally, the rectus femoris, which is part of the quadriceps muscle, also crosses the front of the hip joint and will help to flex the hip (Fig. 1.45). The quadriceps muscle which comprises the rectus femoris, the vastus medialis, vastus intermedius and vastus lateralis extends the knee very powerfully (Fig. 1.46).

For the dancer and all athletes the vastus medialis portion of the quadriceps muscle is particularly important and contracts powerfully during the last fifteen degrees of extension of the knee. After any injury the medialis is the first part of the muscle which tends to waste and is usually the most difficult to build up again. Flexion of the knee is carried out by the hamstring muscles which lie at the back of the thigh (Fig. 1.47). These also pass behind the hip joint and therefore act additionally as hip extensors. When the knee is semi-flexed the biceps femoris portion of the hamstrings can rotate the tibia externally. Internal rotation of the tibia is brought about by the popliteus muscle which lies deeply behind the knee. Neither external or internal rotation of tibia is a strong movement. Rotation of the tibia at the knee plays no part in rond de jambe en l'air. When the knee is fully extended, no rotation is possible between the tibia and the femur in the normal knee.

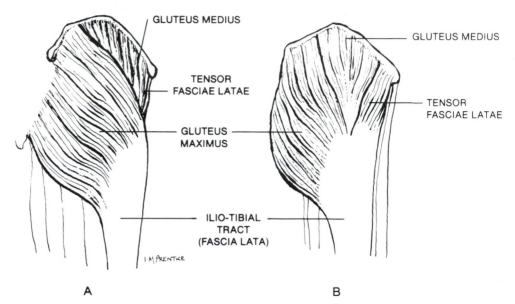

A   B

1.41   Muscles of the Right Hip.   A. From behind.   B. From the side.

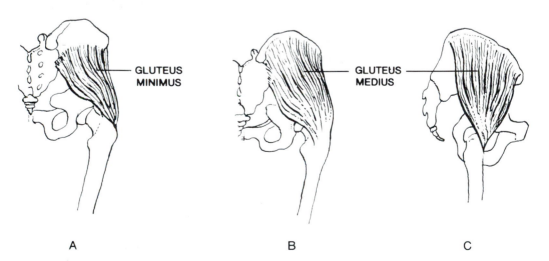

A   B   C

1.42   Muscles of the Right Hip.   A. From behind, showing gluteus minimus with gluteus medius removed.

                                       B. From behind, showing gluteus medius.

                                       C. From the side, showing gluteus medius.

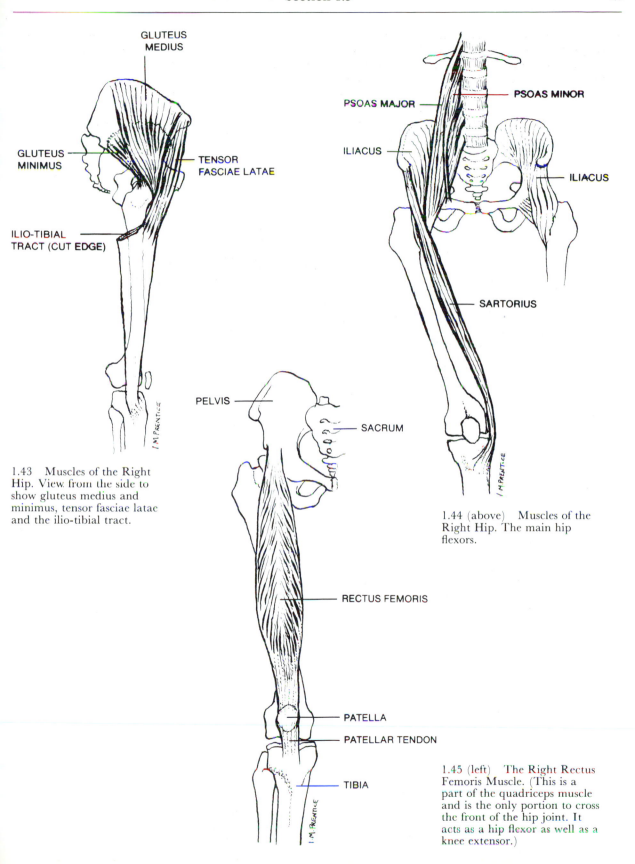

GLUTEUS
MEDIUS

GLUTEUS
MINIMUS

TENSOR
FASCIAE LATAE

ILIO-TIBIAL
TRACT (CUT EDGE)

PSOAS MAJOR

PSOAS MINOR

ILIACUS

ILIACUS

SARTORIUS

1.43   Muscles of the Right
Hip. View from the side to
show gluteus medius and
minimus, tensor fasciae latae
and the ilio-tibial tract.

1.44 (above)   Muscles of the
Right Hip. The main hip
flexors.

PELVIS

SACRUM

RECTUS FEMORIS

PATELLA

PATELLAR TENDON

TIBIA

1.45 (left)   The Right Rectus
Femoris Muscle. (This is a
part of the quadriceps muscle
and is the only portion to cross
the front of the hip joint. It
acts as a hip flexor as well as a
knee extensor.)

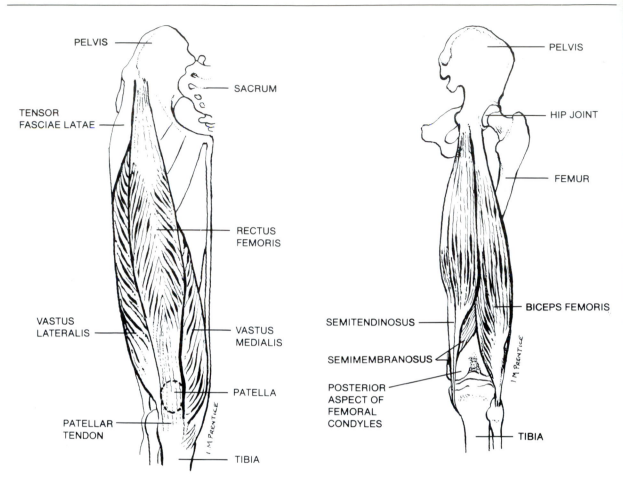

1.46   The Right Quadriceps Muscle. The vastus intermedius is hidden by the rectus femoris.

1.47   The Right Hamstring Muscles.

Below the knee (Fig. 1.48) in the anterior compartment or front of leg are the muscles which extend or (as is more commonly called) dorsi-flex the ankle, foot and toes. At the back of the leg are the calf muscles (Fig. 1.49), consisting of the gastrocnemius and soleus muscles. These join together at their lower ends to form the Achilles tendon. This is responsible for the powerful plantar-flexion of the foot. The gastrocnemius muscle has two heads proximally which pass behind the knee joint to take origin from the the back of the lower end of the femur. It also helps to flex the knee. The soleus muscle lies deep to the gastrocnemius muscle and its origin is in the leg below the knee joint. Twisting the foot into inversion is carried out by the combined action of the tibialis posterior and the tibialis anterior, lying respectively, as their name suggests, at the back and the front of the leg. In simple dorsi-flexion and plantar-flexion they help to reinforce these movements, tibialis anterior dorsi-flexing and tibialis posterior plantar-flexing the ankle and foot.

In the lateral part of the leg (Fig. 1.50) the peroneal muscles are responsible for twisting the foot outwards (eversion). The long extensors and long flexors of the toes as they cross the front and back of the ankle also assist in ankle movements.

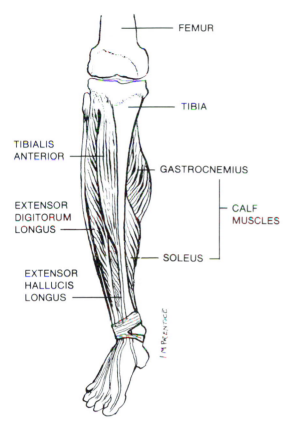

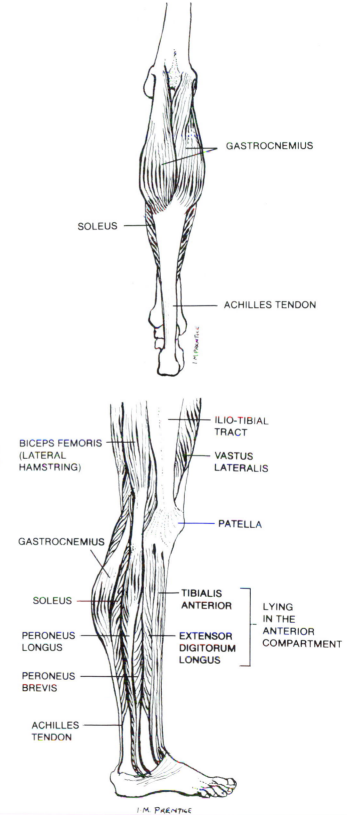

1.48 (above)   The Right Leg, from the front.

1.49 (above right)   The Right Leg, from the back. Note that the gastrocnemius muscle has two heads which cross the back of the knee and therefore help flex the knee as well as plantar-flex the foot and ankle.

1.50 (right)   The Lateral Side of the Right Leg.

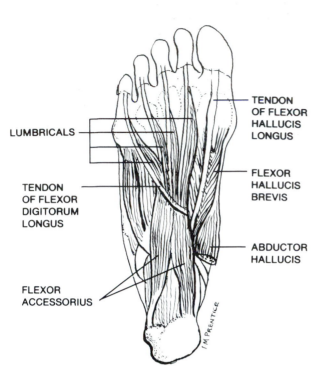

LUMBRICALS

TENDON
OF FLEXOR
DIGITORUM
LONGUS

FLEXOR
ACCESSORIUS

TENDON
OF FLEXOR
HALLUCIS
LONGUS

FLEXOR
HALLUCIS
BREVIS

ABDUCTOR
HALLUCIS

1.51   The Sole of the Right Foot (Superficial Muscles).

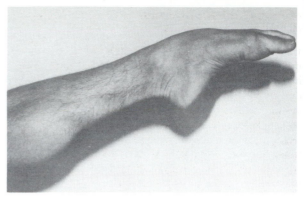

1.53   A Well Pointed Foot. The toes are stretched so that there is maximum stretch at the front of the ankle.

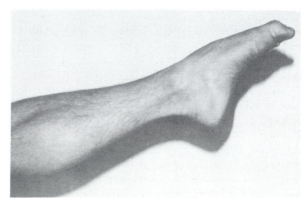

1.54   A Badly Pointed Foot. The intrinsic muscles are weak, so the toes become curled by the unopposed long flexors. As a result there is increased tension along the Achilles tendon and the curled toes prevent the front of the ankle being stretched. Note also the absence of a contraction in the soleus muscle which in Fig. 1.53 is visible below the marked bulge of the contracting gastrocnemius muscle.

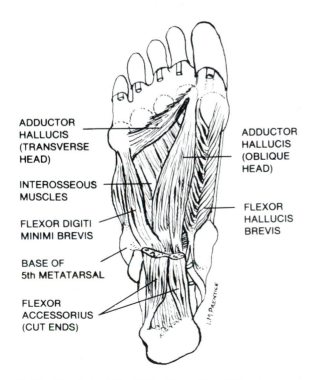

ADDUCTOR
HALLUCIS
(TRANSVERSE
HEAD)

INTEROSSEOUS
MUSCLES

FLEXOR DIGITI
MINIMI BREVIS

BASE OF
5th METATARSAL

FLEXOR
ACCESSORIUS
(CUT ENDS)

ADDUCTOR
HALLUCIS
(OBLIQUE
HEAD)

FLEXOR
HALLUCIS
BREVIS

1.52   The Sole of the Right Foot (Deep Muscles).

Within the foot itself are the intrinsic muscles of the foot (Figs 1.51 and 1.52); these are made up of the interosseous muscles and the lumbrical muscles. Although small, they are of the utmost importance to the dancer as strength there helps to maintain the transverse metatarsal arch across the foot. They are solely responsible for keeping the toes straight when the foot is pointed hard (Fig. 1.53); without the action of the intrinsic muscles the long flexors cause the toes to curl when the foot is pointed (Fig. 1.54).

Muscles which Move Individual Portions of the Body

In this section will be described the more important muscles which move joints which are of particular interest to dancers. It would be totally unrealistic to describe all the muscles in the body and their actions and it would be equally unrealistic in considering any particular joint to mention or expect any readers to memorise the names of all the muscles concerned. We are, therefore, going to consider only the main muscles; those that are particularly important for the dancer are printed in **bold** type.

Starting centrally we will consider the head and trunk followed by the upper and lower limbs.

HEAD AND TRUNK

The trunk is symmetrical and if split down the centre into left and right halves each side would be a mirror image of the other as far as the muscles and skeleton are concerned. The muscles therefore occur in pairs with one on either side of the body. When both sides act together the spine will be either flexed or extended. If one side alone acts, then it will either flex the spine laterally or rotate it or carry out a combination of flexion and rotation. The spine as a whole is capable of flexion, extension, lateral flexion in each direction and rotation in each direction. The most mobile portions of the spine are in the cervical and lumbar regions. The dorsal (thoracic spine) has a very much more limited range of movements. In the neck, flexion is brought about by the sterno-mastoid and extension by the splenius and the semispinalis capitis. In the rest of the spine extension is brought about by the **sacrospinalis** (erector spinae) and the **quadratus lumborum**. Flexion is brought about largely by the abdominal muscles, the **rectus abdominis** and the **external** and **internal obliques**. Flexion is helped by the **psoas major** which crosses the front of the hip joint and the psoas minor. The psoas major is also a flexor of the hip and an internal rotator of the hip. All these muscles when acting on one side alone will laterally flex and/or rotate the spine and trunk. The quadratus lumborum in particular has the added function of steadying the bottom rib which, through the additional action of the various muscles of the rib cage, has the effect of steadying the whole rib cage.

THE RIB CAGE

The external and internal intercostal muscles, which are the equivalent of the external and internal oblique muscles of the abdominal wall, both help to raise the ribs. This action is assisted by the **serratus posterior superior**. This latter muscle can play an important part in creating tension in dancers if they are breathing incorrectly. It runs from the 2nd to the 5th ribs upwards and backwards across to the mid-line to the large ligament (the ligamentum nuchae) at the back of the neck and to the spinous processes of the upper three thoracic vertebrae. The intercostals, as their name implies, lie between the ribs. There are eleven pairs, corresponding to the intercostal spaces between the twelve ribs, and the muscles run from one rib to the next. They play an important part in respiration because by raising the ribs they increase the capacity of the rib cage thus helping to draw in air. This combined with the action of the diaphragm produces inspiration.

THE SHOULDER JOINT

This as a whole is an extremely complex joint. The muscular control is therefore equally complex. Movement of the shoulder takes place at two sites:
1. at the ball and socket joint between the humerus and the scapula;
2. by the scapula sliding over the chest wall at the so-called scapulo-thoracic joint. This is not a genuine joint but as the scapula is only attached to the trunk by muscles it is able to move relatively freely in relation to the rib cage.

Movements of the shoulder are usually by a combination of movements at these two sites. As a result the range of the shoulder is very free. Flexion (to the front) and abduction (sideways) both have a range of 180°. It is possible to elevate the arm from hanging vertically at the side to vertically above the head, either by bringing the arm forwards and upwards or by moving it sideways and upwards. Flexion and abduction both end up with the arm in the same position. Extension (backwards) and rotation are very much more limited. In the use of the arm in heavy work, e.g. for the boys when they are lifting in double work, stabilisation of the scapula itself is extremely important. The muscles which move the scapula are also responsible for stabilising it. The largest of these muscles is the **trapezius**. This muscle takes origin from the base of the skull and all the thoracic vertebrae and is inserted into the spine of the scapula and the clavicle. The **serratus anterior** is also a large muscle that passes from the ribs anteriorly around the rib cage and deep to the scapula to be inserted into the medial (or spinal) border of the scapula. If it is weak it allows winging of the scapula, that is, the medial border of the scapula stands out away from the rib cage, particularly when the arm is used to push something. The **rhomboid major** and **rhomboid minor** are also important in stabilising the scapula. All these muscles as well as stabilising the scapula do, of course, play a part in actual movements of the scapula. Stabilisation is achieved by a balance of forces between the different muscles contracting and pulling in their various directions.

Around the actual shoulder joint are what is known as the short rotators. These are the **subscapularis**, **teres minor** and **infraspinatus** muscles, all of which play a part in rotating the arm. The **supraspinatus** does not actually rotate the arm but plays a small part in abducting it. However, the most important action of all these four muscles is in stabilising the head of the humerus in the glenoid cavity. As given in the earlier description of the shoulder joint, the glenoid cavity or socket is, in fact, very shallow, like a saucer, and has little or no inherent stability of its own. Therefore, during movements of the humerus in relation to the scapula, these four muscles act in order to steady the head of the humerus in the glenoid. They have been referred to as adjustable ligaments and their action is far more like this than the action which is generally associated with muscles. Of the larger muscles, that which actually flexes, abducts and extends the humerus in relation to the scapula is the **deltoid** muscle. The front portion of this muscle will flex the arm forwards, the middle portion will abduct the arm sideways and the back portion will extend the arm backwards.

The **latissimus dorsi** is an extremely important muscle. It takes origin from the bottom six thoracic vertebrae and indirectly from all the lumbar vertebrae and from the iliac crest. It is finally inserted into the humerus where it acts as an adductor of the arm but, on the way, it passes a very significant slip to the inferior angle of the scapula. This plays a very important role in the stabilisation of the shoulder girdle. As as adductor of the arm it is helped by **pectoralis major** and **teres major**. The pectoralis major also pulls the arm forwards and medially. The pectoralis major and latissimus dorsi are the most important muscles when lifting the body, for example – if the body is being lifted by the arms from an armchair or when pulling the body up when climbing.

THE ELBOW

The elbow is essentially a hinge joint, although rotation of the head of the radius against the lower end of the humerus takes place in order to give pronation and supination of the forearm. Normally, full extension occurs when the arm and forearm are in a straight line. However, hyperextension or swayback elbows are not particularly uncommon and when excessive can amount to as much as 25°. Flexion is from the fully extended position to approximately 140°. It is limited by the forearm coming up against the upper arm. As a result, an increase in muscle bulk or fat will decrease the possible range of flexion by the interposition between forearm and arm of the soft tissues.

Extension of the elbow is achieved by the **triceps** muscle, so called because it has three heads of origin. It is the only muscle lying at the back of the arm and is the main extensor of the elbow. Extension is helped by a small muscle, the anconeus, which lies just at the back of the elbow. Flexion is achieved by the **brachialis**, which lies deeply in the front of the arm and the **brachioradialis**, most of which lies below the elbow and extends along the forearm. More superficially in the arm lies the **biceps** (biceps brachii is its correct name, to distinguish it from the biceps femoris which is the lateral hamstring muscle) which stands out so obviously when the supinated forearm is braced in flexion. As well as flexing the elbow it has the additional function of supinating the forearm. The muscle also helps to flex the arm in relation to the scapula as it takes origin from the scapula.

Lower down and lying in the forearm the **supinator** muscle helps the biceps to supinate the forearm. Pronation is carried out by the **pronator teres** and the **pronator quadratus**. The muscles lying more distally in the forearm need not really concern dancers greatly. They are responsible, of course, for flexion and extension of the wrist and flexion and extension of the fingers. The movements of the fingers are also aided by the small intrinsic muscles of the hands.

THE HIP

The hip is a very stable ball and socket joint. The socket is deep with a round head, thus resisting dislocation in any direction, unlike the shoulder joint where the socket is extremely shallow. As the socket is deep the joint is not as fully mobile as the shoulder joint. However, to a certain extent what would otherwise be a more marked limitation of movement has been overcome by offsetting the head by means of a femoral neck which leads down at an angle to the upper end of the femoral shaft. As a result the hip can be flexed to a very much greater extent than would otherwise be possible. Flexion is only limited by the thigh coming up against the anterior wall of the trunk, extension is, however, limited by tension in the capsule, ligaments and other soft tissues. In addition to flexion and extension, rotation is relatively free as well as abduction and adduction.

Although the muscles of the lower limb are of much greater importance and interest to the dancers in many ways than those in the upper limbs we will still try to simplify matters by concentrating only on the major muscles. It is important to remember that these muscles which are described are nearly always being aided by several other muscles which have not been referred to by name. It must also be remembered that several muscles in the lower limb cross more than one joint and an individual muscle may therefore act as a flexor or extensor of both joints or as a flexor of one joint and an extensor of another.

At the hip joint (as in the shoulder joint) there are several small muscles known as the small rotators. The **obturator internus**, the **gemellus superior** and **gemellus inferior**, the **pyriformis**, the **quadratus femoris** and the **obturator externus** all have an action in externally rotating the femur. However, the actual movements produced by these muscles are relatively weak. Their great importance is in stabilising the hip joint and, just as in the case of the short rotators of the shoulder joint, they act more as adjustable ligaments. Their function is also of great importance in limiting the medial rotation of the femur which would otherwise take place during the action of the large strong flexor muscles as these are also medial rotators. The also help to prevent excessive internal rotation. They may therefore be strained on a bad landing and the pyriformis subsequently can go into painful spasm.

The most important hip flexor is the **ilio-psoas** muscle. This is made up of the psoas major and the **iliacus**. Both these muscles are inserted into the lesser trochanter of the femur so, as well as flexing the hip, they will rotate the femur medially and it is this latter movement which is opposed by the short rotators.

The most important lateral rotator of the femur at the hip joint is the **adductor** group of muscles (see **Section 1.11** Turn-out, page 54). The three adductors are large strong muscles occupying most of the inner side of the thigh. As their name implies they also adduct the thigh, pulling the two thighs together aided by gracilis. When the dancer is standing on one leg they help to stabilise the pelvis by acting against the abductors. It is the balance between these two groups of muscles, the adductors and abductors, plus the balance between the flexors and the extensors, which stabilises the pelvis when the dancer is working, particularly the supporting leg. It is only by achieving a really stable pelvis in relation to the lower limb on the supporting side that the working leg can relax sufficiently to produce the necessary fluidity of action. Weakness in any of these groups leads to instability, muscle tension and muscle injury. Abduction of the femur is carried out by the **gluteus medius** and **gluteus minimus** both of which are inserted into the greater trochanter of the femur. The **tensor fasciae latae**, which is inserted into the very stout band of fascia lata running down the outer side of the thigh and ending in the upper part of the tibia, also helps to abduct the hip. Additionally, the tensor fasciae latae helps to extend the knee. If tight, it can play a significant part in lateral tracking of the patella and the production of anterior knee pain (see **Section 3.30**). The **gluteus maximus** has in the main a different function from the other two gluteii and is the most important hip extensor. It also helps to tense the fascia lata and has a much lesser function therefore in helping to abduct the femur. As it is a hip extensor, when the dancer has the trunk flexed forwards at the hips the gluteus maximus rotates the pelvis in order to lift the trunk upright again.

THE KNEE

The knee joint is, in practice, a hinge joint. When it is fully extended there is no rotation possible between the lower end of the femur and the upper end of the tibia. With the knee slightly flexed there is some rotation possible between the femur and the tibia but this only amounts to about 15° in either direction. Extension of the knee, although normally occurring fully when the thigh and leg are in a straight line, is very frequently greater than this, giving a certain amount of hyperextension producing the familiar swayback knees. Flexion is, in most people, limited by the calf muscle coming up against the back of the thigh. Strong collateral ligaments prevent any abduction or adduction of the knee.

The movement of extension is achieved by the **quadriceps** muscle. As its name implies this is made up of four parts. The **rectus femoris** takes origin from the pelvis above the acetabulum and crosses the front of the hip joint to be inserted via the combined quadriceps tendon, patella and patellar tendon into the upper part of the front of the tibia. Therefore as well as extending the knee it will help to flex the hip. The **vastus lateralis**, **vastus intermedius** and **vastus medialis** all take their origin from the shaft of the femur. They do not cross the hip joint. They, together with the rectus femoris, join together at their lower ends to form the quadriceps tendon. This is inserted into the patella, which at its lower pole gives origin to the patellar tendon which is inserted into the front of the upper end of the tibia. The vastus medialis is particularly important in dancers and other athletes. It is largely responsible for the final 15° of extension. It also opposes the lateral tracking of the patella which would otherwise take place by the action of the vastus lateralis and the tensor fasciae latae, the latter through the intermediary of the fascia lata itself. In any knee injury the vastus medialis is the first portion that weakens and wastes and in rehabilitation is the most difficult to build up again. Its importance is referred to on many occasions in **Section 3**.

Flexion of the knee is brought about by the hamstrings. These are the **semitendinosus** and **semimembranosus** lying on the medial side of the back of the thigh and the **biceps femoris** lying on the lateral side of the back of the thigh. As well as flexing the knee they also act as hip extensors as they cross the back of the hip joint taking origin from the pelvis, apart from the short head of the biceps which takes its origin from the back of the femoral shaft. When the medial (semitendinosus and semimembranosus) hamstrings and lateral (biceps femoris) hamstrings are not balanced up in strength, either following an injury or due to incorrect working, they can produce uneven rotational forces at the knee when the joint is anything other than fully extended. In the semi-flexed situation injury is more likely to occur.

Flexion of the knee is aided slightly by the gracilis and the **sartorius**. The latter also acts as a flexor of the hip. It helps to abduct the hip and rotate the femur externally. As a result of these actions if the dancer is straining to overturn the feet, pushes back on the knee and gets into the weightback situation, a great deal of strain occurs at the upper end of the sartorius and this muscle then becomes a frequent site of the so-called groin strain. As will be seen in **Section 5**, groin strains are usually a result of incorrect weight placement.

At the back of the knee is a small muscle called the popliteus, which helps to flex the knee and it also will rotate the tibia medially (internally). When the knee is flexed the medial and lateral hamstrings will also aid in rotating the tibia at the knee, the medial hamstrings (semitendinosus and semimembranosus) helping to rotate the tibia

medially, and the lateral hamstrings (biceps femoris) helping to rotate the knee laterally. However, as has been mentioned earlier, when the knee is fully extended there is no rotation possible at the knee joint. The ligaments lock it in order to prevent rotation, therefore any excessive rotational force will produce damage within the knee. As the knee starts to flex, then an increasing amount of rotation is available between the tibia and the knee but this only amounts to about 15° in each direction at the maximum. It is not until the knee reaches about 45° of flexion that significant active rotation of the tibia in relation to the femur occurs. At less than this amount of flexion, the movement is extremely weak, although this is not to imply that the rotational movement even at 45° of flexion and greater, is particularly strong.

THE ANKLE, FOOT AND TOES

These joints are considered together because many of the muscles concerned will act on all the joints. The **gastrocnemius** is the superficial muscle at the back of the calf and leads us into this section from the knee, because it takes its origin from the lower end of the femur above the back of the knee. It therefore acts as a knee flexor assisting the hamstrings. As it passes through the leg it joins with the **soleus**. These two together form the Achilles tendon which is inserted into the back of the os calcis or heel bone. The gastrocnemius and soleus together act as plantar-flexors of the ankle. The **plantaris** is a small muscle which also arises from the back of the lower end of the femur. It has a very long tendon and is also inserted into the os calcis. It acts in a similar fashion to the gastrocnemius by helping to flex the knee and to plantar-flex the ankle. Plantar-flexion is helped by the **long flexors of the toes**.

Due to the arrangement of the bones in the hind foot and foot as a whole, when the ankle is plantar-flexed it takes with it the whole of the foot, because the mobility of the foot within itself in the direction of dorsi-flexion and plantar-flexion is not very great. Therefore, when one considers dorsi-flexion and plantar-flexion of the ankle, one can consider the movement of the whole foot in those two directions.

Dorsi-flexion of the ankle and foot is carried out by the actions of several muscles, the **tibialis anterior**, the **extensor hallucis longus**, the peroneus tertius and the **long extensors of the toes**. However, all these muscles have other actions in addition.

Inversion and eversion of the foot take place in the tarsal bones or hind foot. Essentially, the talus remains fixed in the ankle joint as far as inversion and eversion are concerned, merely moving as a hinge in dorsi-flexion and plantar-flexion. Inversion and eversion take place along a line through the axis of the talus, the movement occurring mainly in the sub-taloid and talo-navicular joints, although to a certain extent there is some inversion and eversion in the mid tarsal joints in the middle of the foot. Inversion of the foot is obtained by a combined action of the **tibialis posterior** and the **tibialis anterior**. Eversion of the foot is carried out by the action of the peroneal muscles. The long extensors of the toes, as they cross in front of the ankle, do have an action as mentioned in dorsi-flexing the ankle and at the same time in extending the toes. Extension at the foot and ankle is synonymous with the expression dorsi-flexion, the latter expression being more commonly used when applied to the ankle and foot. The long flexors of the toes cause them to curl as they flex at both the metatarsophalangeal and the interphalangeal joints. Additionally, the long flexors of the toes will help to plantar-flex the ankle and foot, plantar-flexion here being synonymous with flexion when applied to the ankle and to the foot.

Additionally, in the foot as in the hand, there are many small muscles which are known as the **intrinsic muscles**. These are responsible for opposing the clawing effect of the long flexors of the toes, so that when the toes are flexed at the metatarsophalangeal joints, the intrinsic muscles by their action will help to keep the interphalangeal joints straight. Thus in a well pointed foot, we see the plantar-flexors of the ankle and foot working and assisted by the long flexors of the toes but the actual flexion effect of the last group of muscles on the toes is counteracted by a strong action of the intrinsic muscles, keeping the toes straight in the pointed foot. Some of the intrinsic muscles also have an effect in maintaining the transverse arch across the forefoot. If the transverse arch drops due to weakness of the intrinsic muscles, then pain can develop under the heads of the metatarsals (known as anterior metatarsalgia).

1.4 The Nervous System

The nervous system comprises the brain, the spinal cord and peripheral nerves. The nervous system is further sub-divided into two parts:

1. that part associated generally with the muscles moving the body and limbs and the associated sensory perceptions, and
2. the other part, known as the automonic nervous system, which supplies the nerves to involuntary and cardiac muscles and to glands.

However, these two systems are closely related; reflex arcs are involved in both systems and the higher senses of control of each are in the brain. The nervous system, as all other systems, is based upon individual cells known as neurones and, unlike other cells, they have extensions from the cell (Fig. 1.55). One type of extension is called the dendron; this may be single or multiple and passes impulses towards the cell body. The other type of extension known as the axon conducts impulses away from the cell body. The voluntary nerves and those associated with sensation are surrounded by a

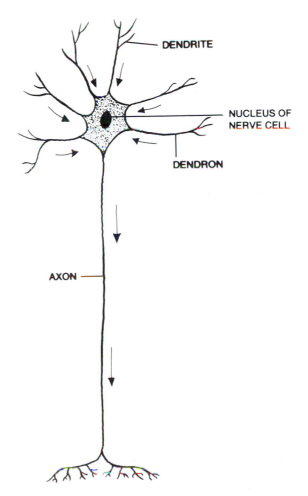

DENDRITE

NUCLEUS OF NERVE CELL

DENDRON

AXON

1.55 A Typical Nerve Cell. The arrows show the direction of the electrical impulses in the nerve.

fatty sheath and are known as medullated nerves or white fibres; whereas the autonomic nerve fibres do not have this fatty layer and are known as non-medullated or grey fibres because of the actual colour difference. The neurones all have a specific function; sensory neurones are those which receive stimuli and pass them centrally to the spinal cord and from there, where necessary, to the brain. Motor neurones are those which pass impulses from the brain and from the spinal cord to the muscles.

The sensory nerves not only receive and perceive what we would consider sensations, such as hot, cold, pain, etc. but also they are responsible for transmitting messages concerned with tension within muscles, tendons and ligaments and information regarding co-ordination and spacial relationships. It is the combination of these mechanisms which enable you, for instance, to place the tip of your finger on your nose or any other part of your body without the necessity of watching it in motion.

The Voluntary or Somatic Nervous System

The term voluntary, although commonly applied, is not a particularly satisfactory name for this portion of the system but it is used to distinguish the major part of the nervous system from the autonomic nervous system (vide infra). Somatic nervous system is a better though less used name.

It is probably easier when considering the action of the nervous system to start peripherally, rather than centrally. If we consider a case where an individual nerve is divided, this will cut through both sensory and motor nerves; the result will be that no sensation of any sort can reach the spinal cord or the brain. The part will feel numb and there will be no appreciation of where it is in space. Division of the motor nerve will prevent any movement at all in the distribution of that divided nerve; the muscles supplied by the nerve will lose all tone as no electrical impulses can travel across the division in the nerve. This therefore will produce what is known as flaccid paralysis, in other words the muscle will be completely soft and toneless to the observer's touch.

Now take a case of a division across the spinal cord itself; the spinal cord will be normal, both above and below the level of division, but there will be no conduction in either direction across the division. We have therefore intact nerves going from the spinal cord to the muscle and from the muscle, skin and other tissues back to the spinal cord. Within the spinal cord there are some nerve connections directly between the sensory nerves and

the motor nerves. These three pathways between them produce what is known as a reflex arc. In primitive creatures where there is little or no brain, the entire organism functions by means of these very simple reflex arcs. Taken at its simplest a reflex arc consists of

a)   a sensory receptor;
b)   a sensory neurone;
c)   a synapse (which is where one nerve ending makes contact with another nerve ending);
d)   a motor neurone, and
e)   an effector cell.

The drawing (Fig. 1.56) shows a simple reflex arc from a sensory receptor (e.g. pain appreciation) to the spinal cord, via an intermediate neurone known as an internuncial neurone to the motor neurone which will supply a muscle fibre causing a contraction. In the simplest reflex arc the internuncial neurones may be missing.

There are reflexes within the spinal cord, passing impulses up and down to leave at higher or lower levels, as well as those going in and out at the same level. There are also more highly developed reflexes going up and down the spinal cord to and from the brain.

Reflex actions play a vital role in

a)   control of the internal organs;
b)   controlling the tone in voluntary muscles;
c)   producing controlled inhibition of antagonistic groups of muscles;
d)   causing protective reactions.

In the division of the spinal cord in a higher animal such as a mammal, the animal is reduced below the level of the division to a primitive type of state. Although the brain cannot receive or transmit any messages, certain functions still occur below the level of division. Muscle tone, for instance, is actually increased in these reflex arcs, because of the lack of modification from the higher centres. Although voluntary movement has been abolished and the muscle is paralysed in that sense, the increased tone produces what is known as spastic paralysis because the affected muscles tend usually to be in spasm because of the increased tone. Various reflex arcs can be initiated by stimuli. For example heat, cold or pain will produce a withdrawal reflex without the brain perceiving anything. In the absence of injury these primitive reflexes are modified by nerve impulses transmitted from the higher centres. In the normal animal there are innumerable reflex arcs not only from the periphery to the spinal cord and brain but also within the different sections of the brain itself, continually modifying, altering and controlling all aspects of function.

1.56   Illustration of a Reflex
Arc in the Nervous System.

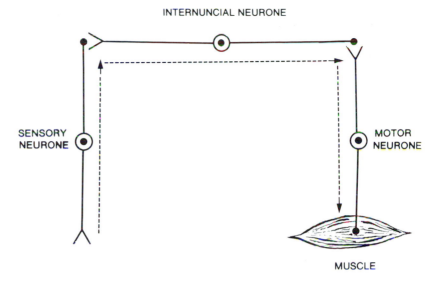

INTERNUNCIAL NEURONE

SENSORY
NEURONE

MOTOR
NEURONE

MUSCLE

The neurological system as a whole is extremely complicated, but in what is possibly an over-simplification, it might be considered that development from primitive life to the human state has progressed from below upwards, starting with a reflex arc and proceeding with the development of the portion of the brain nearest the spinal cord, the hind-brain, the cerebellum and mid-brain and finally to the cerebral hemispheres or fore-brain. The brain and cerebellum have a very wrinkled or convoluted surface in order to increase the available surface area of the brain. With the higher mammals, and particularly with primates, increasingly complicated series of movements can be learned consciously, and once mastered can be reproduced without obvious conscious thought about each individual part of the total complex action. This does not, however, mean that once learnt, these complex actions are then brought about in the lower levels of the spinal cord. These actions are still initiated and controlled within the brain and it is a misnomer to refer to these complex actions as reflex actions.

The Autonomic Nervous System

Once again this is not a very satisfactory name as it implies by the name autonomic that it is self-controlling, whereas it is in fact closely linked with the somatic system and its highest centres are in the brain.

This is the system that controls the involuntary and cardiac muscles and the glands. The autonomic system itself is divided into two parts – the sympathetic system and the parasympathetic system. The two systems act against each other and are therefore called antagonistic. The sympathetic system is a stimulatory system and acts with adrenalin to prepare the body for action. Initially this was, of course, to either fight an enemy or flee from him, but in the more modern situation it will produce the keyed-up feeling required for social confrontations such as examinations, performances or arguments with other people. It is the sympathetic system and the adrenalin which increase the pulse rate and blood pressure on these occasions and produce a feeling of 'butterflies' in the stomach by diverting the blood supply, from the alimentary tract in particular, to other areas which are needed for the 'figurative fight'. The parasympathetic system is inhibitory in type and tends to produce rest and relaxation in the body and aids digestion by increasing the blood supply to the abdominal organs. The sympathetic and parasympathetic systems have their main nerve supplies outside the spinal cord, starting in what is know as ganglia and then running up and down inside the trunk. Parasympathetic and sympathetic nerve fibres travel with the ordinary motor and sensory nerves to the limbs and muscles.

The Sensory System

There are three types of sensory endings:
1. those which can detect stimuli coming from outside the body. These are known as exteroceptors.
2. endings which sense stimuli from within the body, particularly the internal organs, such as the alimentary tract. Known as enteroceptors.

3. those which can detect the tension in the
    muscles and tendons. These are known as
    proprioceptors.

Stimulation of the exteroceptors produces a
conscious awareness of the type of stimulus.
However, we are not normally aware of the
stimulation of enteroceptors and proprioceptors
except for a feeling of hunger or unless it reaches
the point where the stimulus is so great that it is
interpreted as a feeling of pain. The exteroceptors
are responsible for producing a variety of conscious
effects; these are sight, taste, smell, touch,
temperature, pain, hearing and balance. The latter
two are both detected within the ear.
Over-stimulation of touch, temperature and even of
hearing may be interpreted as pain.

SKIN SENSATION

Temperature and pain are protective types of
sensation. Touch is largely connected with the use
of the limbs and movement. A person with a numb
hand or even a numb finger finds that the use of
the hand in picking things up and particularly in
fine and skilled uses is seriously impaired. They will
not know that they are holding something or how
tightly they are holding it and they therefore tend
to drop objects. They will frequently be under the
misapprehension that the hand is weak, although
this is not in fact the case. Loss of sensibility to
touch in the feet produces a stamping gait because
the person cannot feel the feet touching the ground
and therefore the necessary stimulation to initiate
the reflex arcs is absent. As far as the dancer or
athlete is concerned we can pass over the taste and
smell modalities.

AURAL SENSATIONS: SOUND AND BALANCE

Although the appreciation of music in both pitch
and rhythm is important to a dancer, hearing
problems are not something upon which we need
dwell in a work such as this. Balance is, however,

extremely important. The organs of balance are
situated in the inner ear: there are three
semi-circular canals lying in different planes to each
other (Fig. 1.57). The cells inside the canals have
hair-like processes and the canals themselves are
filled with fluid. Hearing appreciation takes place
in the cochlea.

The movement of fluid within the canals
stimulates the hair-like processes and it is this
interpretation of the stimuli which produces a sense
of balance. Diseases of the inner ear can produce a
sensation of falling or dizziness, known as vertigo.
This is often temporary in nature and frequently
associated with a cold and possibly a middle ear or
inner ear infection. The ability to balance is a
combination of the information received from the
inner ear, the information received from the
proprioceptors in the muscles and also the
information received from the eyes. The eyes are
the least important as the normal person has no
difficulty in walking or standing in total darkness.
However, if there is damage to the inner ear, then
the visual reflexes can take over to a certain extent.
In these circumstances if the person then closes his
eyes there will be a tendency to fall over.

VISUAL SENSATION

Visual defects with which one is born are most
commonly caused by too long or too short an eye
ball and these defects can be corrected by
spectacles or by contact lenses. As there is a small
distance between the eyes, the actual field of vision
in each eye is slightly different and it is this slight
difference in field of vision which the brain can
interpret to produce a stereoscopic or 3-D effect.

This gives an accurate judgment of distance,
allowing objects to be touched or picked up
extremely accurately. In a person born with
monocular vision the brain compensates extremely
efficiently for this defect and such a person is

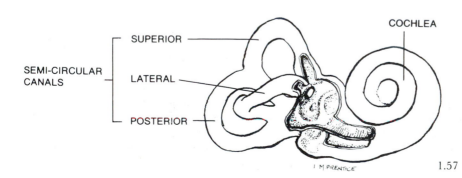

1.57   The Inner Ear.

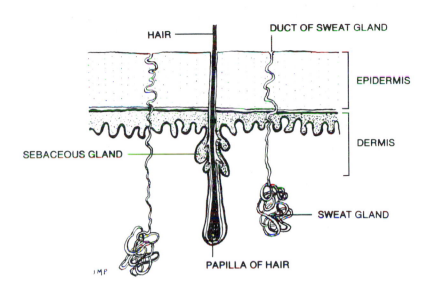

HAIR

DUCT OF SWEAT GLAND

EPIDERMIS

DERMIS

SEBACEOUS GLAND

SWEAT GLAND

PAPILLA OF HAIR

1.58   Diagram of a
Cross-section of the Skin.

usually only at a disadvantage in rapid ball games. However, if vision is lost in one eye later on in life the individual has far greater difficulty in compensating. As a result there can be problems picking up objects and driving vehicles.

1.5 The Skin

The skin comprises two layers of tissue (Fig. 1.58): the epidermis, which is the superficial or outer part and the dermis which is the deeper part. The dermis contains nerves and blood vessels; the epidermis has neither nerves nor blood vessels. In the deeper layers of the epidermis are living cells which proliferate, pushing the more superficial cells towards the surface. As they get nearer to the surface they become flattened and then die, giving layers of dead, horny cells. The epidermis is being constantly renewed by growth from the deeper layers and the superficial horny cells are constantly shed. This is particularly well demonstrated when a part has been encased in plaster of Paris and the dead, horny cells are then only too apparent where they have not been worn away but are still lying in place, giving the appearance of a scaly reptile-type skin. Friction and pressure both stimulate the growth of the cells of the deeper part of the epidermis, thickening up the epidermal layer. This is normal on the soles and the palms, particularly in those who walk bare-footed or who do heavy manual labour. In certain areas this thickness may be localised, producing a callosity.

The skin is not permeable to water. This is not to prevent the rain from getting in but to prevent water being lost from the body. The epidermis is also a protective mechanism that prevents the entry of germs.

The skin contains two types of glands (Fig. 1.58):
1. the sweat glands – the chief function of which is to help cool the body. When the temperature of the body rises the sweat glands secrete sweat; this covers the skin and evaporates. In order to be turned from a liquid into a gas, i.e. evaporate, energy has to be absorbed; this is done in the form of heat absorption from the body and thus the production of the cooling effect. The sweat contains various types of salt and some waste materials from the body. The sweat can be looked upon as playing a minor part in the excretion of these materials. However, in a hot climate where sweating is profuse the body is able to regulate the amount of electrolytes or salts in the sweat and decrease the loss to practically nil. Were this not the case there would be a serious depletion of essential electrolytes in the body.
2. the sebaceous glands, which produce an oily secretion known as sebum which lubricates the horny epidermal cells and the hairs to prevent them from becoming brittle. (Mammary glands which produce milk are specialist forms of sebaceous glands.)

The skin contains nerve endings which perceive temperature and touch. Pain endings are at a deeper level.

1.6 The Cardio-vascular System

This system comprises the blood which circulates around the arteries, veins and capillaries, the heart which pumps the blood through the blood vessels, and the arteries, veins and capillaries themselves.

The Blood

The blood consists of two portions: there is a liquid part which accounts for just over half the volume of the whole blood and a cellular part which accounts for just under half.

The cells themselves are of two main types – the red cells and the white cells. The red cells do not have nuclei by the time they enter the blood stream. They are responsible for carrying the oxygen and give the blood its red colour. There are about four and a half to five million red blood cells in each cubic millimetre of blood. The red pigment in the red blood cells is haemoglobin; this can combine very easily with oxygen and equally easily can shed the oxygen again and it is by this method that oxygen is transported around the body, taking it from the air in the lungs to release it where required in the tissues. The red blood cells only exist in the blood stream for three to four months before being broken down. They are mainly produced in the red bone marrow which contains what is known as erythropoietic tissue – the red marrow in adult life is largely confined to the flat bones, e.g. the pelvis and the scapula, and the ends of the long bones. In childhood most of the bones contain red marrow but this quantity decreases in adult life. In these inactive sites, the red marrow becomes yellow marrow which does not contain erythropoietic tissue. However, if demand suddenly becomes great, even in adult life the yellow bone marrow can revert to red bone marrow and start producing the red corpuscles once more. This may be stimulated by chronic blood loss, e.g. when blood is lost gradually over a long period as in a bleeding ulcer, etc.

When the cells are broken down after three to four months the iron is retained in the body and is stored in the liver to be used again for making further red corpuscles. The other products from the breakdown of the haemoglobin are excreted in the bile which passes into the alimentary tract and hence out of the body in the faeces. The white blood corpuscles, which are also known as leucocytes, are fewer in number than the red corpuscles. There are four thousand to ten thousand per cubic millimetre of blood, but various diseases can produce a very marked increase in the number of white cells. The white cells themselves are divided into two types: polymorphonuclear leucocytes or granulocytes 60–75% and mononuclear leucocytes or non-granulocytes 25–40%. The granulocytes have large irregular nuclei which are lobulated. They are subdivided by their staining characteristics when examined microscopically: neutrophils 60–70%, eosinophils 2–4% and basophils 0.5–2%. The neutrophils are those most concerned with the attack on bacteria and foreign particles. They rapidly collect at any site of infection or invasion by foreign matter, where they act by surrounding these particles or organisms by what is known as amoeboid movements. In this action the individual cells come up against the foreign body or particle and then surround it – the cell membrane breaks down and the foreign particle is taken into the cell itself and the cell membrane reforms. The eosinophils increase in numbers as a result of allergic reactions. The basophils manufacture heparin, which helps to prevent blood clotting in the blood vessels and histamine which causes the small blood vessels to dilate, usually as a result of local injury. The basophils are, however, by no means the sole source of either heparin or histamine.

The other group of white cells are the mononuclear leucocytes, each having a large round nucleus. They form some 25% of the white blood cells; the majority of these are lymphocytes which are associated with immunological responses.

There is a third non-liquid component to blood. These are the platelets; they are very small and are not cells. The blood platelets are associated with the clotting of blood. The mechanism of blood clotting is extremely complex and there are a large number of factors involved; it is the interaction of these various factors which produces clotting at the proper time. If one or more of the factors is missing then blood clotting may not occur. This happens in diseases such as haemophilia. In a greatly over-simplified scheme, clotting is produced by the production of thrombokinase from blood platelets and injured tissue, this then acts with a substance called prothrombin in the plasma, forming thrombin. This action can only take place if there is calcium present in the blood as is the normal state of affairs. The thrombin then acts with a protein in the blood known as fibrinogen producing fibrin. This fibrin will form a net which gradually becomes denser with the formation of more fibrin. The red and white corpuscles get caught up in this net and form the clot. Serum is the liquid that remains after a clot has formed, i.e. when all the clotting factors and cells have been removed.

The blood is the transport system of the body and as such has a variety of different functions:

1. It carries gases around the body. Oxygen is carried mainly in combination with haemoglobin in the red blood cells and is required by the tissues as part of their metabolism. A small amount of oxygen is actually dissolved in the plasma. Carbon dioxide is returned from the tissues to the lungs in both the red cells and the plasma. Nitrogen is also carried around the body dissolved in the plasma. This is an inert gas and forms the bulk of the air that we breathe. It is this nitrogen in the blood stream which causes the problems with deep sea diving; with an increased air pressure being breathed, a far greater amount of nitrogen becomes dissolved in the blood. If the diver is brought to the surface and therefore to a reduced pressure too rapidly, the nitrogen will no longer remain dissolved in the blood because of this decrease in pressure and it will form bubbles in the blood stream. These bubbles can block the small capillary vessels and this results in death of the tissues which would normally be supplied by these capillaries.

2. Food products are carried to the tissues of the body and waste material from tissue metabolism is carried either as carbon dioxide to the lungs or as other waste products to the kidneys where it is excreted in the urine. Various salts and electrolytes are carried around the body in the plasma. Many of these are required by the cells although they cannot be looked upon as a true food item.

3. White blood corpuscles are constantly transported around the blood stream so that they can be readily available as part of the defence system against infection or the penetration by any foreign material.

4. Heat is carried to the skin for removal by a combination of sweating and radiation.

Circulation of the Blood

Obviously in order to perform the functions that have been described the blood has to travel around the body. The heart pumps the blood down through the arteries into gradually decreasing sizes of vessels until the capillaries are reached. The arteries and the smaller arteries (arterioles) have muscular walls which stretch and contract (Fig. 1.59). The capillaries have extremely thin walls which are only one cell thick, so that salts,

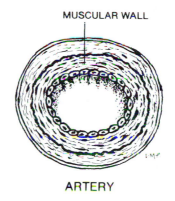

MUSCULAR WALL

ARTERY

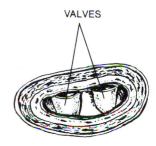

VALVES

VEIN

1.59   Cross-section of an Artery and a Vein. Note the muscular wall in the artery which is absent in the vein.

electrolytes, food substances and gases can pass through the walls into the tissues and waste substances can pass back again. The capillaries then gradually join together to form venules and veins. These have rather thicker walls than the capillaries but are very much thinner than arteries (Fig. 1.59). The veins have very little muscle in their walls and are far less elastic than the arteries.

As can be seen from the schematic diagram (Fig. 1.60) of the circulation, the heart (Figs 1.61 and 1.62) is a double pump. Each pump is divided into two parts, an atrium which receives the blood which it then passes through to a ventricle which gives the powerful contraction to push the blood around the circulation. Blood returning from the main part of the body enters the right atrium and passes from there to the right ventricle; from the right ventricle it is pumped to the lungs via the pulmonary artery and then around the capillaries of the lungs where it can get rid of the carbon dioxide and absorb oxygen. The blood going to the lungs is de-oxygenated and full of carbon dioxide; the blood leaving the lungs has lost most of its carbon dioxide and is loaded with oxygen. From

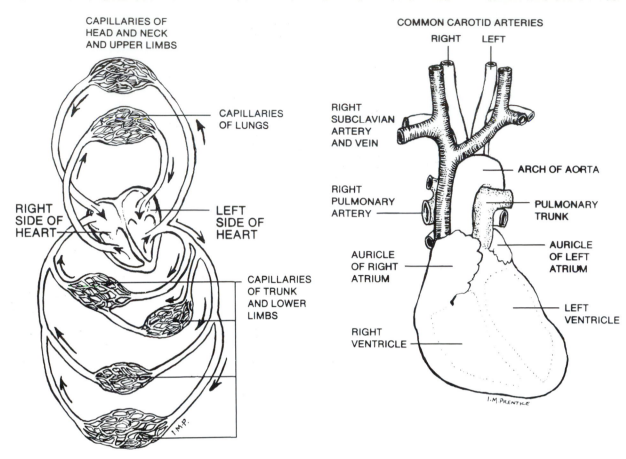

CAPILLARIES OF
HEAD AND NECK
AND UPPER LIMBS

CAPILLARIES
OF LUNGS

RIGHT
SIDE OF
HEART

LEFT
SIDE OF
HEART

CAPILLARIES
OF TRUNK
AND LOWER
LIMBS

COMMON CAROTID ARTERIES
RIGHT   LEFT

RIGHT
SUBCLAVIAN
ARTERY
AND VEIN

RIGHT
PULMONARY
ARTERY

AURICLE
OF RIGHT
ATRIUM

RIGHT
VENTRICLE

ARCH OF AORTA

PULMONARY
TRUNK

AURICLE
OF LEFT
ATRIUM

LEFT
VENTRICLE

1.60   Diagrammatic Representation of the Circulation.   1.61   The Heart.

the lungs, via the pulmonary veins, it enters the left side of the heart in the left atrium, passes from there to the left ventricle and is then pumped around the systemic circulation, as it is known. The circulation going through the lungs is known as the pulmonary circulation. Far greater effort is required from the heart to pump the blood round the very much larger systemic circulation, so the left side of the heart has thicker muscle than the right side. In its pumping action the atria first contract, filling the ventricles which expand to accept the blood. The ventricles thereafter immediately contract, giving the familiar heart sound of 'lub-dup', these being the contractions of the atria followed by the ventricles. There are valves at the entrance to each of the four chambers of the heart in order to prevent the blood being pushed back in the direction from which it came by the contraction of the heart muscle.

The rate of the heart beat is controlled by a special area of cardiac muscle known as the sinu-atrial node. This produces a rhythmic contraction and it acts completely in isolation. The wave of contraction of the muscles spreads through the atrial muscles causing a complete contraction of each atrium; it does not spread directly to the ventricle but the impulses go via another special node of cardiac muscle, known as the atrio-ventricular node, and then down a special bundle called the atrio-ventricular bundle. This causes the stimulation of the ventricular muscle which begins at the apex of the ventricle, squeezing the blood up into the aorta and on into the arteries. Although the sinu-atrial node has its own completely independent rhythmic contraction this is modulated by stimuli from the sympathetic and para-sympathetic nerves. Para-sympathetic stimulation causes a slowing in the rate of the heart beat and sympathetic stimulation causes an acceleration of the heart rate.

From the left side of the heart the blood is squeezed into the major artery which is known as

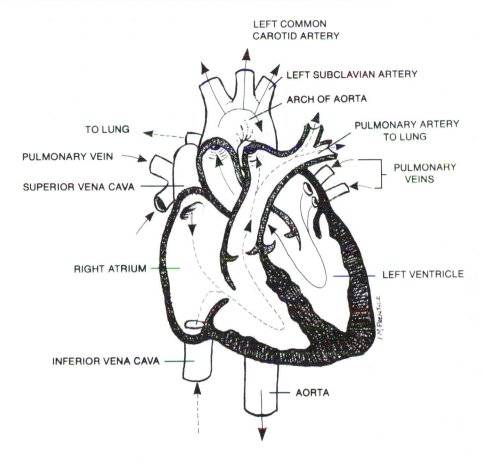

LEFT COMMON
CAROTID ARTERY

LEFT SUBCLAVIAN ARTERY

ARCH OF AORTA

TO LUNG

PULMONARY ARTERY
TO LUNG

PULMONARY VEIN

PULMONARY
VEINS

SUPERIOR VENA CAVA

RIGHT ATRIUM

LEFT VENTRICLE

INFERIOR VENA CAVA

AORTA

1.62   Diagram of the Circulation of the Blood within the Heart and Great Vessels.

the aorta; this then sub-divides into the lesser arteries and arterioles and then the capillaries, as described earlier. As the ventricle contracts the pressure in the aorta rises and this pressure is, of course, transmitted down through the rest of the circulation. To accommodate the blood the aorta and arteries expand; when the ventricle ceases to contract, valves between the aorta and the ventricle close due to the pressure of the blood in the aorta. Following this the muscles in the walls of the arteries contract as a direct result of the stimulus of the stretching of the vessel walls. This then acts as a secondary pump, squeezing the blood further out to the periphery. It also has a secondary effect of maintaining a pressure in the arteries in between the ventricular contractions. If this did not occur the pressure would rise during the ventricular contractions and then drop away to nothing when the ventricles ceased to contract.

It is this combined mechanism which gives the two readings which are obtained when the blood pressure is taken with a sphygmomanometer during a medical examination. The top pressure of about 120 millimetres of mercury, which is the average in a healthy adult, is the pressure which is reached at its maximum when the ventricle is contracting. When the ventricles relax pressure falls to about 80 millimetres of mercury and it is the combination of elasticity and muscular contraction in the walls of the arteries which maintains the pressure from falling below this level at the time of the heart muscle relaxation. The wave of pressure passing down through the arterial tree is detected as a pulse at various sites in the body where an artery can be compressed between an examining finger and some firm, but deeper structure. The pulse rate corresponds to each contraction of the heart muscle, so in this way the heart rate can be measured very simply.

In the normal, undiseased heart the pulse rate, that is the heart contractions, are completely regular and only the rate changes. The rate is increased by the sympathetic nervous system or the release of adrenalin into the blood system and is a natural response to an increase in demand by the rest of the body for oxygenated blood. The increase in heart rate is particularly apparent on exercise but everyone has been equally aware of an increase in heart rate during periods of stress and nervousness. This latter increase is produced by sympathetic nervous stimulation. Irregularity of the pulse, which reflects irregularity of the heart beat, occurs only in a diseased heart, notably in those people who have suffered from heart attacks or coronary thrombosis. This can cause damage to the very special portions of cardiac muscle, the sinu-atrial node and the atrio-ventricular node and the conducting pathways, thus interfering with the normal stimulation of the cardiac muscle.

In normal, healthy people there is a variation in heart rate corresponding to inspiration and expiration during respiration. On inspiration the heart rate will increase slightly and on expiration it will decrease a little. It is possible to detect this very easily in oneself by breathing deeply and slowly with a finger on the pulse.

The circulation through the lungs via the pulmonary arteries and capillaries and back by the pulmonary veins is mechanically very similar to the systemic circulation through the aorta, arteries and major veins. However, the pressures within the pulmonary circulation are less than those on the systemic side.

In the systemic circulation the blood flows from the aorta, arteries and arterioles to the capillaries which form what is known as the capillary bed, a gigantic mesh-work of minute vessels where the actual exchange of oxygen, carbon dioxide, food and waste products occurs.

From the capillaries the blood passes into tiny veins or venules and from there into gradually larger veins, and so back via the vena cava to the right side of the heart. During the heart beat the pulse wave is lost in the capillary system. Therefore the pressure within the veins remains at a far more constant level. There are, however, three totally separate factors which affect the pressure within the veins; the first is gravity – in the standing person from the level of the heart downwards there is the height of the column of blood above the level at which it might be measured in any one particular vein, thus in the veins of the feet there is a column of blood about four feet high in a six-foot person. Quite a lot of pressure is therefore required to push this column of blood up towards the heart. This is aided by valves within the veins preventing the blood from flowing in the wrong direction along

the veins. If the valves become incompetent and fail to hold the blood back the veins become very distended and it is this factor which produces what is known as varicose veins. Above the level of the heart there is of course negative pressure as the blood drains downhill from the head and neck towards the heart.

The second factor which aids the flow of blood along the veins is muscular contraction; many veins pass in between muscles in the limbs and trunk and as these muscles contract and tighten they will squeeze the blood along in one direction, i.e. towards the heart. This one-directional flow is brought about by the presence of the valves in the veins, as already mentioned, which only allow the blood to pass in one direction. This effect of the body muscles in aiding the circulation is sometimes referred to as the peripheral pump.

The third factor associated with the circulation is respiration: when inspiration takes place, that is breathing in, the contraction of the diaphragm and the contraction of the muscles between the ribs increases the size of the chest cavity, this produces a negative pressure within the chest cavity, sucking air into the lungs; at the same time this negative pressure will also affect the large veins within the chest producing a slight negative pressure within them, helping to draw the blood up from the peripheral circulation.

The Lymphatic System

While not strictly part of the cardio-vascular system the lymphatic system may be considered in this chapter as the lymph finally drains into the general circulation.

In the capillaries of the general circulation the walls are extremely thin so that some of the liquid portion of the blood can pass through. Once outside it forms tissue fluid, or interstitial fluid, lying between the cells in tissue spaces. Much of this passes back into the blood stream but the lymphatic system serves to drain any excess. It will also remove any particulate matter and large molecules, such as protein, which cannot pass directly into the blood because of their size. These particles or molecules are carried in the lymph. The lymphatic system starts as very fine capillaries which open directly into the tissue spaces so there are no walls for the tissue fluid and small particles to pass through. Once gathered into these capillaries the fluid is known as lymph. The lymph capillaries join together to form lymphatic vessels which, like veins, have valves, though they are far more numerous. The lymph vessels will join together and along their course will pass through lymph glands or nodes. These lymph nodes tend to become grouped together in various parts of the body notably the groins, axillae, inside the trunk along the base of the vessels coming from the alimentary tract and in the central part of the chest. These lymph nodes act as filters to prevent unwanted matter, such as bacteria, from gaining access to the blood stream. If they intercept a significant amount of infected material containing a large number of bacteria the lymph glands themselves can become painful, swollen and inflamed. This is particularly well shown in tonsilitis because the tonsils themselves are little masses of lymph gland tissue. After passing through the lymph nodes in the lymph circulation the lymph vessels converge and gradually produce larger lymph vessels which finally drain into the large veins before they reach the heart.

1.7 The Alimentary Canal and Digestion

The Alimentary Canal

This runs from the mouth as a continuous tube to the anus (Fig. 1.63). Food is taken into the mouth, where the particle size is broken down by chewing before the ball of food, or bolus, is swallowed. When this happens the back of the nasal cavity is closed by the soft palate. The roof of the mouth is made up of two portions, the front half being the hard palate which is fixed, and the back half being the soft palate, which is movable. This latter palate can be lifted up, closing the nasopharynx so that food cannot enter this area. At the same time the larynx, which lies at the beginning of the respiratory tubes or trachea, is pulled upwards and forwards and is closed by a fold of tissue known as the glottis. This prevents food entering the trachea. From the pharynx the bolus enters a tube known as the oesophagus which extends from the oro-pharynx (mouth and throat) down through the chest cavity and through a hole or hiatus in the diaphram to enter the stomach. The stomach acts mechanically as a large receptacle to contain the mass of food from a meal before it is passed on for further digestive processes, as well as initiating some of the chemical digestive processes. Following the stomach there is a short length of small bowel known as the duodenum. Leading into the duodenum is a duct (or tube) which is made up of

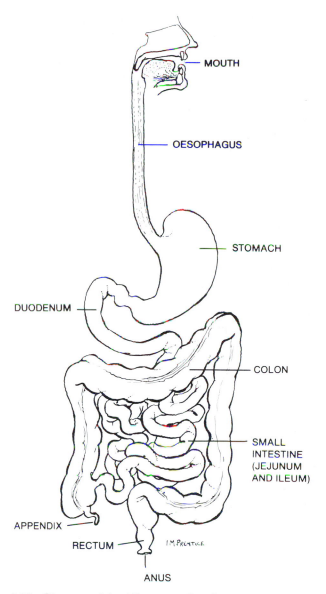

1.63   Diagram of the Alimentary Canal.

two other ducts which have joined together just before entering the lumen of the duodenum. These are

a)   the bile duct coming from the gall bladder and the liver to bring bile and bile salts, and

b)   the pancreatic duct which brings digestive enzymes from the pancreas.

Following the duodenum there is the remainder of the small intestine comprising the jejunum and then the ileum. The latter leads into the caecum, which is the beginning of the large bowel and from which the appendix arises. The remainder of the large bowel is made up of the ascending, transverse and descending parts of the colon which lead into the rectum. The rectum is another reservoir, this time for the residue of the food which forms the faeces.

Digestion

Digestion commences in the mouth. The contents of the alimentary tract are propelled along by waves of muscular contraction known as peristalsis. This peristaltic wave starts at the beginning of the oesophagus and is not under voluntary control. If the peristaltic waves become excessive as in an infection such as gastro-enteritis, they are perceived as severe spasms of pain or colic. At other times the peristaltic wave is not normally felt.

During the mechanical breakdown of food by chewing, saliva is mixed with the food. This helps to lubricate the food bolus so that it can be swallowed more easily and it also contains the first of the digestive enzymes – ptyalin. Ptyalin is the only digestive enzyme acting in the mouth and its role is to start the breakdown of starch, although its effect is not very significant in the overall process of starch digestion. If some starchy food such as bread or potato is chewed and moved around the mouth for a short period the breakdown of starch can be detected by the slight sweetening of the chewed material as the starch is changed to simple sugars. An enzyme is a complex chemical and acts as a biochemical catalyst. Digestive processes are brought about by various enzymes in order to break down the large complex food molecules into much simpler molecules which can be absorbed through the wall of the digestive tract and pass via the blood stream to the liver. Various enzymes enter the alimentary tract at different levels.

Each enzyme is very specific in its action and can only initiate or control one chemical process. Individual enzymes can only act in a very narrow range of pH (the measure of acidity or alkalinity). They all act optimally at body temperature and are destroyed by heat, thus cooked foods have all the enzymes that they may contain destroyed by the cooking. Food substances all have to be absorbed through the wall of the alimentary tract in order to give any benefit and large complex molecules cannot pass through. Without the necessary enzyme this molecular breakdown cannot occur. For example, human beings, although omniverous (eating flesh and vegetables), have no enzyme to break down cellulose which as a result passes straight through the bowel as roughage. Therefore humans could not live off grass, whereas herbivores do produce such an enzyme and can break down cellulose to produce usable carbohydrates.

In the stomach the food is temporarily stored and at the same time mixes with further secretions from the wall of the stomach. Part of the secretion is acid in order to adjust the pH of the contents and allow the gastric enzymes which are also secreted to work at the correct degree of acidity. There is little absorption of food substances through the stomach wall apart from possibly some simple sugars and alcohol. Food substances are passed in small quantities at a time from the stomach into the duodenum. Separating these two areas is a muscular valve or sphincter which opens periodically in order to allow further food to pass into the duodenum from the stomach.

In the duodenum further enzymes are introduced to the food. Intestinal juice containing a variety of enzymes is produced by the glands in the duodenal wall. Bile which is produced in the liver enters via the combined biliary and pancreatic ducts. The bile contains bile salts and bile pigment. Bile salts are concerned with the emulsification of fats and they assist in the absorption of the breakdown products of the fat, particularly fatty acids. The bile pigments are waste materials which have been produced by the liver, largely from the breakdown of red blood cells. Their injection into the small bowel at the duodenum is one of the methods by which they are removed from the body. Through the same combined opening in the duodenal wall, pancreatic juice is introduced into the duodenum. This contains enzymes which help further with the digestion of fat and enzymes which aid in the breakdown of sugar and proteins.

The function of the pancreas does not cease with the enzymes which are introduced into the bowel; within the substance of the pancreas are what is known as endocrine glands. These are glands which produce substances which are secreted directly into the blood stream. In the pancreas the endocrine glands are present in what is known as the Islets of Langerhans. These islets produce two hormones, insulin and glucagon. The insulin lowers the level of sugar in the blood and helps the body cells to store it as glycogen. Glucagon raises the level of sugar in blood by stimulating the breakdown of glycogen back into simple sugars. It is the lack of insulin due to a fault in the pancreas, which causes diabetes mellitus.

In its passage through the rest of the small bowel, enzymes continue to act on the food products, gradually breaking them down. When this breakdown has progressed sufficiently the nutrients are slowly absorbed into the intestinal wall. Most of this absorption has taken place by the time the food has reached the caecum and most of what remains then are waste products in a semi-liquid state. The main function of the large bowel is the absorption of water from the food residues in order to prevent too much being lost from the body. This also reduces the bulk of the waste matter to a solid form so it takes up less space. Only a very small amount of absorption of remaining nutrients from the digested food takes place through the large intestine walls. The amount absorbed is relatively insignificant.

Functions of the Liver

The liver is extremely complex and has many functions which can be considered under three main headings.

SECRETORY

Bile is produced by the liver and contains bile pigments and bile salts. The bile pigments are largely produced by the breakdown of aged red blood cells. They enter the duodenum and are then largely removed from the body in the faeces, but a small quantity is re-absorbed through the wall of the small intestine and enters the general blood circulation from which it is removed in the kidneys and excreted in the urine. Bile pigments are largely responsible for the yellow colour of the urine.

The bile salts also reach the duodenum along the bile duct and their role is to emulsify fats to aid further breakdown and absorption. Once bile has been formed in the liver, most of it is concentrated and stored temporarily in the gall bladder which is a pouch formed as an off-shoot of the bile duct. It is in the gall bladder that stones can form. These may comprise an excess of bile pigments or they may be crystaline deposits of bile salts.

Heparin is also produced by the liver but passes directly into the blood stream. Its function is to help prevent clotting of blood as it passes round in the normal circulation of the body.

STORAGE

a) Glycogen is stored in the liver. It is formed from glucose and is the chemical form in which it is stored. It can be made extremely quickly and broken down to glucose again equally rapidly when required. Glycogen is also stored in the muscles. When glucose is required as a result of exercise or fasting (both of which will produce a fall in the blood-sugar level) glucose is very rapidly formed by the re-conversion of glycogen. After a meal, glucose which is produced from the digestion of carbohydrate and is not immediately required for

metabolism is stored as glycogen. This replenishes the glycogen stores which may have become depleted between meals.

b) The liver is a storage site for vitamins A, the B complex and D. Originally the vitamins are absorbed from the food as they cannot be manufactured in the human body. From the storage depots in the liver the vitamins can be released as and when required.

c) Iron is stored following the breakdown of old red blood corpuscles; it is then released for the synthesis of haemoglobin which is required for new red corpuscles.

METABOLIC

The liver is responsible for the utilisation of proteins, fats and carbohydrates for the general nutrition of the body. These substances, which are mainly in a very complex form when they are taken as food, have to be broken down into far simpler substances to make them suitable for utilisation by the body. Following the breakdown of proteins into amino acids which are very much simpler chemical chains, the liver will then synthesise new proteins as and when required for the various physiological functions of the body. Although the human liver can also synthesise many of the necessary amino acids from basic simple molecules, there are certain amino acids which it cannot produce. These are known as 'essential amino acids'. They must be present in the diet either as amino acids or as more complex protein forms, otherwise the body will come deficient in them and will not function.

If too much glucose is present and the glycogen stores are full, the excess carbohydrate is converted into fat by the liver and is then stored elsewhere in the body. Most poisonous substances which are taken with the food are detoxicated by the liver. Detoxication means that the liver changes the chemical structure of these substances so that they are no longer poisonous. Following that they may be passed back into the blood stream to be removed by the kidneys or they may be excreted in the bile and through the bowel. In addition there are some potentially poisonous substances which are produced as a result of normal protein metabolism in the body. For example, ammonia is immediately converted into urea by the liver. The urea then passes into the circulation and is excreted by the kidneys in the urine. During the process of detoxication the liver cells can be damaged by various poisonous substances which have been ingested. Although new cells can be produced sometimes this does not always take place and the dead liver cells are replaced by fibrous tissue, thus gradually destroying the functional capabilities of the liver and leading to liver failure.Probably the commonest substance which can cause these problems in the liver is an excess intake of alcohol. Various drugs and some industrial chemicals also cause liver damage.

1.8 The Respiratory System

The respiratory system includes the anatomical structures which allow oxygen to be introduced into the body and carbon dioxide to be removed from the body as well as the actual chemical and physiological processes of respiration.

Anatomy of the Respiratory System

As can be seen from the diagram (Fig. 1.64), air enters via the nose. There, small hairs filter out much of the particulate matter and the air is moistened and warmed. From the nose it passes via the naso-pharynx through the larynx into the trachea. The trachea divides into right and left bronchus, each of which supply one lung. Each bronchus branches into bronchioles and continue to branch, decreasing steadily in size until each terminal branch leads into a little air sac or alveolus (Fig. 1.65). The walls of the alveoli are very thin so that oxygen (and other gases) can pass through into the blood stream and carbon dioxide can pass back from the blood into the alveoli and hence be expelled through the nose to the outside.

During breathing, inspiration and expiration are normally reflexly controlled but they can up to a certain point be modified voluntarily. Beyond this point the reflexes can no longer be suppressed by the voluntary centres of the brain and will once more take over. Inspiration is brought about mechanically by a contraction of the diaphram which descends towards the abdominal cavity, increasing the available height within the chest cavity. The intercostal muscles between the ribs contract at the same time and as a result the ribs swing outwards and upwards increasing the diameter of the chest cavity. This increase in the chest capacity sucks air into the lungs through the respiratory passages.

Expiration is normally brought about by a passive elastic recoil of the diaphram and the rib cage when contraction of the muscles ceases and they relax. Forcible expiration begins to occur when physiological demands bring about an increased rate and depth of respiration. Although quiet inspiration involves mainly the diaphram and intercostal muscles, deeper inspiration or panting involves in addition the muscles around the shoulder girdle and some of the muscles in the back. These additional muscles are sometimes referred to as the accessory muscles of respiration. Forceful expiration involves a very strong contraction of the muscles of the abdominal wall. The latissimus dorsi and serratus posterior muscles are those mainly involved in the back. The lungs cannot be completely emptied even by a very forceful expiration and the residual air amounts to about one litre. On maximum inspiration about a further three and a half litres of air can be drawn into the lungs which will then mix with the residual air. Normally, at rest, about half a litre of air is inspired and expired on each cycle.

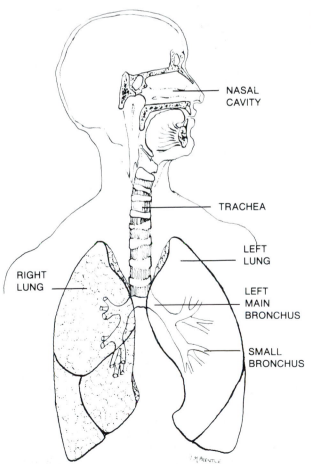

NASAL CAVITY

TRACHEA

LEFT LUNG

RIGHT LUNG

LEFT MAIN BRONCHUS

SMALL BRONCHUS

1.64   Diagram of the Respiratory Passages.

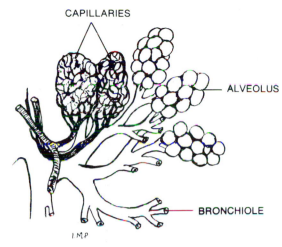

CAPILLARIES

ALVEOLUS

BRONCHIOLE

I M P

1.65   Alveolus in Lung. This shows the terminal part of the air-passage (the alveolus) with the mass of capillaries in close proximity which allows the interchange of gases between the air in the alveoli and the blood in the capillaries.

Respiration

Respiration may be considered in two parts:
1.   external respiration;
2.   internal or tissue respiration.

EXTERNAL RESPIRATION

External respiration takes place in the lungs. Air which contains the oxygen required for tissue metabolism is carried to the lungs through the respiratory passages, ending up in the alveoli. The walls of the alveoli have a large number of capillaries containing blood and the separation between the blood stream and the air in the alveoli is about two cells thick. At this point oxygen passes from the alveoli into the deoxygenated blood which is being brought from the right side of the heart. At the same time the carbon dioxide from the blood passes in the opposite direction from the blood stream through into the alveoli. The expired air therefore contains a decreased amount of oxygen and an increased amount of carbon dioxide compared with the inspired air.

INTERNAL OR TISSUE RESPIRATION

Internal or tissue respiration takes place in every living cell of the body. It is the mechanism which provides the energy which is required for all bodily activity. The commonest energy-producing material to be oxidized is carbohydrate in the form of glucose. The glucose combines with oxygen to give

carbon dioxide, water and energy. This reaction is aided by an enzyme. Substances other than the carbohydrates may also be oxidized. These require different enzymes as all enzymes are extremely specific in their action. If fat is oxidized, rather more oxygen is required than if carbohydrate is oxidized.

Transport of Oxygen and Carbon Dioxide

In the alveoli in the lungs the oxygen in the air becomes dissolved in a thin film of moisture on the cell walls. It then passes by diffusion through the cells into the blood plasma. Most of the oxygen which diffuses through combines with the haemoglobin in the blood to form oxyhaemoglobin with a very small amount remaining dissolved in the blood plasma. The presence of the haemoglobin allows about seventy times as much oxygen to be carried around the blood stream as oxyhaemoglobin than would take place by a simple solution of oxygen in the blood plasma. At the cells where the oxygen is utilised carbon dioxide is produced. This carbon dioxide dissolves to form carbonic acid, which is carried mainly as bicarbonate in the plasma. There is also a small amount of dissolved carbonic acid and some of the carbon dioxide will combine with the haemoglobin once the oxygen has been displaced in order to produce carbaminohaemoglobin.

When the deoxygenated blood returns to the lungs the carbaminohaemoglobin breaks down to liberate carbonic acid. Some of the bicarbonate will also break down to liberate further carbonic acid which diffuses across the cell membrane into the alveoli of the lungs and hence to the outside air.

Control of Respiration

The control of the rate of respiration is largely reflex although it can be modified to a certain extent voluntarily. The main controlling factor is the acidity of the blood as determined by the level of carbonic acid. The greater the amount of carbon dioxide being produced in the tissues, the higher the level of blood carbonic acid and the more acid the blood. This alteration in acidity is detected by the respiratory control centres and the depth and rate of inspiration and expiration will be increased to allow the extra carbon dioxide to be removed through the lungs. A decrease in oxygen level of the blood will also stimulate reflex centres and cause an increase in rate of depth of respiration, but a fall in oxygen level is much less of a stimulus than an increase in carbon dioxide in the form of carbonic acid. By far the most important factor is the acidity as reflected in pH level of the blood.

Incidentally, there are two forms of oxide of carbon. Carbon monoxide is produced by exhaust gases and when carboniferous fuels are incompletely oxidized. Carbon monoxide is extremely poisonous because it combines with the haemoglobin in the blood, preventing the combination of oxygen, and thus kills by depriving the tissues of the oxygen they require. Carbon dioxide is formed when carboniferous fuels (which of course includes glucose and other foods) are completely oxidized.

It is not itself poisonous as it is easily displaced by oxygen at the haemoglobin molecule. However, inhalation of very high levels of carbon dioxide will produce very rapid and severe changes in the pH of the blood. This increase in acidity due to the increase in carbonic acid totally upsets the acid base balance in the body and death may follow very rapidly.

Smoking cigarettes produces a significant amount of carbon monoxide. This combines as described with the haemoglobin, interfering with oxygen transport. Therefore the smoker will be less able than the non-smoker to provide the muscles with the necessary increase in oxygen demanded by any athletic activity, including dancing. As a result his performance will be a little less good than it would have been if he were a non-smoker.

1.9 The Excretory System

The excretory system is made up of two kidneys, two ureters, a bladder and an urethra (Fig. 1.66). From each kidney there is a ureter which goes down to the urinary bladder, from which the urethra carries the urine to the outside. The kidneys lie within the upper part of the abdominal cavity behind the liver and stomach. However, they are surrounded by fat and are not free-floating within the abdominal cavity. The ureters run down the posterior abdominal wall to enter the bladder which lies within the pelvis. The actual excretory functions only take place in the kidneys. The ureters, bladder and urethra are there to transport and store the urine and allow intermittent discharge externally. Without the storage capacity of the bladder there would be a constant drip of urine occurring.

Blood is carried to each kidney by a large renal artery and is returned from the kidney by a renal vein on each side. Within the substance of the

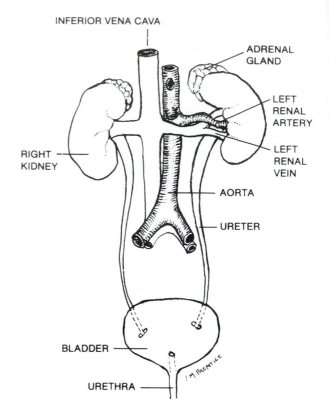

1.66   The Excretory System.

kidney the arteries divide to form smaller vessels. The point where excretory activity occurs is known as the glomerulus (Fig. 1.67). This is a knot of capillaries. The vessel supplying this knot is wider in diameter than the vessel carrying the blood away. As a result the blood within the glomerulus is under increased pressure. At this point some of the fluid component of the blood is filtered through the cells walls into a collection portion known as Bowman's capsule. The cell membranes between the blood stream and Bowman's capsule are such that the blood corpuscles and the blood proteins are unable to pass through and so remain within the blood. The fluid which passes through to Bowman's capsule is made up of water with small amounts of various salts and nitrogenous waste products produced by the breakdown of proteins. This latter is largely in the form of urea. At this point there is also some sugar, water-soluble vitamins and various other substances that are normally present in the blood stream.

The liquid passes from Bowman's capsule to the first convoluted tubule where all the sugar, vitamins and some of the other substances and some water are absorbed again (Fig. 1.68). From there it passes through the Loop of Henle where further water is

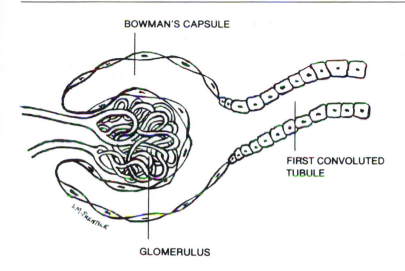

BOWMAN'S CAPSULE

FIRST CONVOLUTED
TUBULE

GLOMERULUS

1.67   A Glomerulus and Bowman's
Capsule.

absorbed. It is at this point that the amount of
water which is absorbed will vary in order to adjust
the osmotic pressure of the blood correctly.
Following the Loop of Henle is the second
convoluted tubule where the pH is adjusted. Urine
is normally on the slightly acid side. Following the
second convoluted tubule is the collecting duct.
This will join with other collecting ducts from other
convoluted tubules. Finally all joining together they
form the pelvis of the kidney, leading into the
upper end of the ureter at the point where it leaves
the kidney. The kidneys are extremely efficient at
stabilising the water and electrolyte balance in the
body, which is only able to tolerate very small
variations from the normal ratio between the
various electrolytes and the water. The control is
via hormones. The pituitary gland produces a
hormone which encourages water retention while
the hormones of the adrenal cortex encourage the
retention of sodium and an increased loss of
potassium. If a great deal of fluid is taken by
mouth the urine increases in quantity and becomes
very dilute. This is achieved by a decrease in the
absorption of water from the Loop of Henle.
However, in hot climates when there is a
considerable amount of perspiration the urine
output decreases in quantity and becomes very
much more concentrated. The sensation of thirst is
brought about by a very small increase in the
osmotic pressure of the blood affecting certain cells
in the brain.

The kidneys have an additional function
inasmuch as they produce two hormones, renin and
erythropoietin. Renin affects the maintenance of
blood pressure. If pressure within the renal artery
decreases then some quantities of renin are released
in order to stimulate an increase in the blood

1.68   Diagram of a Renal Tubule.

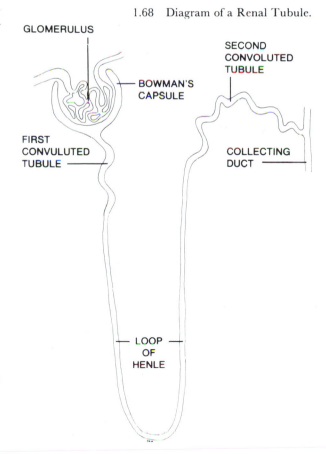

GLOMERULUS

SECOND
CONVOLUTED
TUBULE

BOWMAN'S
CAPSULE

FIRST
CONVOLUTED
TUBULE

COLLECTING
DUCT

LOOP
OF
HENLE

pressure. Should the blood pressure fall below a certain level, as may occur in states of surgical shock where there has been a considerable loss of blood, then filtration from the glomerulus into Bowman's capsule ceases and the person enters a state of renal failure. Unless this is corrected, death will follow because of the steady increase in the nitrogenous waste products and the total upset of the salt and water balance of the body.

The second hormone, erythropoietin, helps to control the production of red blood cells.

1.10 The Endrocrine System

The endocrine system comprises a number of endocrine organs. These are glands which pass their secretions, known as hormones, directly into the blood stream. The glands have no ducts in which to collect the secretions, unlike those glands which lie in the walls of the alimentary tract. A hormone is a compound formed within the gland. It is carried from the gland in the blood and its action is to influence the activity of another organ or organs. The two regulating systems of the body, i.e. the nervous system and the endocrine system, are very closely linked. In some instances the production of hormones is controlled directly by nervous impulses. The main function of the endocrine system as a whole is to maintain homeostasis, i.e. the constancy of the internal environment of the body.   The mode of action of hormones is biochemically extremely complicated and outside the scope of this book.

The actual endocrine glands are: the pituitary gland, which has anterior and posterior lobes with separate functions and which lies in the base of the skull, closely associated with the brain; the thyroid and parathyroid glands, which are anatomically intimately associated, lying in the front of the lower part of the neck; the adrenal glands, composing the cortex and medulla, with separate functions and lying like little caps on the superior poles of each kidney. Apart from these well localised glands there are scattered areas of cells in various other organs, in particular the so-called Islets of Langerhans in the pancreas, the interstitial cells in the testes and the follicular cells in the ovaries. There are also some cells in the walls of the stomach and small intestine. In pregnancy some cells of the placenta can have a temporary endocrine effect.

The anterior lobe of the pituitary gland is sometimes said to be the conductor of the endocrine orchestra. This lobe is regulated by hormones produced in the hypothalamus of the brain. The hormones secreted by the anterior lobe of the pituitary then in their turn regulate the activities of the various other endocrine organs. Normally it is the concentration of hormones in the blood circulation which will regulate the stimulation or otherwise of the further production of hormone. In other words, if the hormone level is high, this will tend to suppress the stimulatory effects which would encourage the production of further hormone (Fig. 1.69). Conversely, if the level of hormone in the blood stream falls to a low level, this will then stimulate the activity of the endocrine glands to produce more hormone. In most hormones their life in the blood stream is relatively short, sometimes only a few minutes, before being destroyed. This enables the equilibrium to be very accurately and constantly adjusted. The hormones in the blood stream are either de-activated by the liver or excreted through the kidney.

The endocrine glands themselves can be the subject of disease and this may result in either the over-production or under-production of the relevant hormone. Probably the common condition that is seen and with which most people will at least be acquainted, is that of thyrotoxicosis, when the thyroid gland produces an excess of hormone, one of the side effects of which is to produce the staring, pop-eyed appearance of a patient who is thyrotoxic. Additionally, the patient tends to be very overactive, lose weight, and feel hot and sweat freely. In general the over-action or under-action of an endocrine gland also produces changes in the production of hormones from other endocrine organs due to the close relationship that there is between one endocrine gland and another. This means that when there is, for instance, an over-production of hormone by a diseased gland, the clinical picture becomes complicated because of the other endocrine effects which also become manifest, even though the other endocrine glands themselves are not the subject of disease.

The symptoms which are caused by the alteration in hormone level from the diseased gland are known as primary symptoms. Secondary symptoms are those which are produced by the variation in hormone level at the other endocrine glands which are not themselves the seat of the disease. It is this widespread upset in the endocrine pattern produced by an excess or lack of hormone that makes the administration of steroid drugs such as cortisone a potentially hazardous process and not a treatment that should be undertaken lightly and without proper consideration of the potential and grave side effects. It must be emphasised that this

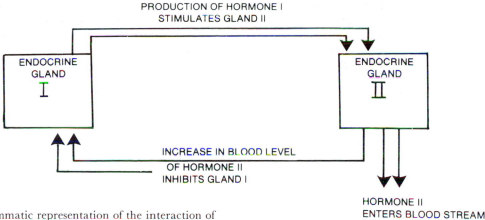

1.69 Diagrammatic representation of the interaction of hormones between two endocrine glands.

only applies when cortisone is given by mouth. The steroid which is used for injection to control local effects during the course of treatment of various local injuries or inflammations does not have these side effects. This preparation of the steroid (usually hydrocortisone acetate) is not absorbed generally into the circulation as it is a suspension and remains where it has been placed. It does, however, have its own complications which are of a local nature and these will be considered later in the section on injury and the treatment of injuries (see **Section 2.5** Medical and Surgical Treatments, page 92).

Actions of the Endocrine Glands

These will be dealt with very briefly as any great detail would be irrelevant to the probable requirements of the reader.

THE PITUITARY GLAND

The anterior pituitary gland produces six hormones. The growth hormone is secreted in greatest quantity during childhood but there is some secretion during the rest of adult life in order to maintain normal body structure and function. Occasionally it is administered clinically in a child who is very small and underdeveloped. However, like the use of any other hormone, its administration is fraught with undesirable side effects and dangers and its use should not be undertaken lightly.

The thyrotrophic hormone stimulates the thyroid, helping to control the level of thyroxin which is produced by the thyroid gland. The adrenocorticotrophic hormone stimulates the cortex of the adrenal gland to produce its hormones. These hormones from the adrenal cortex are associated with the regulation of carbohydrate

metabolism and, less importantly, make sex hormone production.

The follicular stimulating hormone, the luteinizing hormone and prolactin all have activities on the gonads (ovaries and testes), are responsible for the maturation of the ova and spermatozoa, and are associated in part with the development and regulation of menstruation and the post-pregnancy regulation of milk production.

The regulation of the production of anterior pituitary hormones is through the hypothalamus in the brain, which produces stimulating or inhibiting hormones acting on the anterior pituitary. The regulation is also controlled by the level of hormone produced by the other endocrine glands on which the anterior pituitary itself has an effect.

There are two hormones from the posterior pituitary. The most important hormone produced is vasopressin, the chief action of which is as an anti-diuretic hormone. In other words, it acts on the kidney, increasing the amount of water which is absorbed from the collecting tubules, thus preventing excessive water loss from the body. Additionally, it has a very minor effect on the maintenance of arterial blood pressure by causing contraction of the smooth muscle in the blood vessel walls. This latter effect was the first one discovered by researchers, hence the name given to the hormone. The other hormone which is produced by the posterior pituitary, oxytocin, only has an effect in the female during childbirth and lactation. Like the anterior pituitary, the posterior pituitary secretions are controlled by the hypothalamus in the brain.

THE THYROID GLAND

The thyroid gland produces thyroxin and an associated hormone, both of which stimulate cell metabolism. Additionally, the gland produces calcitonin (thyrocalcitonin), which prevents the transfer of calcium from the bones to the blood stream. It thus brings about a lowering of calcium in the blood stream as it still allows the transfer of calcium from the blood plasma into the bones. The control of production of the hormones from the thyroid is by the anterior pituitary.

There are four parathyroid glands, which lie closely applied to the back of the thyroid gland. They produce a parathyroid hormone which is responsible for an increase in the concentration of calcium in the blood. The action is by increasing the absorption of calcium from the urine while still in the kidneys. It increases the breakdown of calcium in the bone, thus pushing it into the circulation, and it also increases the absorption of calcium from the intestine in the presence of adequate quantities of vitamin D.

THE ADRENAL GLANDS

The adrenal glands consist of the cortex and the medulla. The cortex produces hormones which regulate the electrolyte and water balance in the body, sexual function and carbohydrate metabolism, The adrenal medulla produces two forms of adrenalin. The effect of adrenalin is to increase the rate of the heart and increase the capacity of the heart to push the blood through the circulation and therefore raises the blood pressure. It also constricts the blood vessels supplying all the alimentary tract and constricts the blood vessels of the skin. This is the reason why people go pale with fright or in other situations of stress, caused by blood being diverted to the heart and skeletal muscles so as to deal with the emergency which may have arisen. It also has a general arousal function so as to make the person more alert. It is sometimes referred to as the fight or flight hormone because in more primitive conditions it was to prepare someone to either fight the attacker or run away. Under present day conditions, it is the hormone which produces the feelings of apprehension, increased pulse rate and butterflies in the stomach before examinations, performances or times of modern stress. The action of the adrenal medulla is stimulated by nerve impulses through the sympathetic system.

The testes and ovaries are responsible for the production of sex hormones, testosterone in the male and oestrogen and progesterone in the female. At puberty the levels increase greatly and the balance alters. This produces the secondary sex characteristics, the general maturation of the body and the onset of menstruation in the female. In particular, after the onset of puberty and maturity it becomes difficult and probably impossible to stretch fibrous tissue such as there is in the ligaments and capsules.

The Islets of Langerhans in the pancreas produce two hormones, insulin and glucagon. These two hormones are responsible for regulating the transport of glucose and its storage by changing it into glycogen and also the breakdown of glycogen to produce glucose when required (see **Section 1.7 Digestion, page 44**). It is the lack of production of insulin which produces the well-known condition of diabetes mellitus.

1.11 Anatomical Points Relevant to Ballet

The overall use of the muscles is directed at attaining correct stance and weight placement. To this end the muscles can be considered in groups rather than as individuals. Correct use of these various groups starts at the head and shoulder girdle and encompasses all the groups down through the trunk and legs to the feet. It is only when all groups are *working correctly and in balance with each other* that correct stance and weight placement will be obtained and the dancer will be completely stable in all the many and varied positions required during the execution of ballet technique.

Stance and Muscle Groupings (Fig. 1.70)

Trunk stabilisation is achieved by the spine extensors, i.e. the long back muscles assisted by the short muscles between the individual vertebrae, and the trunk flexors which are made up largely of the abdominal muscles. The trunk has to be balanced on the lower limbs. This is achieved by the balance betwen the hip extensors (the gluteals) and the hip flexors, which between them control the tilting of the pelvis.

The knees in many people are relaxed when standing still and stabilisation is achieved by the ligaments alone. However, in most dancers there is usually some degree of hyperextension of the knees (swayback knees) which varies from mild to very marked and in these instances the knee has to be stabilised in neutral by contractions occurring in the quadriceps and hamstring muscles. Of course, it is perfectly possible for a person even with very marked swayback knees to allow them to drop into hyperextension and stand thus, which unfortunately

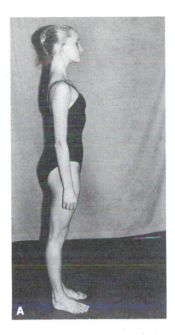

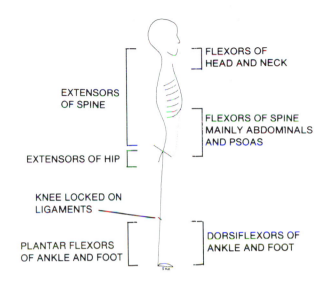

1.70   The main muscle groups controlling posture when standing.

FLEXORS OF HEAD AND NECK

EXTENSORS OF SPINE

FLEXORS OF SPINE MAINLY ABDOMINALS AND PSOAS

EXTENSORS OF HIP

KNEE LOCKED ON LIGAMENTS

PLANTAR FLEXORS OF ANKLE AND FOOT

DORSIFLEXORS OF ANKLE AND FOOT

A. and B. From the side.   B

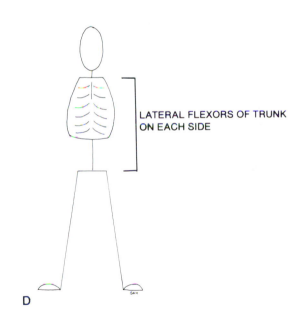

LATERAL FLEXORS OF TRUNK ON EACH SIDE

C. and D. From the front.   D

one frequently sees happening in dancers. However, this position in dance pushes the weight much too far back and leads to technical faults and injuries. The rectus femoris muscle, which is part of the quadriceps complex, and all the hamstring muscles, cross in front of and behind the hip joint respectively so they also play a role in stabilising the pelvis in relation to the thighs.

Below the knee, stability depends upon a constant interaction between the calf muscles which plantar-flex the foot (i.e. a movement in the direction of pointing the foot) and the muscles in the front of the leg which dorsi-flex the foot. In the foot itself the intrinsic muscles are maintaining the longitudinal and transverse arches as well as the general foot posture. Note also that the superficial calf muscle – the gastrocnemius – crosses behind the knee, taking its origin from the back of the lower end of the femur, so it also plays a part in knee posture.

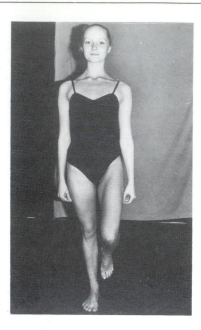

1.71   Standing correctly on one foot, showing the line of centre of gravity falling through the supporting foot. The pelvis and trunk remain aligned correctly.

1.72   Standing on one foot incorrectly. The pelvis and the trunk are mis-aligned and crooked.

As will be seen when standing *correctly* on one foot, the line of the centre of gravity is moved sideways so it falls through the supporting foot (Fig. 1.71).

Note that the trunk and pelvis do not alter. The hip on the supporting leg is adducted and stability is achieved by the interaction between the adductors and the abductors (gluteus medius, gluteus minimus and tensor fasciae latae. Gluteus maximus is a hip extensor).

Unfortunately and only too often the adjustment of the line of centre of gravity is made totally incorrectly and the subsequent rather bizarre posture remains uncorrected (Fig. 1.72).

In the turn-out position the stance remains basically the same but the area of weight bearing on the floor is much narrower from front to back so the postural muscles have to be even more finely and accurately tuned to maintain correct balance with the minimum of effort.

Turn-out (Fig. 1.73)

The constraints which limit the possible range of turn-out at the hip are (a) bony, (b) capsule and ligaments and (c) muscles. The configuration of the bones of the hip joint produce an absolute limitation in the possible range which cannot be

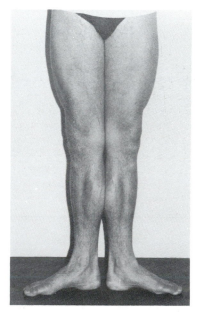

1.73   The turn-out position correctly held.

altered by exercises or stretching. These bony limits
are made up of the depth of the acetabulum (the
socket) and the angle at which the head and neck
of the femur are set on the shaft of the femur.

Surrounding the hip joint is the capsule and
various ligaments. The latter are notably the
ilio-femoral ligaments or Y-shaped ligament, the
ischio-femoral ligament and the pubo-femoral
ligament. Tightness in these fibrous soft tissues will
limit turn-out. It is extremely difficult to stretch
ligaments and, to a lesser extent, joint capsules after
the age of puberty because the fibrous tissue, of
which these are composed, becomes mature and
practically non-stretchable.

Tightness in muscles, usually the adductors, can
play a part in limiting turn-out but if these are
involved in the restriction (which is rare, except
when it occurs secondarily following an injury) they
can usually be stretched out gently.

Control of turn-out is by interaction between the
external rotators and the internal rotators of the
hip joint. The most important external rotator is
the adductor group of muscles. The small muscles
around the hip joint are stabilisers of the joint and
play little part in either external rotation or
internal rotation. They should be looked upon as
adjustable ligaments. The external rotation effect of
the adductors is balanced mainly by the ilio-psoas
muscle aided to a much lesser extent by various
other muscles.

There is no *active* external rotation (turn-out)
possible at any level of the leg below the hip joint.
A small amount of extra turn-out can be obtained
when standing because of friction between the foot
and the floor which can be used to give a *passive*
external rotation force to the whole leg and this can
produce a rotation between the knee and the foot.
This passive external rotation can produce very
damaging results (see **Section 5.7**). When the knee
is flexed there is some active and passive rotation
possible within the knee joint but this does not
occur when the knee is extended.

Plié (Fig. 1.74)

The posture and the pelvis remain unchanged
during a plié. In particular the lumbar spine
becomes neither lordotic nor over-flattened (tucking
of pelvis). The hips are flexed and turn-out is
maintained by the adductors. Hip flexion is
accompanied by knee flexion brought about by a
controlled relaxation of the quadriceps muscles.
The hamstrings play little part as it is gravity which
will be bringing the body down into the plié
position and it is gravity which is opposed by the

1.74 Plié.

From the front.

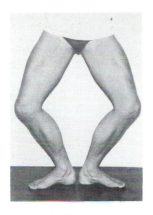

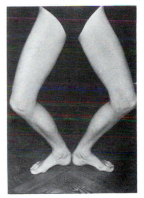

From the side.

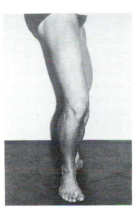

Note that the knee is
reasonably well aligned
over the foot but is not
quite perfect, though
better in the boy. If
there is any degree of
tibial torsion (which is
very common in
dancers) then it will
never be possible to
obtain 'exact alignment
as the foot is externally
rotated in relation to the
knee.

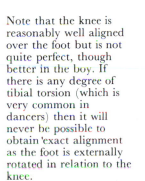

1.75   Plié.

With the knees in front of
the feet and the feet rolling.

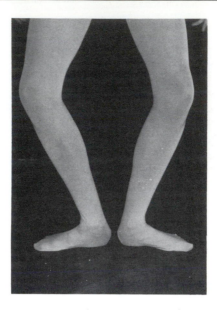

From the front.

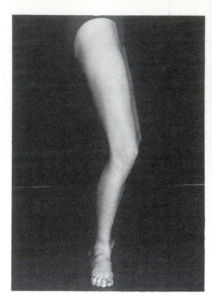

From the side.

quadriceps which are relaxing slowly. Ankle
dorsi-flexion is largely passive and the calf muscles
gradually relax. As the plié progresses to a grand
plié and the heels leave the floor the ankle
dorsi-flexion is still a passive movement. However,
during the whole range of plié the intrinsic muscles
are acting to maintain foot posture in the same
manner as when standing. This is achieved by the
natural maintenance of good tone and strong
intrinsic muscles and not by an active
over-contraction.

Rising from the plié is brought about by active
contraction of the quadriceps and the hip extensors.
This is achieved by pushing down on the floor with
the feet and not merely by straightening the knees.
Turn-out is maintained the whole time by the
adductors. Ankle movements remain passive but the
heels should be allowed to come down onto the
floor as soon as possible and not kept off the floor,
which would require an active calf muscle
contraction and produce strain of the quadriceps.

Care must be taken to ensure that the knees and
feet remain aligned, particularly when going down
as far as a grand plié, as it is only too easy to allow
the heels to swing forward and the feet to roll,
producing an over-turned situation when coming
out of the plié (Fig. 1.75).

On rising from a plié care must be taken to
maintain the weight correctly over the feet
otherwise there is a marked tendency to come up
with the weight too far back. This can occur even
if the weight has been correct at the start of the
plié and while going down into the full plié. There
is a great tendency to push the weight back as the
dancer comes up.

Note: In order to maintain the correct
alignment and weight placement throughout
both the plié and the rise, it is essential that
the dancer feels the contact with the floor
through the feet and that he actually pushes
down into the floor so that he has the
sensation that he is pushing himself up from
below. This is particularly important in
coming up from the plié when the dancer
must *not* feel that he is merely straightening
his knees.

Tendu (Fig. 1.76)

This term means stretched and its main benefit
when correctly carried out is its effect on the feet.
It is very important that the correct placement in
the trunk and supporting leg is maintained
throughout, otherwise the exercise is totally useless.
If the position of these other areas is incorrect and
the weight is back the tendu becomes ineffective
and the muscles in the feet are not stimulated and
therefore do not benefit.

1.76   Tendu.

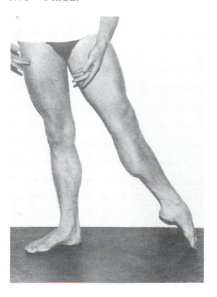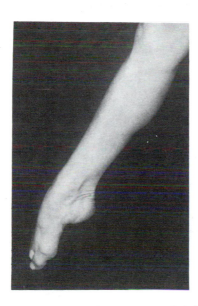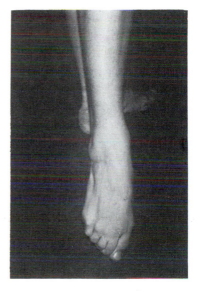

Note that the stretch carries on to
the tips of the toes, which remain
straight.

Incorrect tendu with the toes curled. This is a younger dancer still in training
whose intrinsic muscles have not yet fully strengthened.

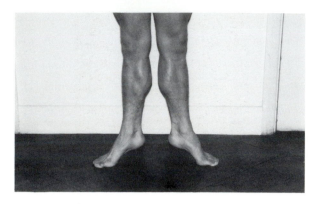

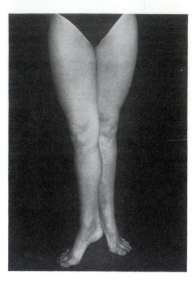

To half pointe (demi-pointe or à demi).

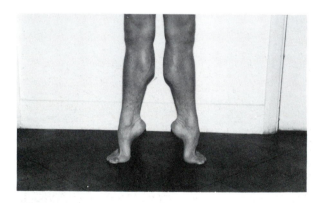

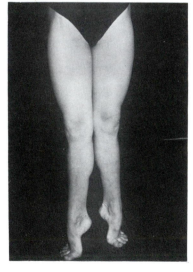

To three-quarter pointe (à trois quarts).

1.77   Rise.

Rise (Fig. 1.77)

The trunk and pelvis move as one and come slightly forward with the line of the centre of gravity, to lie over the toes when the rise is completed. This is achieved by pushing up from the floor with the forefoot in order to maintain correct alignment and weight-bearing. Anatomically, the calf muscles contract, lifting the heel and hindfoot against gravity. At the same time the tone is maintained in the gluteals, the adductors, the hamstrings and the knee extensors (quadriceps) giving the feeling of being lifted up from above and not pushed up from below. In the presence of swayback knees the balance between the quadriceps and hamstrings is exceptionally important in order to maintain correct knee control.

The rise can stop at either half pointe or three-quarter pointe. See *Note*, page 56)

Pointe (Figs 1.78 and 1.79)

To achieve a position on pointe the progression is as
through a rise to half pointe then to three-quarter
pointe and finally to full pointe, using the same
muscles and the whole movement being fully
controlled. Coming down from pointe is just as
controlled and in the reverse order. To maintain
full control throughout necessitates strength in the
intrinsic muscles just as importantly as in the calf
and in the other leg muscles, all of which have to
work much harder to produce the rise.

Once on pointe the base becomes very small so
that weight transference has to be very accurate.
This requires even finer control of total position
and line of head, trunk and limbs.

On pointe, relative strength and stability are the
crucial factors required to maintain the position.
Relative strength does not mean pure brute
strength but rather the accurate and delicate
balance between one muscle group and another.

However, additionally, inherent (rather than
acquired) proprioceptive skills are an essential part
of the maintenance of balance on pointe, although
practise can still and will improve these skills. The
ability to balance, which is a combination of
proprioceptive feedback, efficiency of the balance
mechanisms in the middle ear and to a very minor
degree visual reflexes, is very variable from one
individual to another and a skill which can only be
improved to a limited extent. It is certainly
associated also with the speed of response
(subconscious) to the various stimuli from the
different sources.

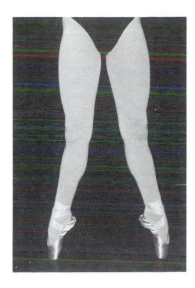

1.78   On Pointe. This is reached by means of a relevé in
which the dancer passes through the various levels of
pointe to reach the full pointe position (sur la pointe).

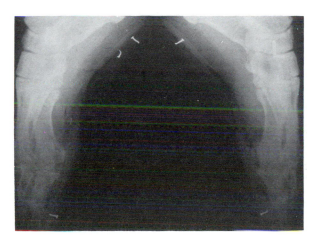

1.79   On Pointe. X-ray of a dancer on pointe.

AGE TO START POINTE WORK

For many years it has been said that twelve is the
age to start pointe work. This is, however, totally
incorrect and there is no particular age at which
pointe work should be commenced. The only factor
which matters is the state of development of the
child and to be dogmatic about an age does not
make any reference to the child's maturity or
immaturity.

There is no shame and certainly no disadvantage
in starting pointe work later rather than earlier.
Starting before the child is physically and
technically ready is potentially very harmful.
Waiting until the correct time, as far as that
individual child is concerned, will have very
positive advantages. There will be far less risk of
injury. She will be able to achieve the correct
technique more readily and accurately and will
progress more speedily, being able to gain

confidence more rapidly than if she started before being physically ready.

Pointe work should not begin until growth has settled in the feet. Strength must have been achieved in the feet and around the ankles with full control of all the relevant joints. However, it does not end with the feet. It is as important for strength to be present and well controlled higher up, in particular children must be able to hold the turn-out at the hips and be generally stable around the hips when on both legs or on one leg alone. Additionally, they must be strong and stable in the trunk. If there is any weakness or inadequate control of the muscles in the trunk, hip and thigh area then they will become extremely unstable and unsafe when coming up onto pointe. Far better results are obtained if the onset of pointe work is deferred until children are ready physically. Certainly, pointe work should be avoided if the feet and body are still soft, very mobile and floppy.

Great caution is required when dealing with any child who has hypermobile feet and ankles. Although this excessively pointed foot can look very pleasing when it is the working leg and the foot is in the air, it is the type of foot that is at greatest risk once pointe work has started. It is at this time that, if allowed to come up onto the over-pointed foot, the child can sustain lasting damage along the dorsum of the foot and the front of the ankle (Fig. 1.80). Before a student with this type of foot can start pointe work safely he or she has to do a considerable amount of work to strengthen all the muscles of the feet and the ankles so that a really well controlled foot is held in the correct and not in the over-pointed position.

There are certainly well-known dancers who were not strong enough to start their pointe work until they were over the age of sixteen and this has proved no handicap in their career.

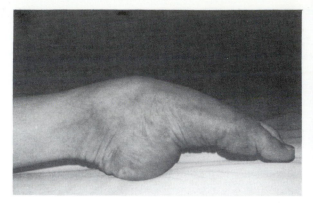

1.80A   An over-pointed foot. To come up onto pointe with the foot in this position places an excessive strain on the capsules and ligaments of the dorsum of the foot as the line of the centre of gravity falls in front of the toes (i.e. in front of the dorsal aspect).

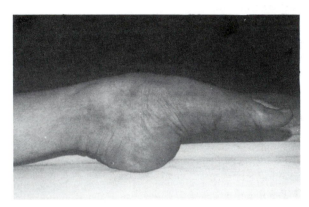

1.80B   The same foot in the correct position for dancing on pointe.

Injuries:
Pathology, Causes, Treatment, Prevention, Nutrition

2.1 Patho-physiology of Injury: Inflammation and Healing

Injuries to tissues can arise from a variety of causes: mechanical, burns, chemical, action of bacteria, action of viruses, etc. However, in this book we are really only interested in injury which is caused mechanically. These injuries include sprains, muscle tears, fractures, bruises and occasionally cuts and abrasions.

Inflammation

Any injury, whatever the cause, produces inflammation. Inflammation is a response which occurs in the surviving adjacent tissues at any injured site. There is a general view that inflammation is something which is undesirable and should be avoided, because the first thing that springs to mind when one considers inflammation is something very painful such as a boil, sore throat or similar infection which has produced an inflammatory response. As bacterial infection of tissue is one form of injury it therefore produces an inflammation, hence the feeling that the inflammation itself is undesirable. However, the opposite is the case, inflammation is a very beneficial thing. It is a natural protective and defensive mechanism which the body has developed in order to deal with any type of injury.

If the inflammatory response is absent dramatic and disastrous effects can arise. Everyone nowadays hears of patients who have been treated with special drugs to prevent inflammation, particularly following various organ transplant operations and also, of course, in a slightly different form in the conditions known as AIDS (Acquired Immune Deficiency Syndrome). Without the inflammatory response, there is a very high incidence of severe infections which can spread extremely rapidly and are frequently lethal. It is this inability of the body to control infections that renders patients so vulnerable when they have had immunosuppressive therapy, as it is known. It is important therefore that it is understood from the beginning that the inflammatory reaction is a desirable condition.

Whatsoever the type of injury to the tissue the result in the normal person is an acute inflammatory response.

THE SIGNS OF INFLAMMATION

The signs of inflammation were described some 2000 years or more ago and have been taught ever since. Until the current century they were always described in Latin as 'calor, rubor, dolor, tumor' and 'functio laesa' or in English 'heat, redness, pain, swelling and loss of function.'

Heat – calor
Heat accompanies the redness of the hyperaemia and is due to the increased blood flow. It is only appreciated at the skin surface because this is usually cooler than the internal body temperature, so with the increased blood supply the skin temperature is raised up to, or nearly up to, the inside of the body, i.e. 37°C. (98.4°F.) There is, therefore, a localised increase in warmth compared with the surrounding skin.

Redness – rubor
The redness appears early. It is due to the dilatation of the arterioles in the area. This allows the capillaries to fill up and become distended very quickly. It is sometimes known also as hyperaemia, which means an increased blood flow.

Pain – dolor
There are various causes for the pain which is associated with an inflammatory reaction as distinct from the pain which is produced by the actual injury, for example a sprain or a fracture, both of which are painful in their own right. The inflammatory pain may be produced by local stimulation of nerve endings due to an alteration in the local pH level (the acid alkali balance) or by the release of certain chemicals such as histamine which also stimulates the nerve endings. Swelling within the inflamed tissues causes pain due to the increase in pressure.

Swelling – tumor
Local swelling always occurs in the presence of inflammation and is due to the spread into the tissues of fluid and cells from the blood stream. This will be considered again shortly.

Loss of Function – functio laesa

Loss of or altered function occurs with inflammation. Pain may well inhibit muscular action and swelling will also limit movements of joints. However, apart from these very obvious causes of loss of function the underlying reason for the alteration in function in the presence of inflammation at other sites is not really understood. The most likely explanation is that the function becomes inhibited to allow the part to rest.

TISSUE CHANGES IN INFLAMMATION

Fluid Changes

As mentioned above, the redness and heat are brought about by the dilatation of arterioles which leads to engorgement of the capillaries. With the dilatation of the capillaries there is an alteration in permeability of the walls of these tiny vessels.

Instead of retaining the large protein molecules within the circulation and not allowing them to cross the cellular barrier of the capillary walls, the permeability of the walls changes and some large protein molecules can pass out into the tissue fluid. As a result the osmotic balance between the tissue fluid and the blood alters and further amounts of water are drawn out into the tissue fluid, producing the local swelling. This increase in vascular permeability is the most important factor in the causation of the swelling. However, there is a less important factor in that the dilatation produces an increase in the pressure of the blood within the engorged vessels and this increased pressure will also aid the pushing out of water into the tissues.

The endothelial cells which line the small vessels and largely form the walls of the capillary vessels act in a physical sense as a semi-permeable membrane. A semi-permeable membrane is any sort of membrane or layer which allows water and small molecules to pass through but keeps back the larger molecules. It acts very much like a sieve. In normal circumstances the plasma proteins in the blood circulation are large molecules which cannot pass through the semi-permeable membrane. The concentration of large molecules on one side of the semi-permeable membrane exerts a force which is knows as an osmotic force, drawing fluid and smaller molecules, depending upon the permeability of the semi-permeable membrane, through into the blood in an attempt to dilute down the concentration of large molecules. This osmotic force is also known as the osmotic pressure. In inflammation, the permeability of the endothelial cells alters and as a result the large protein molecules can pass through so that they enter the tissue fluid. Therefore the difference in osmotic force between the two sides of the semi-permeable membrane alters and, due to the proteins which have been exuded into the tissue fluid, there is now a force there drawing more water out into the tissue spaces. The fluid which passes out into the tissues as a result of the inflammation is known as the exudate.

The lymphatic system also plays an important part in acute inflammation. The lining cells of the very small lymphatics separate a little, allowing material from the spaces in the tissues to drain into the lymphatics. There is thus a very great increase in the flow of lymph draining from an area of inflammation. This lymph is carrying not only normal tissue fluid with the extra plasma protein and blood cells but also various agents which may have caused the inflammation. In an injury, of course, these are only the products of tissue damage but if the inflammation has been brought about by infection or penetration by foreign material, this material or the bacteria will get into the lymph system and will be carried along in the lymphatics. They will then reach the regional lymph nodes which act as filters.

As was decribed in the first section of the book, the lymph nodes or lymph glands filter out any foreign material. As a result the regional lymph nodes themselves can become inflamed. Everyone will have experienced a sore, infected throat at some time in their lives and will have found that the glands at the angles of the jaw become enlarged and tender. This is because the glands at that site are acting as the filters for the lymph which has been flowing from the sore throat. As a result of the infection and the bacteria which the glands have filtered out, they themselves become the site of inflammation but, due to their capability to concentrate the white blood cells, they are able to deal with the bacteria or other materials and prevent them passing through into the rest of the blood stream. Occasionally, if the infection is severe, it can get through the lymph nodes. It then stands an excellent chance of being filtered out by more central nodes but if these nodes are also overcome it can reach the general circulation, producing a generalised infection throughout the body and severe illness in the person concerned.

As far as injury is concerned, there is usually at most some cell debris or breakdown products of blood which have to be filtered out, so any inflammatory changes which may occur in the regional lymph glands are only mild.

Cell Changes

In the early stages of the acute inflammation, the arterioles and capillaries are dilated and the flow of blood into the inflamed area is greatly increased. However, shortly after that, as the fluid passes out of the capillaries and very small vessels into the tissues, the concentration of cells left behind in the blood increases and the blood becomes more sticky, i.e. the viscosity increases. As a result of this, the circulation within the area slows down. With the slowing of the blood flow the white blood cells or leucocytes move to the periphery of the stream adjacent to the lining of the blood vessels. This phenomenon is knows as margination because the leucocytes are moving towards the margin of the blood stream in these small vessels. When the leucocytes reach the linings of the blood vessels, or the endothelium, they tend to stick to the endothelial lining. This is known as pavementing because under the microscope it has an appearance much like that of a cobbled street. The leucocytes then push their way through the walls of these tiny vessels. They penetrate the vessel wall in an amoeboid fashion by inserting a small portion of their tissue through the space between two cells in the lining wall and then gradually squeezing the rest of the cell tissue of the leucocyte through this space. It would be much the same if you picked up a jellyfish from the shore and then started to push it through a small knot hole in a piece of wood. As a jellyfish is so completely mobile, you would push a small portion through and as you went on pushing, the body would narrow down, the jelly fish would slowly go through the hole so that more and more of it appeared on the other side, which would get larger, until finally the last bit went through without any damage at all to the jellyfish (Fig. 2.1). This type of action is known as amoeboid movement because the very primitive cells, or amoebae, move along like this. The portion of cell they initially put out is known as the pseudopodium which, translated literally, means false foot.

Thus the leucocytes or white cells move from the capillaries into the tissue fluid so that they can deal as necessary with the cause of the inflammation. Once through into the tissue fluid, the leucocytes move very specifically in the direction required. This is brought about by chemical stimulation and the process is known as chemotaxis. The chemotactic signals which attract leucocytes can emanate from infectious agents, damage to tissues and substances produced by the proteins which have passed out from the blood stream by osmosis. There are several different types of leucocyte or

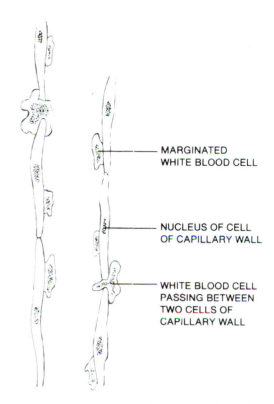

MARGINATED WHITE BLOOD CELL

NUCLEUS OF CELL OF CAPILLARY WALL

WHITE BLOOD CELL PASSING BETWEEN TWO CELLS OF CAPILLARY WALL

2.1 Diagram showing margination of the white cells along the walls of a capillary and two white blood cells passing through the capillary wall. The capillary wall is itself made up of cells each with its own nucleus. The white cell passes out between two cells forming the capillary wall and not through a cell body.

white blood cell and they have different actions. The first cells appearing in large numbers within the exudates at inflammatory sites are the neutrophils, named thus because of their neutral staining characteristics. They are the commonest white cell in the ordinary blood circulation and have a very short life. There are large numbers kept in reserve in the bone marrow which can be released when required. At the site of inflammation, they are able to engulf bacteria or foreign materials by putting out pseudopodia and spreading around the particle and taking it within itself. This process is called phagocytosis. Once it has been enveloped within the cell, the particle or bacterium will be destroyed or digested by various enzymes within the cell. In an acute infection, if a sample of blood is taken and the white cells counted, there will be a greatly increased number of neutrophils per cubic millimetre of blood and this increase is taken as evidence of infection when a blood count is carried out.

The eosinophil is another type of blood cell. It is in much smaller numbers in the blood stream. It becomes dyed a bright red when the stain eosin is used, hence its name. Although it will respond in much the same way as the neutrophils and will kill some bacteria, it is basically a cell which gathers in much larger numbers when the inflammation is of the allergic type. Thus in allergic conditions, the count of eosinophils in a blood sample is increased.

The third type of white blood cell which comes in the group of granulocytes is the basophil. These cells are called granulocytes because the cytoplasm of the cell has large granules. In the basophil these granules stain a dark blue whereas in the other two types of granulocyte the neutrophil stains lavender and the eosinophil stains red. The basophils are only present in very small numbers in exudates. They are stimulated to release the contents of their granules into the surrounding fluid in non-specific and immunological reactions.

The monocyte is a different form of white blood cell and, unlike the granulocytes, the cytoplasm has very few granules. Its life is about four times longer than the granulocytes. Monocytes enter the exudate in small numbers and at a smaller rate than the neutrophils but with the passage of time their number increases steadily. When a monocyte is within the exudate it is usually called a macrophage and during normal circumstances it will often be wandering around through the connective tissue spaces in the body and it is sometimes then referred to as a histiocyte. Basically, these three names refer to the same type of cell. Its functions are very much like those of the neutrophils inasmuch as it is able to absorb particles and bacteria into itself and kill and digest them. When in the tissue, its life cycle is different from the neutrophil in that it can survive for very long periods. The neutrophil, as with the other granulocytes, cannot sub-divide and form new cells. The macrophage or monocyte is, however, capable of cell division when in the tissue fluid and it can also synthesise or build-up a variety of different enzymes within its own cell. Thus it is able to respond and deal with a variety of different noxious agents. Sometimes the macrophages will join together to form one large cell with several nuclei. These are known as multinucleated giant cells.

As mentioned, the macrophages are not only seen in the exudates at sites of inflammation but they are also normally distributed around the body and are not only in the blood stream as monocytes. They may also be fixed and line the vessels in the spleen, the liver and the bone marrow and also the walls of the lymphatic system. Their main function is phagocytic, i.e. the ingestion of particles which would otherwise be harmful to the body as a whole. They act as the street cleaners of the body. They are constantly working because in many aspects of daily life there is a release of a large number of bacteria into the blood stream, for example, eating and teeth cleaning will produce a lot of organisms in the blood stream. These rapidly get removed by the phagocytic activities of the macrophages. As a result, these episodes of what is known as bacteraemia are very short-lived and cause no harm at all.

The last type of leucocyte, which is the lymphocyte, is only present in very small numbers in exudates. However, if the exudate becomes old and the inflammatory reactions becomes chronic, the number of lymphocytes increases markedly. They are seen therefore in chronic infections such as tuberculosis. The functions of lymphocytes are largely in the production of various aspects of the immune reactions and are outside the scope of this book.

It will now have been seen that the inflammation is in fact a good or beneficial thing from the body's point of view. The increased blood supply has brought cells to clear up the tissue damage or infection. It has brought proteins and electrolytes to help with tissue repair and will also in various conditions have brought antibodies. The exudate can also start to form a clot, which is made up of fibrils of protein which work very much like a scaffold as the first stages of tissue repair. This will be mentioned a little later.

Types of Inflammation
There are three different types of inflammatory reaction. The normal one following an injury such as a cut or an infection such as a boil is known as an acute inflammation. The inflammation will develop rapidly with the various aspects which have been described. This will be followed by repair and healing all taking place over a relatively short period. If the infection is one which is known as chronic, then there is an advanced repair process going on but at the same time the inflammatory condition persists, so for a very extended period there is continuing inflammation with continuing attempts at repair alongside this. In chronic inflammation the aspects of acute inflammation are much less marked, i.e. there is less swelling and pain, although both these may persist to some extent as does also some degree of interference with function; heat is usually absent. A sub-acute

infection is an intermediate between acute and chronic infection, where there is some evidence of repair but there is also some inflammation and exudation going on. It is often experienced by the subject as an area which does not seem to get really bad and yet does not seem to get better. When one refers to an inflammation of a particular part, it is usually named by taking the particular inflamed part and adding the four letters 'itis' as in tonsillitis or appendicitis. Arthritis is also well known and applies to an inflamed joint. If it is an injured joint which is painful and swollen, it will often be referred to as a traumatic arthritis, i.e. an arthritis which has been produced by trauma.

Inflammations are also sometimes further described by the type of exudate which is produced. While there is no need to go deeply into this as there are many different types of exudate, it is worth mentioning a serous exudate which is one composed largely of fluid and protein and has very few white cells. For the dancer the most common serous exudate that they will see is the fluid which is present in a blister. The swelling in a damaged joint may be a serous exudate with very few cells, or if the damage has been great and there has been actually some tearing, the fluid in the joint may contain a greater or lesser amount of blood, in which case it may be called an haemarthrosis. Another type of exudate which is well known is, of course, pus. In this the neutrophils are in such great numbers as to colour the fluid and make it white. The pus also contains products of digestion and disintegration of the damaged tissue.

Sequelae of Inflammation

Considering as we are in this book injuries rather than other conditions, we need to consider what happens after the initial acute inflammatory response to the injury. The result will depend largely on the degree of damage to the tissues. If there has been very little or no destruction of tissues, the inflammation will settle and what is known as resolution will take place and the tissues will return to normal. An example of this would be a small blister where the skin gets damaged. The exudate forms underneath the skin to give the actual blister, the skin over the blister breaks, the exudate is discharged, the area dries and heals with the dead epithelium slowly peeling off, leaving once again normal skin at that site.

If there has been a significant degree of tissue destruction then resolution cannot occur, i.e. the tissues cannot return to normal. In this case, the area where the tissue has been destroyed has to be repaired. Repair can occur in two different ways.

The first and best way is by cell regeneration. This occurs when the neighbouring undamaged cells divide and reproduce and proliferate, replacing the damaged tissues with new cells which are identical to those which have been lost, thus replacing the whole area with the same kind of cell. The other method of repair is brought about by the proliferation of fibrous tissue, or connective tissue which produces a scar. Due to the differing abilities of the various kinds of cells and tissues to regenerate, repair is usually by a combination of regeneration and scar formation. The ability to regenerate depends entirely upon the ability of the cells in a particular tissue to sub-divide and produce new identical cells. Tissues such as the skin and the lining of the whole of the gastrointestinal tract can regenerate very well. Some of the internal organs such as the liver and kidney can also regenerate provided that the areas of damage are not too great. Unfortunately for the dancer, regeneration in muscle is normally very limited and healing is largely by scar tissue. Heart muscle cannot regenerate at all and heals entirely by scar tissue. Equally importantly, there is no regeneration at all of damaged nerve cells. Recovery after heart attacks occurs because neighbouring cells and the rest of the heart muscle take over the function. However, if the damage is too great the remaining heart muscle will be unable to cope properly and heart failure will occur. Similarly, in the brain, if cells have been destroyed by a stroke, which is either a haemorrhage or a thrombosis in the brain, they cannot be repaired or regenerate. Any function which does return is by adjacent cells taking over the actual neurological functions of the destroyed cells.

However, repair by scar tissue (fibrous tissue) is a very efficient and satisfactory repair process although obviously not as functionally good as the original tissue. The repair comes about in the following manner. Into the damaged area there is an ingrowth of proliferating connective tissue so that the damaged area becomes what is known as organised, the process being known as organisation. The ingrowing tissue is referred to as granulation tissue. This is made up of proliferating fibroblasts which produce fibrous tissue and proliferating capillary buds which form new capillary vessels, together with some white blood cells from the inflammatory process and the fluid parts of the exudate and loose connective tissue.

Organisation is already occurring within several days of the start of the inflammation. By the end of a week the granulation tissue is still loose so that the wound can be easily pulled apart. However, after about a week the fibroblasts in the granulation tissue produce substances which lead to the formation of the protein called collagen. The collagen appears as fibrils within the granulation tissue. As time passes the amount of collagen is gradually increased and becomes steadily more dense. It is the dense collagen which forms the actual scar and this process takes about two weeks to achieve sufficient strength to hold the wound together. Over the following weeks the collagen continues to increase in strength. The lines of the fibrils that have been laid down in the collagen gradually become more regular so instead of being higgledy-piggledy as will be the state to begin with, they become more arranged upon the lines of tension. In the early days this scar has a high vascularity and therefore looks pink. With the passage of time the scar loses the pink colour and becomes white, the length of time varying from person to person. Also varying in individuals is the amount of scar tissue which is laid down. Sometimes the scar becomes extremely thickened and this is then often referred to as a keloid scar. It may also be very irritating.

Healing of Injuries

There are two patterns of healing. The first is known as healing by first intention, or primary healing. The second type is referred to as healing by second intention. The most desirable form is healing by first intention.

HEALING BY FIRST INTENTION

If we consider a very simple injury such as a wound caused by a clean cut in the skin, where the edges have been brought together, we can see what happens in healing by first intention. Immediately after the wound occurs, there is bleeding, the wound edges are bound together by a blood clot, in which the stringy fibre acts as a binding material. At the edges of the wound an acute inflammatory reaction develops in exactly the fashion that has been described earlier. The various cells pass into the blood clot and the macrophages in particular begin to destroy it. As the demolition of the blood clot takes place, granulation tissue grows into the area and after a few days the wound is crossed completely by the granulation tissue. Obviously the length of time taken to bridge the wound depends upon the size of any gap. However, in primary healing, the gap should be minimal.

During this time, in a skin wound, the epithelium at the surface begins to regenerate and after some days there is a thin layer of epithelium across the wound surface. This epithelium gradually thickens and becomes mature so that it looks like the adjacent skin. In the deeper layers, the granulation tissue has matured to form a scar which is a dense collection of collagen or white connective tissue. In the skin, if the edges have been really well opposed, the final scarring at the surface may be practically invisible. In skin wounds which gape, the reason for putting in stitches is to hold the edges close together so that healing can take place by first intention.

HEALING BY SECOND INTENTION

Healing by second intention is largely similar to that which has already been described. However, it occurs in wounds or injuries where the edges cannot be brought together and opposed. This may happen at the skin level if there is tissue loss or if the wound is gaping and is not stitched up, or it can occur in deeper layers of tissue. In order to fill the gap, very much more granulation tissue is required and at the skin surface very much more regeneration of the epithelial cells. As a result, a very much larger scar is formed. Because the collagen is laid down in the granulation tissue and then matures, this leaves a dense mass of collagen or fibrous tissue. At the skin, this leaves a very obvious scar. It must be remembered that in deeper layers a similar mass of scar tissue will also form in order to fill a gap. As was mentioned above, different tissues have different powers of actual regeneration of cells. Therefore, in many areas where an injury occurs, the damaged area is repaired mainly or totally by fibrous scar tissue. This scar tissue can become adherent to adjacent structures. The presence of the mass of scar tissue in, for example a muscle, can impair the function of the muscle as a whole. It is therefore extremely important when an injury occurs to avoid further damage and hence the proliferation of scar tissue. If an injured part is exercised too early or unwisely, the the amount of scar tissue formed can be increased considerably.

Essentially, healing of any damaged tissue in the body is similar to that which has been described. Local variations occur because of different types of cells and their ability or otherwise to regenerate. Even in·bone, the actual healing process is similar. However, with the formation of the granulation tissue and accompanying the migration of the cells are two types of bone cell – the osteoblasts which are responsible for laying down new bone and the osteoclasts which are responsible for eating away the bone. Initially, in a fracture the broken bone ends are slightly eaten away by osteoclasts and the various minerals are released. This gives a very high level of concentration of the minerals required for bone repair. The healing takes place with the formation of granulation tissue and collagen and along this scaffold that has been laid down, osteoblasts will produce bone. This bone which is put down is done in a totally random manner. With the passage of time and the action of the osteoclasts, this new bone is eaten away and relaid so that the lines of the bony mesh are lying in the right direction. The bone slowly becomes mature and the outline becomes remodelled to a variable extent so that it tends to resume its old shape. This happens particularly well in children before they have stopped growing. The immature bone which is initially laid down during the process of healing of the fracture is relatively soft and springy. The hardness of bone that we recognise is brought about by the various mineral salts in the bone. As the new bone is formed, the mineral salts are gradually brought in and laid down and the bone hardens and becomes solid.

FACTORS AFFECTING HEALING

The most important factor associated with healing is the presence of a good blood supply to the damaged area. If the blood supply is very poor, the inflammatory processes do not take place adequately. This will lead to very slow or inadequate healing and also predisposes to infection because of the deficiency of the body's protective mechanisms, largely due to the inadequate number of white blood cells reaching the area. If the damaged part does not have adequate rest, the newly formed granulation tissue can be repeatedly damaged, which will again affect the blood supply to the area and also increase the amount of fibrous tissue which is laid down. Infection from the beginning, for example in a dirty wound, can also impair the healing processes as can other non-infected foreign material.

Even if healing has taken place normally, the scar tissue itself can cause problems. It may become stuck to local structures fixing them together, producing what are called adhesions. As scar tissue matures, it tends to shorten or contract. As a result, movements of a part may become limited resulting in permanent post-injury stiffness. A scar which contracts in the skin can produce a marked disfigurement and it takes little imagination to realise the limitation of movement which can occur by similar contractures occurring in the deeper tissues when they are damaged. Also, as already mentioned, at skin level an excessive amount of collagen may be formed leading to a very prominent scar which is known as a keloid scar.

This is usually of cosmetic importance only, although at an area where rubbing can occur, the scar can tend to break down repeatedly and become sore. Occasionally, during the process of healing, small damaged nerve fibres can produce a lump of nerve fibres in the area of healing. This is known as a neuroma and a neuroma can produce a very painful or tender area within the scar.

The primary aim of any form of treatment is to obtain healing by first intention. This will produce the shortest recovery time, the minimum amount of scar tissue and hence the maximum return to full and normal function.

2.2 Types of Injury

Having discussed the patho-physiology of injury and how healing occurs we are now going to describe various types of injury with consideration of how the injury affects different parts and structures in the body. Although the general principles outlined above apply to all types of injury, because of differences in the structures in the body, the response to injury will vary between different structures and hence sometimes produce variations in the healing processes.

Joint Injuries

In considering the joints we will include not only the bony parts of the joint but also the capsule and any external ligaments that are supporting the joints, any internal ligaments of the joint, and the synovial lining of the joint. In addition, in the knee there are flaps of cartilage known as menisci or semi-lunar cartilages which stick out in the joint and are themselves subject to injury. The temporo-mandibular joint of the jaw is the only other joint to possess a meniscus.

The commonest injury to a joint is a sprain affecting one or more of its ligaments and usually the capsule and synovial lining in addition. A sprain occurs when the fibrous tissue of the ligament or capsule is stretched and this is accompanied by what are known as micro-tears within the substance of the ligament and capsule. In these micro-tears a varying number of fibres are actually torn. If the sprain is more severe there can be actual lengthening of the ligament as these torn fibres tend to pull out past each other. If the force continues the ligament can rupture and a gap occur.

The first structure to take the strain in an abnormal movement is usually one of the ligaments around that joint. If the stretch continues the adjacent capsule becomes involved and then the underlying synovial membrane lining the joint itself. A sprain produces local bleeding where the various fibres have been torn and this frequently shows superficially as discolouration beneath the skin, i.e. bruising. This particularly applies to joints which have little overlying tissue, such as the ankle. In deep joints (e.g. the hip) this bleeding is not usually visible in the subcutaneous tissues. If there is any damage or irritation of the synovial lining of the joint there will be an outpouring of fluid into the joint, causing the whole joint to become swollen. This fluid is produced by the synovial membrane and represents an attempt to flush away or dilute the irritant source. This is seen in anything more serious than a very minor sprain. Frequently the effusion is merely an excess of synovial fluid secreted by the irritated synovial lining. If there has been any damage to the synovial lining bleeding will occur into the joint, producing an haemarthrosis. An effusion or haemarthrosis is always painful, mainly due to the increase in tension in the joint although the blood itself is an irritant and causes pain. Both are indicative of serious injury. The only way to differentiate between an effusion and an haemarthrosis is to aspirate the joint with a needle and syringe. Sometimes an haemarthrosis is due to a fracture of the bone with the fracture line entering the joint. X-rays are required in order to exclude or to confirm a fracture.

It is very important to determine whether a sprain is relatively minor or whether it has progressed to the stage where there is a complete rupture of a ligament. This may be obvious on clinical examination but sometimes the examination causes too much pain for the patient to tolerate the proper testing of the ligaments. In these cases it may be necessary to administer an anaesthetic in order to test the stability of the joint. X-rays are taken at the same time in order to demonstrate whether there is any instability of the joint when it is strained in one or other direction (Fig. 2.2). In the case of damage to internal ligaments within a knee (the cruciate ligaments) or possible injury to a meniscus of the knee, then arthroscopy is invaluable. An arthroscope is a fine telescope which is inserted into the joint through a small wound, making possible direct inspection inside the joint. It is possible to carry out some operative procedures using the arthroscope; removal of portions of damaged meniscus can frequently be carried out with the help of the arthroscope and without opening the joint widely. However, for most

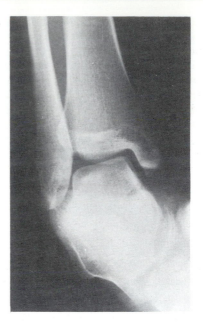

2.2A   An X-ray of an ankle, showing that the talus is tilting during a forced passive inversion.

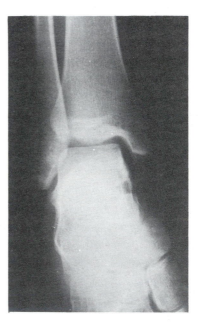

2.2B   The same X-ray without any inversion strain applied, showing that there is a normal appearance despite the presence of ligament damage.

conditions within the knee and certainly with injuries affecting other joints that require surgery, open operations are inevitable.

If significant ligament damage is undiagnosed early, the condition can progress to a chronic sprain or, if the ligament has been greatly stretched, or ruptured, to chronic joint instability.

If there is any instability in the joint, the dancer feels very unsafe on that joint and it tends to give way frequently. This may or may not be accompanied by repeated swelling around the area as well as by pain. Late repair of undiagnosed ruptured ligaments is not very satisfactory and the results are far worse than repair of ruptured ligaments immediately after the injury. By immediate one means within the first twenty-four or at most forty-eight hours. Failure to institute surgery when necessary may result in a degree of instability sufficient to prevent the dancer getting back to full work with confidence. A late repair, although improving the situation, may still fail to give the required stability to enable the dancer to perform fully.

Sometimes a feeling of instability in the joint is due to damage to the nerve ends which lie in the capsule and ligaments. This can be improved by intensive physiotherapy in various forms. The ankle is the most common joint to be affected in this manner and here the balancing board is one of the most vital parts of the rehabilitation programme. (See Figs 3.4, 3.5 and 3.6 on page 107.)

Within the joint itself there can occur occasionally what is known as an osteo-chondral fracture where a chip of the articular cartilage and a small fragment of the underlying bone is damaged and separates from the joint surface. This is uncommon in dancers as it usually follows a direct blow on the unprotected surface of a joint, such as the front of the flexed knee. However, in certain types of inversion injury of the ankle, a fragment can be knocked off the dome of the talus.

Bone Injuries

ACUTE FRACTURES

In bones the common injury is a fracture when the bone is broken. A fracture is merely the medical name for a broken bone (Fig. 2.3). In children these fractures may be of the greenstick type where the fracture is only partial and is accompanied by some bending of the unfractured part of the bone. Sometimes fractures are accompanied by fragmentation of the broken ends and these are known as comminuted fractures. In compound

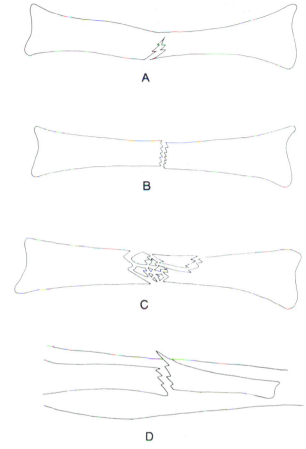

2.3   A. Greenstick fracture.
      B. Transverse fracture.
      C. Comminuted fracture where there are several fragments.
      D. Compound fracture where the bone comes through the skin.

fractures there is a break in the skin and sometimes the bone actually comes through the skin. Severe fractures are uncommon in dancers.

The commonest type of fracture is that affecting the 5th metatarsal. This is produced by a forcible inversion injury. Fractures can take from six weeks to many months to heal. Usually they are immobilised with a plaster of Paris cast. Occasionally internal fixation – plates and screws – is required. There are a few fractures which can be treated by simple strapping. During immobilisation the dancer should spend a great deal of time exercising all the other groups of muscles in the body that have not been immobilised by the plaster. Once the plaster is removed then time has to be spent strengthening up muscles which have become weak as a result of the immobilisation. Many fractures will be the site of aching even though the fracture has united satisfactorily. Although uncomfortable this is not of serious significance and in the long term gradually settles. Frequently the aching becomes more pronounced in cold or damp weather. It does not stop the dancer performing fully and certainly does not mean that there is anything wrong with the healing of the fracture.

Obviously it is of importance to diagnose a fracture early and to this end X-rays are usually required although a clinical diagnosis of a fracture is usually fairly straightforward and only requires X-ray confirmation.

STRESS FRACTURES

These are particularly common in dancers and are more frequently seen than actual acute fractures. They occur as a result of repeated local stress on one area of the bone and come on gradually. If a bone is subjected to recurrent forces or stresses that are somewhat different from those experienced in everyday activities – walking, stair climbing, running relatively short distances, etc. or if these everyday activities are excessive – the area of bone that is being stressed will respond initially by gradually thickening up the hard cortex. This is well seen in dancers, especially in the 2nd metatarsal which, particularly if it is long, can often be seen to be very much thickened on an X-ray. When the stress ends, e.g. when the dancer retires, the stress thickening will gradually disappear and the bone will return to a normal X-ray appearance.

If the stress is more intensive and particularly if it is well localised, small cracks will develop in the bone. The local response is to invoke the inflammatory and healing mechanism. However, if the stress continues the cracking may proceed faster than the healing in which case a stress fracture or even multiple stress fractures (as often seen in the tibia) will occur. This produces a gradual increase in the amount of pain experienced by the dancer. Initially it will only trouble them while they are actually dancing, but as the stress fracture increases the pain becomes more continuous until eventually the pain is present all the time that there is any type of activity, although it will usually disappear when the part is being rested completely. If the presence of a stress fracture is ignored it can progress eventually to a complete fracture of the bone. Additionally, the longer the dancer continues to work with a stress fracture, the longer it will take to heal. The history and examination should enable the diagnosis of a stress facture to be made without much difficulty. Persistent pain on activity, which is

well localised to one area, is suggestive of a stress fracture. When examined, this area, if the bone is superficial, will reveal a local area of warmth, well localised tenderness and palpable thickening. These findings are highly indicative of a stress fracture. Early treatment in the form of rest from dancing activity should be undertaken.

Stress fractures usually do not show up if X-rays are taken in the early days. In the case of the metatarsal it may be two weeks before there is any evidence of a stress fracture. In the tibia (Fig. 2.4) or the pars interarticularis of the spine it may be several months before any X-ray changes are visible. It is most important that treatment is not delayed until there are positive X-ray findings otherwise the length of time for healing and recovery can be lengthened to many months. It is possible to confirm the presence of a stress fracture by a radio-isotope bone scan. The radio-active isotope is concentrated at the stress fracture site, producing what is known as a 'hot spot'.

As with other injuries, during the period of rest from dancing, the dancer can still do a whole series of exercises in order to keep the body in good physical trim. This programme of exercises should be worked out with the help of an experienced physiotherapist so as to ensure that no strain is put on the site of the stress fracture.

Associated with bone but not an actual bony injury is a condition known as a sub-periosteal haematoma (Fig. 2.5). This results from a direct blow to relatively superficial bone such as the shin. Bleeding occurs between the periosteum and the bone, lifting the periosteum from the bone and producing an extremely painful lump. Treatment is symptomatic only. Very rarely the haematoma can become infected, producing an osteomyelitis. This is certainly more likely to happen if someone is injudicious enough to try to put a needle into it to aspirate the blood. An additional sequel to a sub-periosteal haematoma is that the blood may not be completely absorbed and some of this residual blood may be converted into bone, leaving a small bony lump at the site of the haematoma.

Tendon Injuries

Tendons run from the muscle belly to the point of insertion of the muscle. They are present because they enable the pull of the muscle to be taken to the point of the tendon attachment without having the bulk of the muscle going the whole distance. Thus tendons are found, as described in **Section 1**, in areas where bulk is disadvantageous, such as from the forearm to the hand and the leg to the

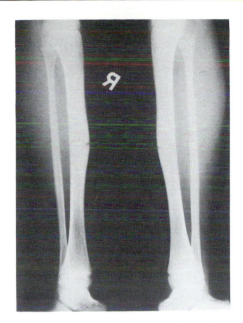

2.4   A stress fracture in the mid-shaft of the tibia.

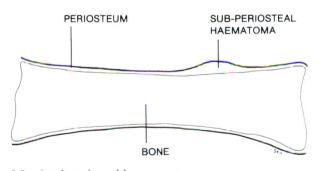

2.5   A sub-periosteal haematoma.

foot. Tendons are very strong. There is very little stretch in them and because they have to slide up and down without impediment they have a poor blood supply.

TENDONITIS

Tendonitis is merely an irritation of a tendon without any significant damage to the fibres. It is caused by unaccustomed exertion. This may take place either in someone who is not in the habit of taking much exercise or in a situation where someone who is physically fit suddenly demands a large number of repetitions of a movement involving one or more tendons repeatedly. If treated by rest this is usually sufficient to allow the symptoms to settle. Sometimes resolution can be speeded up with the use of ultrasound or ice.

TENDON RUPTURE – PARTIAL AND COMPLETE

Partial rupture of a tendon is a more serious injury and is akin to the sprain which occurs in the ligaments. A dancer experiences sudden pain and may actually hear or feel something give way. A partial rupture results in the tearing of some of the fibres of the tendon while other fibres remain intact. There will be local bleeding at the site of the partial rupture and this will manifest itself as a local tender swelling. If the tendon is superficial, an increase in warmth can be felt by the examining fingers. Rest, with or without any immobilisation, is usually all that is required in order to allow healing of the partial rupture to take place. Occasionally however, surgical repair is indicated if it is considered that the partial rupture is fairly extensive or if there is doubt about whether there may or may not be a total rupture of the tendon. If adequate rest is not allowed for healing to take place, then the condition can progress to a chronic state where a combination of healing and further tearing is taking place at the same time. This normally occurs if a dancer does not take the necessary time off to allow complete healing to take place. After the period of rest an exercise programme is required in order to strengthen up the muscles which have been affected by the period of rest.

A total rupture of a tendon in dancers is fortunately very uncommon. In the population as a whole the commonest tendon rupture is where one of the extensor tendons is pulled off the distal phalanx of the finger, causing the phalanx to droop down into partial flexion; this is known as a mallet finger. This also occurs in ball games when the end of the finger is struck. Very occasionally in dancers the major tendons are ruptured, i.e. the Achilles tendon, the patellar tendon and the quadriceps tendon. Almost invariably this happens because of a sudden violent contraction of the muscle. This may take place because the dancer misses his footing or slips from a prop. More commonly it happens in the mature dancer or dance teacher who is demonstrating a large jump or unaccustomed routine which needs a sudden explosive burst of muscle power.

Immediate diagnosis is vital. Initially the diagnosis is fairly obvious but if some hours have elapsed the local swelling may be sufficient to disguise what was earlier an easily felt gap. Urgent repair in the first twenty-four hours is essential if a satisfactory functional result is to be obtained. Even so, the rupture of a major tendon will usually lead to the dancer failing to regain the same level of activity which was pertaining before the rupture. Apart from the immediate and skilful surgical repair, the post-operative physiotherapy plays a vital part in the satisfactory recovery of the patient. The treatment includes a full rehabilitation programme and a great deal of hard work by the patient.

TENOSYNOVITIS AND PERITENDONITIS

The tissues surrounding the tendon can be the site of inflammation and irritation. In those tendons which have a proper sheath the inflammation will affect this tendon sheath producing what is known as tenosynovitis. Some tendons, for example the Achilles tendon and the patellar tendon, do not have a sheath but the soft tissue around the tendon can become inflamed in exactly the same way as the tendon sheath. This is known as peritendonitis. In both tenosynovitis and peritendonitis the condition tends to be triggered off by over-use of the tendon. This can be caused by either faulty technique where the tendon is being repeatedly over-stressed or by too many repetitions of the same movement. Clinical examination usually shows that there is some swelling and tenderness along the line of the affected tendon and sheath. Movements are painful and frequently the examining finger can feel a crepitus or grating/creaking sensation over the moving tendon.

Treatment is by rest which usually produces rapid relief. In other cases ice, ultrasound and physiotherapy measures are required and some form of splintage may assist. In long standing cases, an injection of steroid will be helpful. Only on very rare occasions is an actual surgical decompression of the tendon sheath required. This is only necessary when the condition has become chronic and is not responding to conservative treatment. By then it has usually led to some thickening and scarring of the tendon sheath or the peritendinous tissues. Occasionally, there is a local cause such as pressure on a tendon. In dancers this is sometimes seen at the lower end of the Achilles tendon near its insertion, where badly fitting shoes can cause pressure. In sportsmen the high backs of the shoes or a shoe tab can cause great irritation of the Achilles tendon. Obviously where there is a local cause, this must be removed.

TENDON INSERTION INJURIES

These occur at the site where the tendon goes into the bone and are usually in the form of a strain. Adequate rest is an essential part of treatment. Ultrasound, ice and occasionally steroid injections may be required. Frequently the response to treatment is slow and treatment may be prolonged.

Use of steroids in any type of tendon injury should be confined to chronic injuries only. Many authorities believe that steroid injections can pre-dispose to a total rupture of the tendon. Certainly injections of steroids should never be made into the tendon itself but only into the tissues around the tendon, either within the tendon sheath or in the peritendinous tissues. Repeated injections of steroids should be avoided as this is certainly more likely to lead to a tendon rupture. As at all other sites, steroid injections should not be looked upon as a quick cure to get the dancer back to full performance. After the steroid injection, even if the symptoms are relieved, a proper course of rehabilitation exercises must be instituted to prevent the condition rapidly recurring or progressing to a more serious injury.

Muscle Injuries

Fortunately, serious muscle injuries are not particularly common in dancers although minor muscle pulls and strains are quite frequent.

Muscles may be damaged by direct blows, such as an inadvertent kick or striking a prop or scenery. This can produce bruising with possibly some actual damage to a few of the fibres. A short period of rest accompanied by ice and ultrasound followed by some gentle graduated exercises and stretching usually produces a rapid resolution of the condition.

MUSCLE TEARS

Actual tears of the muscle may occur. Usually, these are only minor and partial, i.e. the tear does not extend right across the muscle and only involves a portion of the muscle belly. It is usually known as a pulled muscle and will occur in most circumstances because of an inco-ordinated contraction of the muscle or part of the muscle, frequently associated with an improper or incomplete warm-up or having to work in an environment which is too cold, possibly standing around between sudden bursts of activity. The tear may be centrally within the substance of the muscle or in the periphery of the muscle. The latter tends to cause less marked pain and interference with use than the former. In a central muscle tear the central swelling which occurs exerts pressure all around the periphery, whereas in a peripheral tear the bleeding is able to disperse and may track along the muscle, appearing at some distance from the site of the tear. However, having said that, it is frequently difficult or impossible to differentiate between the two types of tear. It is often only because recovery is taking very much longer than anticipated that one can come to the definite conclusion that it was a central tear which had taken place. If extensive bruising has appeared, this will be a peripheral tear so the dancer can be confident that recovery will be fairly rapid. A central tear will normally take three or four weeks to heal and allow recovery to take place. Treatment is initially by rest, in order to minimise the amount of bleeding and to prevent any further tearing. Application of ice will help to decrease the amount of bleeding as will also compression by a firm bandage. Elevation of the injured limb will help to decrease the pressure in the injured area.

Early active and passive movements are instituted once it is certain that bleeding has ceased. The degree of exercise must be regulated by pain. Injudicious exercise can aggravate the situation. As the condition settles, a gradual increase in resisted exercises is required to build up the muscle. This is accompanied by regular, gentle stretching so that the scar tissue at the tear does not contract. The more time every day that the dancer can spend on the graduated exercises, the more rapid and satisfactory the recovery. A short period of exercise once a day with nothing in between is not conducive to a rapid recovery.

It is essential that the muscles return to full strength before the dancer is allowed to return to full dancing. However, with care, a gradual return to class can be used as part of the rehabilitation programme.

Occasionally, muscle damage can be complicated by formation of bone within the healing area of muscle. This is caused by damage to the periosteum at the same time as the muscle injury, leading to spillage of bone cells into the muscle haematoma. This bone formation produces a great deal of pain and there is marked limitation of movement. A very firm swelling can be felt deeply within the muscle and this swelling gradually becomes harder. X-rays will show that bone is starting to form in the muscle. The only treatment is to rest the muscle completely. Any sort of activity will aggravate the situation and increase the ossification. No form of physiotherapy helps and is certainly contra-indicated, as treatment is nearly always

detrimental to recovery. Only when the bone has matured and there is no risk of it increasing can active physiotherapy start again. A satisfactory recovery usually occurs if these initial precautions are taken conscientiously. Only rarely is it necessary to remove the lump of bone. Unfortunately, this itself may lead to further spillage of bone cells and the condition can recur, so surgery should certainly not be undertaken lightly.

MUSCLE STIFFNESS

Muscle stiffness usually follows unaccustomed exercise. It is therefore experienced most frequently when the dancer returns to work after a period of holiday. Occasionally it can occur if the dancer has to undertake a sudden increase in workload. The causes of the stiffness may possibly be due to very tiny ruptures of the muscle fibres occurring in the incompletely trained muscle, giving rise to local swelling and causing pain and inflammation. Another possible cause is the accumulation of various waste products which are not removed as rapidly in untrained as in trained muscle. However, neither of these theories has been proved.

Whatever the cause of the stiffness, the treatment is to continue with regular classes and to gradually build up the work. It is important that classes are carried out in a warm atmosphere and that they are designed to give adequate warm-up with a graduated increase in the amount of work. Class should finish with an adequate warm-down.

2.3 Causes and Complications of Dance Injuries

> *All dance injuries are caused by faulty technique.*
>
> *Dance injuries are not an Act of God.*

There is no doubt that this is the most important fact the dancer or dance teacher must understand. When trying to determine the cause of an injury the first question which must be asked by the professional dancer or student, by the dance teacher or by the medical attendant is 'What technical fault has led to this injury?' Once they have started asking this question they are at least part way to making the right diagnosis and instituting the correct treatment and remedial measures. The aim must be a full recovery as rapidly as possible and, equally importantly, the prevention of recurrences of the same injury.

Always remember that the cause or causes of injury may not be apparent except on detailed and meticulous observation and examination.

A small percentage of injuries are best called dance-related injuries and are not dance injuries as such. Under this heading would be included injuries which are sustained during the course of dancing but arising more from the environmental conditions than from faulty technique and occurring in the absence of any fault in technique.

There is also the dancer who is suffering from an injury which is neither a dance injury nor a dance-related injury. If a dancer has been run over by a motor car or has fallen downstairs, he is not suffering from an injury related in any way to his dancing and is merely an injured dancer. Treatment will obviously follow standard lines but, during rehabilitation, which should start from the early stages of treatment, consideration should and *must* be given to the fact that the patient is a dancer and will be required to return to a very high level of activity. Therefore, most aspects of treatment described under that for specific dance injuries can be applied to injuries sustained from non-dance causes. In fact, if medical personnel treating injuries in general were to apply the intensive rehabilitation methods to the average members of the population, they would obtain very much more satisfactory results, given the wishes and dedication of the patient to follow what might be considered a fairly rigorous rehabilitation programme.

Causes of Dance Injuries

INJURIES CAUSED BY FAULTY TECHNIQUE

Anatomical Causes
As most dancers are not anatomically perfect for dance, there will be physical limitations and constraints which may play a part in preventing the development of a perfect technique. Certainly the commonest anatomical cause of potential problems and injuries is limitation of turn-out (external rotation) of the hips.

It is important for the dance student and the teacher of the student to realise and appreciate as early as possible the exact anatomical limitations present so that the student can learn to work within his true physical range. During their early years students must learn to make the best use of all aspects of their physical potential but should not attempt to go beyond that. Reference to **Section 5.7** will enable you to appreciate all the troubles and problems that can arise if dancers attempt to

turn the feet out further than the hips allow, i.e. by attempting to exceed their physical potential or limits.

Lack of Technical Knowledge
During student years young dancers will be more prone to injury as they try to put into effect technique which they are in the middle of learning. Many injuries are seen during this phase of their career, although fortunately they are usually minor, particularly if facilities are readily available for early diagnosis and treatment. If, however, these facilities are not available, it is also at this stage of their lives that the injury can become long-term and persistent. This is usually a result of a failure to appreciate the actual cause of the injury so that the young students do not receive the technical help which is needed to prevent the injury becoming recurrent or chronic.

Bad Teaching
It is in the causation of injury that the bad teacher can excel. They commonly fail to appreciate the anatomical limitations which are being experienced by a student. They fail to recognise areas of weakness which may be exacerbated at some particular time by a growth spurt, by a medical illness such as glandular fever, or by some other extraneous problem. They can fail to notice technical faults which the child is developing and, even worse, they can be teaching technical faults which can bring about injury or compound the ill effects of injuries which have already been suffered. Over turning the feet in relation to the hips is probably the commonest single teaching fault, e.g. demanding a flat or 180° turn-out at the feet which is not matched at the hips. As a general rule the feet should not be turned out further than the available turn-out at the hips. Putting children on to pointe too early and before they are strong enough or pushing them into examinations or other situations with which they are not ready to cope, can also produce very significant problems.

Non-application of Correct Technique
This situation includes professional dancers who are technically fully trained but who for various reasons may allow their technique to slip. This is particularly prone to happen when they become tired. It is seen frequently during the course of a long tour. In this situation, as the tour progresses, the injury rate gradually increases due to a combination of many performances, a great deal of travel with insufficient rest between performance venues and frequently, inadequate conditions for performance and of hotel-type facilities.

In this sub-section should also be included injuries which are produced by bad choreography, where the choreographer may, during the never ending search for something totally new, embark on a routine which is so bizarre or awkward that it is incapable of being carried out with any type of established technique. In this situation dancers may become injured while they are trying to develop a technique in order to carry out the required routine, or injury may follow the sudden unaccustomed use of an area of the body, e.g. muscle group or type of movement, which has been little used in the past and would, if it were to remain injury free, require gradually increasing use and development.

ENVIRONMENTAL CAUSES OF INJURY

These causes will produce what might be termed dance-related injuries, although the environment may in fact contribute to genuine dance injuries themselves. Over most of these environmental causes the dancer personally will have little or no control, although the experienced professional should be able to recognise the potential dangers and at least make representations for an improvement or correction of whatever defect is present.

Among the environmental causes are inadequate facilities. This particularly applies to a lack of daily class opportunities as pertains in many stage shows which involve a great deal of dancing, as opposed to professional dance companies where the daily class is part of the routine working of the company. In a large town it may be possible for the dancer to go out and join an open class if one is available. However, in some areas adequate classes may not be held and it is in this situation that the management, if they fail to provide facilities for their dancers to carry out a daily class of their own, would be creating an environmental cause for the development of injuries among the dancers concerned. If the dancer has no access to a space large enough for him even to construct his own daily class, he will be in the situation where he has to go into the show each evening without any adequate preparation earlier in the day. It is at times such as this that injury rates can be seen to rise steadily. It is certainly in the management's own interest either to provide the actual facilities for a daily class for all their dancers including, if possible, someone to take the class, or else to make arrangements for the dancer to have the opportunity to attend an outside class. This failure on the part of management and promoters is probably as much due to their lack of appreciation of the requirements of their dancers as any deliberate disregard of these necessities. From this point of view the dancers themselves, together with their representatives, must take some of the blame for not insisting on the provision of adequate facilities.

Among the genuine environmental causes which may predispose to injury are (a) temperature (b) floor.

Temperature

The ambient temperature in which the dancer is expected to take class, rehearse or perform must be such that they do not become chilled before, during or after any of these activities. The ambient temperature should not be allowed to fall below 68–70°F. As has been mentioned in the causes of injuries (**Section 2.2** Muscle Tears, page 72), muscle injuries in particular are far more likely to occur if the dancer is inadequately warmed-up. Excessively high temperatures, although not predisposing directly to injury, have their own complications, notably the production of excessive sweating leading to loss of water and electrolytes (mainly salt). If this loss is adequately replaced then no harm will accrue. However, there is a tendency for the dancer to inadequately replace the fluid loss and this can lead to muscle cramps and spasms as well as more serious medical problems if it occurs over a longer period.

The Floor

This is an extremely important factor in environmental causes of injury. The actual floor construction is of the greatest importance to the dancer. Unfortunately, in many modern theatres and in studios which are not purpose-constructed the underlying foundation for the floor is reinforced concrete. The sight of a wooden floor should not delude the dancer into thinking the wood has been sprung. Only too frequently it has been laid directly on a concrete surface, or upon rolled steel joists. The lack of spring can produce many injuries, notably foot problems, injuries in the lumbar region of the spine, in the muscles which are associated with take off and landing and in the bones, mainly the tibia and the metatarsals, which can be the site of stress fractures. Floor construction is a complicated subject and outside the sphere of this book. However, it does appear that provided classes and rehearsals are carried out on a floor which is completely suitable for dancing, then occasional performances which are carried out on inadequate floor constructions may be acceptable provided the inadequate floor is covered with two layers of special cushioned vinyl. Although this is the current thinking, further experience may indeed show that even this covering of a solid floor is, in the long term, inadequate, particularly if performances are regularly held on that type of surface as opposed to a short series in one particular theatre or television studio.

A second factor in floor construction applies to stages. Many touring companies will find that they have to work on a heavily raked stage. While this is eminently satisfactory for normal theatrical productions in giving the audience a far better view, it does pose great problems for dancers. The presence of a rake not only predisposes to the development of injuries but it can also delay recovery from minor injuries which are insufficient to stop the dancer from working. Predominantly, a raked stage will cause a weight back situation with all its associated problems (see **Section 5**). Additionally, moving *across* a rake poses different problems. Unfortunately, there is nothing that can be done about the presence of a raked stage but it behoves the dancer and the medical attendants to be aware of the possible dangers.

Finally, when considering the floor, the actual surface is important. The difficulties associated with a slippery surface are obvious. Less obvious, however, is the over-use of rosin. Unless the floor is cleaned regularly, the rosin can build up, frequently in irregular and uneven patches. This can result in a dancer suddenly finding that his foot is sticking to the floor with potentially disastrous consequences if he is in the process of a turn, when the transmitted twist between the fixed foot and the moving body can produce serious injury at the ankle or knee.

General Complications of Injury

EFFECTS ON THE WHOLE BODY

Decrease in Cardio-respiratory Fitness
As a result of the enforced decrease in activity following an injury, the cardio-respiratory fitness of the dancer will decline. In other words, when he returns to exercise, he will get out of breath more rapidly, his pulse rate will increase to a higher level and he will feel his heart pounding for a given activity. These effects are largely brought about because the stroke volume of the heart will have decreased. In other words, the amount of blood pumped out on each contraction of the heart will be less, hence to get the same amount of blood to the various organs, in particular the muscles, the heart will have to beat more quickly. In the trained person, the heart will on each stroke pump out a

larger volume of blood than in the untrained heart, therefore the athlete can maintain an increased blood flow to the muscle by a combination of increased volume from the heart on each stroke as well as an increased stroke rate. In the untrained heart, the demand for more oxygen and a greater requirement for the removal of carbon dioxide will result merely in an increase in heart rate, with little ability to increase the volume of blood on each stroke. This at the limit will produce a situation where the heart will reach such a rate that inadequate time is given for the heart to fill between each contraction so that a further increase in rate would be self-defeating. During the course of training the heart responds by a greater relaxation between each contraction, which allows a greater volume of filling, thus increasing the quantity of blood pumped out on each contraction. On the respiratory side, the chest capacity and lungs will undergo a similar adaptation so that the volume of air which is breathed in and out on each occasion becomes very much greater.

Generalised Muscle Wasting
This comes about due to inactivity. As a result of the lack of demand the bulk of the muscles will gradually decrease (muscle wasting), the tone will go down, as will also the strength of contraction of each muscle. If the inactivity is prolonged, the muscles will become increasingly flabby. During this period they will also tend to shorten a little, thus slightly decreasing the available range of movement.

Increase in Body Weight
This is by no means inevitable. However, eating patterns are in general psychologically based rather than occurring as a result of demand. Therefore, although the calorie requirements are greatly decreased as a result of the decrease in activity, the calorie intake will probably remain very much the same. These extra and superfluous calories will inevitably be laid down as fat as they cannot be metabolised. If eating is controlled sensibly following an injury, then this weight increase need not occur, although at the same time an adequate balance of nutrients must be maintained in order to facilitate rapid healing (see **Section 2.7**).

Psychological Effects
These may be more or less noticeable depending upon the mental make-up of the individual dancer. However, if the injury is such that the dancer has to be off work, a general feeling of depression is not uncommon. This seems to reach its peak when dancers have been off about five weeks, at which

time most of them will become very depressed, will sleep badly and generally feel that no progress is being made at all. If this is anticipated and the dancer strongly reassured, he will usually get over this period without very much difficulty. If it is known beforehand that he is going to be off for a period of many weeks, then it can be helpful to warn him that he is going to feel like this in due course but that it is a perfectly normal reaction that happens to all dancers and that he will weather it perfectly satisfactorily.

LOCAL EFFECTS

Persistent Swelling

Although swelling follows most injuries, it will normally settle fairly rapidly. Not unusually, the swelling may be such that it has disappeared when the dancer gets up each morning but then gradually recurs during the day. This type of swelling can be helped by elevation from time to time during the day but will gradually lessen and disappear during the course of treatment and the normal healing processes. The dancer merely needs reassurance. However, the swelling may become more permanent. If it is still present first thing in the morning, particularly if the dancer has been elevating the foot of the bed, it may have more serious significance. In the early days the swelling will be due to retention of fluid locally and this can drain away. If, however, drainage is for any reason inadequate, either because the part has not been elevated sufficiently or because there has been more local damage than had been realised, the swollen area may become invaded with fibrous tissue and permanent thickening and scarring can result, hence the importance of the early elimination of swelling as part of the initial and continuing treatment process.

However, this invasion with scar tissue will not take place if the situation is such that the swelling has always disappeared after a night's rest with elevation of the injured part. Permanent thickening, although it may be inevitable if the injury is serious with considerable soft tissue damage, can unfortunately occur just as commonly as a result of inadequate treatment and advice to the dancer. It is in these latter circumstances that it is totally avoidable and to allow it to develop is unforgivable.

Local Vascular Effects

These may play a part in the development of persistent swelling. There may be damage to the local small vessels, particularly the capillaries and lymphatics, which interfere with the resorption of tissue fluid. Elevation of the injured part becomes even more essential in order to aid the drainage of tissue fluid by the use of gravity. With the passage of time, damaged vessels will usually reform themselves and blocked channels will become reopened or new ones will develop. During this part of the healing phase, assistance can be given to the normal body processes by minimising swelling and aiding resorption of the fluid by ice and elevation and other local methods.

Less common are local aberrant vascular responses resulting in greatly increased blood flow with flushing or constriction of vessels with blanching. These effects may be caused by the nervous system but normally will settle spontaneously. At the periphery of the upper or lower limbs there is a rare vascular phenomenon (Sudek's dystrophy) where the bones of the hand and wrist or foot and ankle become partially de-mineralised. The skin becomes tense and shiny and the tissues tend to be swollen. The exact causes for the onset of this syndrome are unclear but there is no doubt that it can be aggravated by immobilisation. Unfortunately, because of persistent pain associated with the condition there is a tendency to prolong the period of immobilisation and this makes the situation very much worse. It can be helped by active movements and use and therefore activity of the part is to be encouraged provided that this is compatible with the healing of any underlying fracture. Fortunately, the condition is normally self-limiting and recovery will be spontaneous, though possibly slow.

Local Muscle Wasting

The causes of this are the same as described above for general muscle wasting. However, due to the local inactivity of the injured part, the muscle wasting in this area will be rather greater, particularly if the limb has had to be immobilised because of a fracture. The muscle wasting will occur rapidly and can be noticeable within two to three days of an injury. By the end of this time the decrease in tone of the muscle can be easily felt by the examining fingers and there can even be a measurable difference when compared with the other limb. Muscle wasting and weakness can be minimised by exercising as much as the injury or immobilisation will allow. It is very important to try to develop some sort of suitable exercise routine which can be initiated early and applied throughout the rehabilitation period (see **Section 2.5**).

Stiffness of Joints

Following inactivity the whole body will tend to

feel rather stiffer. If there has been immobilisation of a joint or joints during the course of treatment then, once the immobilisation is discontinued, the joints will be found to have stiffened up to a greater or lesser extent. This stiffness occurs in the soft tissues around the joint, i.e. the capsule and the ligaments, in the soft tissue planes between the various structures and within the muscles themselves which may have very slightly shortened. Additionally, a weaker muscle is usually less able to relax and lengthen than a trained muscle, so this will also contribute to some loss of movement range. In the normal course of events, provided the joint itself has not been the site of damage, this post-immobilisation or post-inactivity stiffness will wear off fairly rapidly and full mobility will be regained. Once again, exercise is the most important factor in the regaining of a full movement range, together with general strengthening of the muscle groups which control the joints. If, unfortunately, there has been some damage to the joint itself, particularly within the joint, then some restriction of movement may be permanent.

2.4 The Treatment of Injuries – General Principles

The most important fact to recognise is that treatment itself does not heal injuries. Injuries heal by the processes described in **Section 2.1** and are entirely brought about by the body alone.

Treatment can be considered as having primary and secondary aims.

The Primary Aim of Treatment

It must, in essence, be the provision of the optimum conditions so that the body's natural processes of healing can work in the most efficient and rapid manner. These optimum conditions are rest, maintenance of a good blood circulation and a ready supply of the necessary nutrients.

REST OF THE INJURED PART

The rest will allow healing to proceed unimpeded. Movement may cause damage to the granulation and other healing tissue, thus resulting in the end in a great increase in the amount of scar tissue that is formed.

Disadvantages of Rest
If the area rested is too widespread, for example involving the whole limb or even the whole person,

then this will have a three-fold undesirable effect. First, there will be a decrease in stimulation of the circulation. Second, unnecessary muscle wasting will occur. Third, if rest is very prolonged the bones become de-mineralised. Ideally, therefore, the actual area of injury alone should have rest and all the other areas should be encouraged to remain active.

Effects of Immobilisation
The collagen and other tissues of the fibrous network, such as areola tissue, become hard and dense with loss of suppleness during periods of immobilisation. It will start to occur after a few days. The time taken to recover mobility depends on the length of the immobilisation. However, the recovery time to regain full motion is not a simple arithmetical progression but a geometrical progression. This means that immobilisation for, say, four weeks, will not take merely twice as long to recover from as immobilisation for two weeks but will take four to five times as long.

MAINTENANCE OF ADEQUATE CIRCULATION

A good blood supply is essential as has been explained in **Section 2.1**. The blood stream is responsible for bringing most of the necessary cells, proteins, minerals and other requirements for satisfactory healing to take place. Therefore, a good circulation of blood is to be encouraged and factors which can interefere with the blood supply have to be eliminated as far as possible. Probably the most important factor which interefers with the blood supply to the injured part is local swelling. Following the injury there is a great outpouring of blood and fluid into the tissues. This should become absorbed by the lymphatics and circulation. However, this reabsorption can become impaired and the swelling can become greatly aggravated by the effects of gravity and by local inactivity. The heart will have no difficulty pumping blood to the injured part in normal circumstances but drainage via the veins or lymphatics can be greatly hindered by increased pressure due to local swelling and by the effects of gravity. If the swelling increases too greatly it can actually restrict the flow of blood *into* the part and therefore interfere with healing. This can occur to such a degree that the areas adjacent to the damaged tissue can start to die from lack of blood supply and this produces what is known as tissue necrosis. Two important and relatively simple measures can be used to help to decrease this local swelling and maintain an adequate circulation.

a)   *Elevation*   If the injured part, usually the foot or some other portion of the lower limb in the dancer, is elevated, gravity can be used to advantage to help the swelling drain away from the injury.

b) *Ice*   Local application of ice packs or cold packs help to reduce the swelling. NB. Care should be taken with the use of ice packs, particularly if they have been stored in a deep freeze where the normal temperature is 0°F (minus 18°C). (See **Section 2.5** Technique of Application, page 81.)

The measures which are taken to minimise bleeding and swelling at the site of injury are not a contradiction of the statement that a good *circulation* must be maintained. Blood circulation implies that the blood is taken to a part and then removed again via the veins. If there is bleeding at a site of an injury this blood is lost to the circulation as well as increasing local swelling. The ideal is to ensure that there is minimum bleeding following the injury but also then to maintain the maximum circulation.

c) *Pressure bandaging*   The purpose of this is to minimise bleeding at the injury site. The compression should aim to apply enough pressure to control the blood loss into the tissues but at the same time not to be so excessive that the circulation becomes impaired. Less pressure is required to impede or stop the venous return than to impede or stop the arterial inflow. If the venous return alone is impaired then the effect will be to increase rather than decrease swelling because the arterial blood will continue to be pumped into the area. Unless properly applied, compression is better avoided. It is only of value until local bleeding has stopped and should then be discontinued.

Elevation and ice are easily instituted by the patient or helpers and, if carried out immediately, can play a great part in the rapid recovery from an injury. These simple measures, accompanied by a short period of rest for the injured part, may be all that is required to allow satisfactory resolution to take place.

In achieving the primary aims of treatment (i.e. rapid healing with minimum scarring) the physiotherapist has a part to play by the use of ultrasound, etc. This will be described later.

ADEQUATE NUTRITION

This may sound a strange statement when applied as it is to a society affluent enough to afford to maintain dance companies and similar 'luxuries'. However, as will be described in **Section 2.7** on Nutrition, many dancers (as well as other athletes) have very bizarre ideas of what they should be eating. These faulty eating patterns are frequently associated with very undesirable attempts to achieve a weight far lower than is healthy. Without an adequate supply of nutrients the body cannot properly repair tissue damage from injury or even maintain tissues in the best condition following the normal cycles of cell breakdown and repair that constantly occur in all living organisms. During the whole of life various tissues in the body are in a state of change and replacement. There is a continuous change over of the constituent parts of cells. The various body proteins are being broken down and rebuilt, the minerals are being moved around and cells that die are being replaced daily by the million. This is one of the characteristics which makes a living organism as opposed to something like a lump of rock which, however chemically complex it may be, does not alter within itself.

The Secondary Aim of Treatment

This is so to arrange a rehabilitation programme that, while the primary aims of treatment are not jeopardised, the rest of the body can be kept in the best possible physical condition. This includes maintaining cardio-vascular and respiratory fitness as well as ensuring that all possible muscle groups are kept strong and active and are not allowed to waste or weaken. To this end the most important action is to construct an exercise programme for the particular dancer for his or her particular injury.

It must be recognised that rehabilitation, if it is to achieve the greatest success, starts immediately following injury and it is not something which is commenced days or weeks later.

2.5 Specific Treatments of Injuries

Although most forms of treatment have to be administered by a physiotherapist or in the case of more sophisticated treatments, by an orthopaedic surgeon, there are certainly some measures which can be applied satisfactorily by the dancer himself. These are cold therapy or ice, elevation, rest of the injured part and exercise. The latter, of course, can only be carried out by the subject and no third party can do exercises for him.

First Aid Measures

In most acute injuries, i.e. an injury which happens

suddenly as opposed to a chronic injury which comes on very slowly and insidiously and is usually the result of recurrent minor traumas, there are certain measures which should be carried out as soon as possible by the dancer. If carried out immediately they can have a very beneficial effect in dramatically decreasing the time during which the dancer will be partially or wholly incapacitated.

ICE

As soon as the injury has occurred, ice should be applied to and around the injured area. The actual technique of application will be described a little later under the specific physiotherapy treatments (see page 81).

ELEVATION

The icing should be accompanied by elevation of the injured part in order to discourage swelling. As most dancers' injuries occur in the lower extremities, gravity plays a very important part in increasing the amount of swelling. If the leg is elevated then gravity will assist in the drainage of fluid from the injured area.

REST

Rest will encourage early healing to take place without extra disturbance of the damaged tissues. In other words, don't carry on with the class or performance if the injury is anything other than of a trivial nature. Take a taxi home rather than walk a long distance or stand on public transport. Once home, continue with the ice and elevation. These simple measures promptly applied can frequently halve the length of time for recovery.

COMPRESSION

Firm bandaging to compress the injured area is often advised. The purpose is to arrest the local bleeding which occurs at the site of any injury. While theoretically advantageous it can have undesirable complications. In order to arrest the local bleeding the pressure must be sufficient to compress the vessels. If this compression is maintained for too long, or if too extensive, then interference with essential blood supply can occur and there may be local tissue necrosis (death). If used, it should be for a relatively brief period. Once bleeding at the site of injury has ceased, compression can no longer be of any benefit.

In the case of a mild strain it might well be possible to continue class or performing with the use of supporting bandaging or strapping. However, it is important to be certain that there is no serious underlying injury before this action is

taken. Immediately after an injury the damaged part can rapidly become slightly numb and during this period the injured person may not be aware of the possible serious nature of any damage. To continue activity in the presence of a fracture can greatly prolong the actual recovery period or even do more significant damage.

In this short section on first aid measures, a cautionary word against the use of pain-killing tablets or even more powerful pain-killing injections would be in order. If the pain is sufficient to interfere with a performance then nine times out of ten disguising the pain with tablets or injections to allow the performance to continue is merely going to hide temporarily a significant underlying injury. To perform in that state is going very greatly to increase the period of recovery and may indeed cause such further damage that the dancer's career may be ruined – either because he will never be physically capable of returning to dance or because the recovery is so prologed that he may lose his job.

Never forget that pain is a protective mechanism provided by nature in order to stop further damage taking place and to allow recovery to take place in the shortest possible time. Another protective mechanism which some people will try to abolish without due consideration of the consequences or of the next steps in the progress of treatment, is muscle spasm. Muscle spasm is nature's way of providing splintage to an injured part. The muscles around the damaged area will tighten up in order to attempt to immobilise the area. In other words, to provide local rest to the part in order to permit healing to take place as rapidly and successfully as possible. The abolition of muscle spasm by drugs or other methods without due regard to what is taking place underneath and without proper consideration of the next line of treatment can be almost as damaging as the injudicious use of pain-killing drugs. The abolition or relief of muscle spasm at the correct time, i.e. during the course of proper treatment, is highly desirable, but certainly not in order to allow the dancer to continue performance regardless of consequences.

The dancer should always remember that following injury the responses of the body that have been provided by nature have been developed by evolutionary processes to provide the optimum conditions for healing of the injured part. It is only when *adequate* treatment is provided that nature's own protective mechanisms can be removed. It cannot be over emphasised that far too many dancers and other athletes have had their convalescence unnecessarily prolonged by unwise treatment provided either by themselves or by their friends or by ignorant advisors.

It is obviously in the dancers' and their employers' greatest interest that the injury should cause the shortest possible time off work or classes and that recovery should be as complete as possible. An incomplete recovery can be very troublesome as it usually leads to recurrent injuries, either of the same part or elsewhere.

Physiotherapy Treatments

COLD THERAPY

This is usually loosely referred to as ice. However, the cold can be applied by various methods as described under the Techniques of Application on this page. The uses of cold therapy are for
a) relief of muscle spasm;
b) mechanical trauma;
c) pain relief;
d) arthritis;
e) burns.
The last two – arthritis and burns – are not relevant to this book.

In Muscle Spasm
The use of cold therapy in muscle spasm can decrease the actual tone in the muscle itself, provided that the muscle temperature is lowered. If the muscle temperature is not lowered then the tone is not decreased and the muscle spasm is not relieved. Cooling of the skin alone may, in fact, increase the spasm. It may take from ten to as long as thirty minutes, depending upon the amount of fat present, to produce a decrease in the temperature of the muscle. However, the effect, once achieved, is long lasting due to the insulating effect produced by the vaso-constriction in the fat layer. The fat itself is an excellent insulator and the insulation effects are improved by the vaso-contriction of the blood vessels in the fat, i.e. the shutting down of the blood vessels.

Decreasing the spasm in an antagonistic muscle will free the protagonist and can enhance its performance by up to 50%. The effect on the muscle can also help facilitation techniques.

In Mechanical Trauma
Cold therapy can be used advantageously in mechanical trauma. The trauma should be acute, i.e. of recent onset, but it should not be used in severe trauma. The cold works by vaso-constriction (shutting down) of the blood vessels which in turn reduces swelling and bleeding. To this end it is as well to remember the great benefits of applying ice

as soon as possible after the injury and before there has been very much swelling or bleeding. The vaso-constriction is produced by its effect on the sympathetic fibres and also directly by lowering the temperature of the blood within the blood vessels.

In Pain Relief
Pain relief by the use of cold therapy is brought about by several pathways. The pain may be decreased by a direct effect on the sensory endings of the nerves and on the pain nerve fibres. It also works by relieving muscle spasm, which can itself be causing pain within the muscles. Additionally, pain can be relieved indirectly by decreasing swelling. The presence of swelling will cause pain because of increased tension (pressure) within the tissues. Finally, the relief by the use of cold can take place because the cold is acting as a counter-irritant. Pain relief by a counter-irritant has been used for thousands of years and is usually the basis for the various analgesic ointments, balms and linaments that are rubbed into the skin.

Technique of Application
Compresses can be used. These are usually of terry towelling which is soaked in melting ice and water. This mixture gives a temperature of 0°C. The terry towelling is rung out and then placed on and around the affected part.

The part itself can be immersed in the ice and water mixture. Massage using blocks of ice can be carried out. Gel packs can be frozen in a freezer compartment of a refrigerator. They are particularly useful because, when frozen, they do not become solid and can be moulded around a part.

Note: Great care must be taken with massage with blocks of ice or with gel packs. The freezer compartment of a refrigerator or deep freezer is normally set at minus 18°C (0°F) for the adequate preservation of food. Therefore ice straight from a freezer will be at that temperature. Ice does not reach 0°C (32°F) until it starts to melt. Hence the great safety and value of a mixture of ice and water. The surface of a block of ice which is very cold may well adhere to the skin and cause damage unless the surface of the ice has reached the temperature of 0°C and has started to melt. Gel packs are just as dangerous because, as they are malleable, it can be very easily forgotten that they are at a very low temperature. They should not therefore be applied directly to the skin straight from a deep freeze. Before application they can be placed in a bowl of cold water, although this is an uncertain method of raising their temperature. When applied to the patient some terry towelling can be put on the skin first and then the cold pack applied on top of that. Alternatively, the skin can be oiled before the cold pack is applied. The oil will prevent any adherence and will also act as a very slight insulating layer. Over-cold packs can produce frostbite (cold burns). Once a cold pack has been applied it should be lifted from the skin every minute to make certain that the skin is not being blanched, indicating that cooling is excessive.

The skin itself cools rapidly but there is a very much slower reduction in muscle temperature. This rate of drop will depend largely on the thickness of the fat layer. It will take at least ten minutes in a thin person and up to half an hour in an obese person to begin to cool the underlying muscle.

When cooling is applied in trauma it should be carried out early before any considerable swelling has developed. It can with advantage be combined with elevation of the part and also sometimes with simultaneous compression. Once swelling and bleeding are minimised and are not likely to recur, further cooling application of the part serves no purpose. (This, of course, does not apply when cooling is being applied for the relief of muscle spasms.) Cooling over an excessive period may retard healing because of the vaso-constriction of the blood vessels. It was seen in **Section 2.1** that one of the prerequisites of satisfactory healing was an adequate blood supply. Bleeding into an area must not be confused with blood supply. The bleeding produces no satisfactory purpose and merely increases the tension within the tissues. Blood supply implies that the blood is not only brought to the part with the necessary cells and nutrients but also that metabolites and other substances are being removed from the area, i.e. for a good blood supply you need not only an adequate arterial flow and supply but also an adequate venous drainage. Swelling and increase of pressure within the injured part will interfere more with the venous and lymphatic drainage than it will with the arterial supply which is coming in at a far greater pressure.

HEAT THERAPY: METHODS AND EFFECTS

Methods of application of heat are sub-divided into those that heat the superficial tissues only and those that heat the deeper layers. Hot packs, infra-red and similar radiant heat sources heat only the superficial tissues while shortwave diathermy, microwave and ultrasound all heat deeply. All these different modalities work by producing temperature elevation but the reasons for their individual choice comes from the fact that they will selectively heat different areas of the body and will produce a peak of temperature in different locations.

It is important to remember that none of these forms of heat is a cure in itself but it can be extremely valuable in association with other therapies.

The most important factors in determining the intensity of the reactions of the body are

a) *the level* of the tissue temperature attained. To obtain therapeutic benefit the range of temperature lies between 40° and 45°C;

b) *the duration* at which the temperature remains elevated to gain therapeutic benefit; this should be from 3 to 30 minutes;

c) *the rate* at which the temperature rises within the tissues being treated;

d) *the size* of the area that is heated.

The physiological responses to heat therapy are as follows:

1. A rise in temperature increases the extensibility of collagen. The heat will produce changes in the fibrous tissue which makes up tendons, joint capsules, ligaments and scars. This enables them to be stretched very much more easily. In order to attain this the heating needs to be by one of the deep methods of application; pure skin heating is useless. The heating has to be vigorous in order to produce an adequate rise of temperature in the area to be stretched. A steady stretch is very much more effective than intermittent stretching or short term stretching. It is for exactly the same reasons that stretching should be done towards the end of a class when the body is warmed up rather than at the beginning of a class or before a class. Certainly stretching should never be carried out when the person or part is cold. In those circumstances, instead of stretching, the tissue will tend to become torn.

2. Heat will decrease joint stiffness, in part by its effect on the fibrous tissues around the joint and in part by its effects within the joint itself.

3. Heating produces pain relief by its effect on the peripheral nerves and nerve endings.

4. Heating will decrease muscle spasm by its direct effect on the muscle spindles which makes them less sensitive to stretch stimuli. This is also another reason for only stretching when the muscles are warm.

5. Heating will increase the blood flow by the

direct effects of temperature on the blood vessels as well as by reflex mechanisms.

6. Heating assists in the resolution of the inflammatory swelling and exudates by its effect on the tissue and on cellular function.

Distant Reactions to Heating

If the skin in one area is heated an increase in blood flow is produced in other parts of the body, although this increase in blood flow will be less than in the heated area. If the underlying muscle itself is not heated its vessels may actually constrict because blood is being diverted from inactive organs to the skin for heat exchange and body temperature control. Of interest is the observation that has been made that when heat is applied to the abdominal wall the lining of the stomach blanches (whitens because of a decrease in blood supply) and there is a fall in acid level in the stomach. Heat on the abdominal wall also causes relaxation of the smooth muscle in the gastro-intestinal tract and in the uterus, hence the beneficial effects on pain by the use of a hot water bottle on the abdomen at times of abdominal pains from the gastro-intestinal tract and in dysmenorrhoea.

Heating may be vigorous or mild. In vigorous heating the tissue temperature in the deeper structures is elevated and it is particularly indicated when scar tissue is to be stretched. Although superficial heating tends to be mild, if it is applied to a very small part such as a finger, the temperature of the whole part can become very significantly elevated.

Contra-indications to the Use of Heat

1. In anaesthetic areas damage may be caused by heat because of the inability of the person being treated to detect any over-heating. In most instances the physiotherapist relies upon the patient to inform her if the part is becoming too warm.
2. Regions with an inadequate blood supply should not be heated because the increase in warmth will also increase metabolic demand. If there is an inadequate vascular response, as would be the case with poor blood supply, the increase in metabolic demand may in fact lead to ischaemic necrosis (death of the tissues due to inadequate blood supply).
3. Any bleeding tendency is increased by heating because of the increase in blood flow and vascularity.
4. If an acute inflammatory response is present, this will be aggravated by vigorous heating but may be helped by mild heating.

5. Heat is also contra-indicated in many acute mechanical problems. For instance, an acute prolapse of an intervertebral disc, when the rise in temperature produced by an increase in heat will result in an increase in local swelling. If a nerve is already under pressure from the disc prolapse, the pressure on the nerve will be increased, possibly with serious results. However, in an acute mechanical problem, mild superficial heat may help by relieving secondary spasm.

While gentle superficial heat is unlikely ever to do any harm, none of the deep heat modalities should be applied except by a fully trained physiotherapist. Severe and lasting damage can be caused by any of the sophisticated deep heating methods, some of which also have non-thermal effects. In no circumstances should the dancer be tempted to use one of these machines either on himself or on a friend.

SELECTION OF MODALITY OF HEAT

Superficial Heating

This can be applied by hot packs, paraffin wax baths, infra-red or heat tunnels. However, it is as well to remember that a very small part such as a finger may, even with superficial heat, have a rise in temperature of the whole part, merely because of the small bulk of tissue.

Hot packs may be obtained by wringing out terry towelling in hot water and then applying to the part. However, they have the disadvantage of cooling rapidly. Gel packs can be used hot as well as cold and these have the advantage of retaining their heat for a very much longer period. Paraffin wax baths have traditionally been used for many decades for the treatment of hands and feet. They are particularly beneficial in the treatment of hand injuries and rheumatoid arthritis but have little application in the treatment of sports and dance injuries.

Infra-red or radiant heat is produced by special bulbs or heating elements. It uses the red end of the spectrum, going into the adjacent infra-red wavelengths. It has very superficial penetration, reaching the skin and only the most superficial parts of the subcutaneous tissues.

The Effects of Superficial Heating

Benefit can be derived for pain relief by being a counter-irritant. It can also produce some deep responses reflexly but these are of little value or significance although there can be some relief of muscle spasm. In the main, superficial heat will produce a feeling of comfort and relaxation in the patient and will help from that point of view.

Contrast Baths

These really fall in a section of their own, using as they do both hot and cold. They achieve their benefit by producing a hyperaemia (an increase in blood flow) by alternately submerging the part in hot water and in cold water. In sports and dance injuries they are particularly useful for feet and ankles. The hot water should be at a temperature of between 40° and 44°C and the cold water at between 15° and 20°C, although some authorities recommend a much lower temperature than this for the cold bath.

The contrast baths are used by immersing the part in the hot water for ten minutes initially and then transferring to the cold water for one minute. The cycles are then continued with four minutes in the hot bath and one minute in the cold bath for a period of half an hour. Contrast baths are something that can be very safely and satisfactorily carried out at home by the dancer. They are very effective and achieve their results by increasing the blood supply. End with the cold bath.

DEEP HEATING

Diathermy is a name which covers a variety of different methods of heat production, all acting in the deeper layers. Energy is converted into heat at an interface, for instance between subcutaneous tissue and a muscular layer or between a muscle layer and bone.

The pattern of heating will vary between the different diathermy modalities. The temperature distribution is also modified by the different physical properties of the various tissues, e.g. by their specific heat (this is the amount of heat energy which is required to elevate that particular tissue by 1°C – tissues and all other matter have varying specific heats) or by their differing thermal conductivities (some substances, e.g. metals, conduct heat very quickly and effectively, whereas others such as wood conduct heat very slowly).

Short-Wave Diathermy (S.W.D.)

This is the application of high frequency currents for therapeutic purposes. All S.W.D. machines have three components, namely, a power supply, an oscillating circuit and the patient's circuit. The allowed oscillating frequencies are 13.66, 27.33, and 40.98 megaherz (MHz). The most commonly used frequency is 27.33 MHz which is equivalent to a wavelength of 11 metres. The patient's own electrical impedence (resistance to the passage of an electrical current) forms part of the patient's circuit. Therefore the machine has to be tuned for each individual patient. The actual current flow

through the patient can then be regulated after tuning by varying the inductive coupling of the high frequency oscillating circuit and the patient's circuit. It is not possible to measure the high frequency current flow through the patient. The physiotherapist is guided by the feeling of warmth on the part of the patient. Low warmth indicates a low dose. A high warmth up to the limit of tolerance is required for a high dose, hence the importance of having normal sensibility in the part being treated. An anaesthetic area is a very definite contra-indication to the use of S.W.D.

Basically, the treatment is applied by the part being treated lying between two capacitator plates. These can vary in shape and flexibility.

There are certain precautions which must be taken. Metallic objects will undergo selective heating, so all watches, jewellery, etc. are removed before treatment starts. The patient must be treated on a wooden and not a metal couch. If the circuit is not tuned correctly, small movements of the patient may alter the impedence of the circuit, causing resonance. As a result, there may be a surge of increased current flow and possibly burns of the patient. Internal metal such as pacemakers or artificial joints (unlikely in dancers) and metal plates or screws used to fix bygone fractures (quite possible in dancers or athletes) are definite contra-indications to short-wave diathermy and must be reported to the physiotherapist before treatment starts, if the physiotherapist has not already made enquiries about their possible presence. However, surgical implants such as plates and screws, if far removed from the site of treatment, do not impose any particular risk. Contact lenses may cause hot spots and although normally nowhere near the area of treatment, it is advisable to remove them before treatment starts.

Microwave

These are very high frequency currents and are usually either 2456 MHz or 915 MHz in medical application. The latter are rather better and produce heating more deeply. These very high frequency currents are selectively absorbed by water and hence allow selective heating of certain tissues such as muscles which contain a lot of water, but relatively little heating of bone which contains very little water. (Hence the use of microwave in cooking, when the food – all of which has a high water content – is heated and cooked, while the dish remains cold until it is warmed by direct conduction from the hot food.)

Therapeutic Effects   Microwave can selectively and easily heat the musculature and can also selectively heat a joint, provided it has only a little soft tissue covering.

Side Effects   The eyes, which contain a great deal of water, can be selectively heated and must be carefully avoided. Microwave can produce a decrease in bone growth. It should not be used in anaesthetic areas or in the presence of buried metal.

Non-Thermal Effects   Microwave may also have some non-thermal effects but these are not fully understood and must therefore be discounted for therapeutic purposes.

Ultrasound

The ultrasound machine produces a high frequency alternating current of 0.8 MHz to 1.00 MHz. This is converted by a crystal transducer into mechanical sound waves – acoustic vibrations. The sound beam produced by the ultrasound head is almost cylindrical in shape. The intensity is expressed in watts per square centimetre (watts/cm2). The maximum that should be used is four watts/cm2. Most commonly, the application is at less than one watt/cm2. Like audible sound waves, ultrasound waves are propagated by compression waves. Therefore propagation depends upon the presence of a medium capable of being compressed. As the wave passes through the tissues it produces powerful mechanical forces, among the effects of which may be the production of small, gas filled cavities from dissolved gases. These cavities then collapse, causing shock waves. As the sound is passed through the tissues it becomes absorbed and converted into heat. Remember a basic law of physics, i.e. that energy can neither be created nor destroyed. It is therefore converted from one form of energy to another form of energy, in this case from sound to heat, although initially it was electrical energy which was converted to sound.

The penetration of ultrasound into muscle is very satisfactory. The temperature distribution produced by ultrasound is different from the other modalities – short-wave diathermy and microwave. Ultrasound causes very little superficial temperature elevation and has a greater depth of penetration into the muscles and soft tissues than S.W.D. or microwave. The ultrasound selectively heats interfaces between tissues of different acoustic impedence because of reflection, formation of sheer waves and selective absorption. Even the temperature in joints covered by a great depth of soft tissues can be raised therapeutically by ultrasound. (For example, in the hip, which is not greatly affected by either short-wave diathermy or microwave.)

Effects of Ultrasound   These are due to the heating effects of ultrasound and are similar to the effects produced by the other agents, although as mentioned, ultrasound can penetrate far more deeply.

Non-Thermal Effects   Ultrasound increases the permeability of tissue membranes. Cavitation can be produced and this can cause tissue damage. It is evidenced by petechial haemorrhages (small red spots on the skin) but these only occur at high intensities of ultrasound and a poor application technique. However, with a poor technique, cavitation can be produced at even one to two watts/cm2. With good stroking technique, intensities of up to four watts/cm2 are safe although usually quite unnecessary. In certain situations ultrasound can speed up healing processes but this mainly occurs in chronic rather than in acute lesions.

Side Effects   Ultrasound can cause nerve damage due to a concentration of heat at the interface with the nerve and also within the nerve at the interfaces between the nerve fibres.

Ultrasound is, however, the only deep heating method that can be used safely with buried metal because although there is an increase in heat at the metal interface due to reflection, the metal carries away the heat more quickly than any effective or damaging rise in temperature that can be produced.

It must be stressed again that none of these pieces of apparatus, short-wave, microwave or ultrasound, should be used by a patient or by anyone other than a fully qualified physiotherapist. Ultrasound in particular can seem very innocuous and the dancer may be tempted to apply it himself with very unfortunate results. Also there can be no excuse whatsoever for any physiotherapist, however busy, who allows a patient to apply the ultrasound himself, even when under partial supervision. Despite using a low wattage a poor application technique or use at a site overlying a very sensitive structure, such as a nerve, can produce damage.

INTERFERENTIAL THERAPY

Two medium frequency currents between 4000 and 4100 Herz generate low frequency impulses between 0 and 100 Herz in the area in which the medium frequency currents are superimposed. At this site they produce an interference pattern.

Depending on the low frequency current wavelength produced the result can be analgesic (pain killing), can stimulate muscle contractions or can increase the blood supply. The selected results can be used to make the active form of treatment, e.g. exercises, more easily carried out by either pain relief or by stimulating muscles. The hyperaemic effect can be of value in increasing the rate of healing, including the stimulation of the healing process in stress fractures. In competent hands interferential therapy is safe and effective and can be used in the presence of buried metal. However, in the hands of the careless or unskilled it is at best useless and at worst can cause the patient considerable discomfort; either by producing electric shocks by allowing the machine to surge or by causing the muscles to go into very painful spasms by over-stimulation. Like the other machines it should not be used by the untrained person.

FARADISM

This is the direct stimulation of the nerve endings in the muscle itself by the use of electric currents at the make and break phases in order to produce muscle contractions. Its use is re-educative, as by making a muscle or group of muscles contract the patient will appreciate in the conscious part of the brain not only the movement that is required but also the sensation engendered by the muscle contracture. This sensation is brought about by a combination of sensory responses to stretch in the muscle tendons and by proprioceptors affected by joint movements. The patient must be encouraged to reinforce the contraction by voluntarily copying the contraction produced by the stimulating current. The stimulation can be decreased and then discontinued in due course but the patient will still be able to reproduce the contraction actively. It is only by active contraction of a muscle that it can be significantly strengthened. Mere passive contraction by faradism alone has little effect in strengthening muscles. Its commonest use is in faradic foot baths where, try how he may, the average patient with poorly functioning intrinsics is quite unable to voluntarily produce the desired movements. Once the patient 'gets the feel' of what should be happening by using faradic stimulation he can then begin to reproduce the same contraction voluntarily. It is important that the patient realises that for it to be effective he must work *with* the stimulating current; little benefit will accrue if he remains completely passive.

Faradism can be of help in initiating muscle contractions in other areas of inhibition, e.g. the quadriceps after a knee operation. Here as elsewhere it is re-educative and not a definitive treatment. Many dancers find it advantageous to own their own small faradic machine, enabling them to carry out regular faradic foot baths in order to keep the intrinsic muscles working

efficiently and under control. It is surprising how easy it is to lose the conscious control of these muscles to the point that, however much the dancer puts in mental effort and tries to get them to work, there seems to be a complete loss of continuity between brain and muscle. This is probably because from an evolutionary point of view these muscles are on their way out as we no longer use the feet for gripping, as do the apes. It is in the maintenance of conscious control that the faradic machine plays a vital role.

In passing, it must be said that faradic stimulation does not produce weight loss, reduction of fat in selected areas or redistribution of fat. There are machines sold commercially to the public which claim just these benefits. They are expensive and quite useless for their alleged purposes.

TRANSCUTANEOUS NERVE STIMULATION (T.N.S. BUT T.E.N.S. IN THE USA)

This is carried out by a very small battery-operated machine which can be worn on the belt or carried in a pocket. Electrodes at the end of wires are stuck to the skin and apply small electric currents in order to stimulate the nerves and relieve pain. (Mode of action – It is thought to work by closing a neuro-electrical 'gate' in the spinal cord, thus preventing pain impulses from ascending the spinal cord past this point and hence failing to reach the level of consciousness. An alternative theory is that it works by stimulating the production of endorphins. These are analgesic substances which occur naturally within the body. Recently they have been arousing a great deal of interest and have been referred to as naturally produced morphine-like substances. The action of the T.N.S. may be a combination of these two theories.) By its repeated use it can gradually produce longer periods of pain relief, leading in the end in many cases to the complete relief of pain, enabling the T.N.S. machine to be discarded. As the electrodes are stuck onto the skin, there is no invasion of the body and it has no attendant risks.

ACUPUNCTURE

This probably works in a similar fashion to T.N.S. However, because of the possibility of the transference of viruses such as hepatitis or even AIDS, if the needles that are used are not completely sterile, it is less safe than T.N.S.

ACUPRESSURE

This is by the external application of pressure to the acupuncture points. It works in a similar manner but is probably less effective. As it is non-invasive it is safer than acupuncture and carries no risk of infection.

TRACTION

Traction, or a pulling on a part, can be applied either manually or through a machine. Commonly, a machine is used for cervical and lumbar spinal traction. It is more effective and easier to apply than manual traction, which rapidly tires the physiotherapist who cannot maintain a heavy pull for very long. In the cervical spine, the traction is exerted through a halter which grips the back of the head and the chin. In the lumbar spine, traction is applied by means of a pelvic corset. Heavy weights can be applied for a short period of time to an out-patient but if a patient is to have continuous traction in bed, as in an acute neck or lumbar condition, then the weights have to be relatively low, about $2\frac{1}{4}$ kilograms in the cervical region and about $4\frac{1}{2}$ to 7 kilograms in the lumbar region, otherwise they cannot be tolerated for any length of time.

Traction probably exerts its beneficial effects by the stretch which is applied to the soft tissues. A continuous gentle stretch will tend to abolish muscle spasm. It may very slightly open up the facet joints between the vertebral bodies (see **Section 1.2** for facet joints). By relieving pressure from within the small facet joints, pain will be eased. Traction is particularly beneficial in various pains originating in the cervical spine, whether from the intervertebral discs or from the soft tissues and in the lumbar region from symptoms originating in the lumbar discs, especially if there is referred pain down one or more nerve roots producing sciatica.

During the course of treatment, traction is frequently applied to various other joints. This is merely part of a general stretching of the soft tissues and really should be considered more under the heading of passive stretching rather than genuine traction.

We now come to those treatments where machinery is not required.

MASSAGE

This is undoubtedly the oldest of all remedial treatments and was certainly being used more than 3000 years ago. Even without being looked upon as a definite treatment, massage is instinctively used by both man and animals who will naturally tend to rub a painful area.

Effects of Massage
1. Reflex –
   By stimulation of the peripheral receptors which transmit impulses to the spinal cord and

brain to produce sensations of pleasure or relaxation. The relaxation is both of muscle and of mental tension.
2. Mechanical –
   a) It increases blood circulation by assisting the return of blood and lymph if the massage is applied with the greatest pressure towards the centre of the body.
   b) It can produce intra-muscular motion and may be effective in stretching adhesions between muscle fibres.

It is very important to remember that massage cannot build up muscle strength, nor can it dissipate fat. Overall, apart from producing a pleasurable relaxation, the effects are minimal. However, with care, it is quite harmless.

Contra-indications
Massage must be avoided in local infections and in any case of thrombo-phlebitis or suspected thrombo-phlebitis.

MOBILISATIONS

This is a term used for gentle, non-violent passive movements of joints. It is applied to areas of the spine as well as in the more peripheral joints. The useful results are produced by a gentle repetitive stretching of capsules and ligaments which will gradually diminish or abolish the painful impulses being transmitted from nerve endings within those structures. These impulses are often reflexly causing muscle spasm so a secondary benefit of mobilisations is the relief of this spasm. The mobilisations (also called Maitland mobilisations) are applied by oscillating passive movements without forceful techniques. In the spine their use is very much safer and has a much more localised effect than the violent manipulations used by osteopaths amd chiropractors.

MANIPULATIONS

This term (together with expressions such as Thrust Techniques and Grade V) is used to describe a forceful passive movement of small amplitude and high velocity. The proponents of manipulation do not agree about its use or its mechanism (as examination of the literature will show). However, provided that one can accept that its use is empirical and not anatomically specific, particularly in the spine, it can sometimes be useful in relieving acute pain. It has nevertheless significant risks attached to its use. In the spine, manipulation is just as likely to increase a disc prolapse with the unfortunate production of nerve damage, as it is to relieve pain. Fractures can occur with fragile bones and joint instability can be increased. It should never be used in the presence of inflammation or in suspected or possible malignant disease.

There are some people who have a sense of increased mobility and well-being after manipulation of a normal joint or joints, although others will feel stiff and sore. In the former group, the prophylactic use of manipulation in the hope that injuries will be prevented has no foundation of proof. Continued manipulation of a normal joint is considered by many to be harmful in the longer term and may possibly lead to the onset of osteo-arthritis in these joints. It is well recognised that osteo-arthritis frequently occurs early in joints subjected to the repeated stress of certain activities or sports and so-called prophylactic manipulation probably falls into this category. The dancer should certainly beware of those who recommend weekly manipulations as a routine. Managements or others in authority who send their dancers off for this type of treatment must also be aware that they could be legally liable for any damage that ensues in the short or long term.

STRETCHING

Stretching can be passive, assisted active or completely active. As has already been mentioned, stretching is effective if the tissues to be stretched are warm (see **Section 2.5** Deep Heating, page 84). To be most effective, the stretch should be prolonged and steady rather than intermittent or frequent, short-term stretches. Any stretch has to be applied with care in order to avoid damage to the tissues. If tissues are torn during stretching, then healing has to take place. As was described in **Section 2.1**, all healing is by scar tissue, i.e. fibrous tissue. With the passage of time scar tissue tends to contract and this may well make the tightness, which the stretching was originally aimed to relieve, worse than before the stretching started. Certainly any forcible stretching can only be harmful and will tend to be totally counter-productive.

The aim of any stretching is to gain an elongation of the tight tissues without any bleeding into the tissues. This can only be produced gradually over a period and must never be rushed. After an injury, the tissues, even though apparently healed, can still be very sensitive in the early stages and may respond very badly to stretching. This can lead to further contracture rather than to the desired stretch. It is important, therefore, that following injury stretching does not take place until the appropriate time in the convalescent period which will tend to be later, rather than sooner. It is quite impossible to lay down any general time scale and it is here that the advice of a physiotherapist

experienced in the treatment of sports and dance injuries is invaluable.

Passive stretching is, as its name implies, carried out entirely by the therapist. Active stretching is that carried out by patient or dancer alone. Assisted active stretching is a combination of stretch applied by the physiotherapist and by the patient. Again it must be emphasised that the dancer must be aware of what he is trying to achieve and the best way to go about it. The essential points are:

1. the dancer must be warm;
2. *gentle* stretching should be carried out after the pre-class warm-up and again during the course of class once the muscles are really warm, e.g. at the end of barre;
3. the stretch should be steady and prolonged and not forcible;
4. sudden forcible stretches, jerking, bouncing and similar stretching effects are undesirable and usually counter-productive;
5. a weak muscle should never be stretched. Stretching in this case must be deferred until the muscle has been adequately strengthened. Stretching must always be accompanied by exercises to strengthen the muscles;
6. Stretching must be in the longitudinal direction of the fibres in the tissue being stretched. Stretching across the fibres achieves nothing and may cause tearing. Stretching of tight areas is frequently not best carried out in the direction of the apparent tightness. Consideration must be given to what particular structures are causing the tightness and in which direction their fibres run. Only then can the stretch be carried out in the correct direction. A joint which seems tight in one particular direction (e.g. tightness of turn-out at the hip) may need individual stretching programmes in two or more different directions in order to obtain the desired increase in mobility.

Specifically, two of the worst things that can still be found happening from time to time is seeing a dancer, commonly a student, lying in the frog position with someone standing on their knees trying to push them apart and down to the floor. Quite apart from the damage that this is going to do to the soft tissues, the turn-out in the frog position bears no relation at all to the turn-out at the hips when the legs and hips are straight in the working position (see **Section 5.8**). The other abomination is to see a girl student with her forefeet (toes and metatarsal region) under a piano or radiator leaning back in order to 'improve' her pointe. There are, unfortunately, still some older teachers around who advocate this as the only method of improving the pointe. These two different actions can be at best useless and at worst actively harmful. They will certainly produce no benefit on either turn-out or pointe.

EXERCISES: THEIR VALUE

In both dance and sports injuries, a suitable programme of exercises is by far and away the most important part of treatment and rehabilitation. All earlier physiotherapy treatments that have been described, although effective in many conditions and aiding the healing processes, cannot in themselves in any way produce a full return to normal function and strength. Only exercises can strengthen muscles. Only exercises can help to mobilise joints satisfactorily and permanently. Those treating dancers, as well as dancers themselves, must realise the importance of proper exercise programmes. If treatment is confined merely to something easy and quick to relieve the current symptoms and pain, this will leave any underlying weakness or weaknesses that have developed as a result of the injury or have been the cause of the injury to remain uncorrected. As a result the injury is likely to recur or further injuries at other sites will be likely to occur.

After any sort of injury the muscles involved in that part, as well as more distant groups, are going to weaken. This is the natural response of the body when muscles are not used for however brief a period. Every injury will increase the weakening and as the weakening itself increases, so will the liability to further injuries.

THE AIM OF EXERCISE

Cardio-respiratory Fitness

Any form of general exercise benefits the cardio-vascular and respiratory systems. It produces what is known as cardio-respiratory fitness, i.e. it stimulates and strengthens the heart, the general circulation, the respiratory capacity and the way the body can deal with metabolites (the by-products of tissue metabolism which are increased in exercise). Hence it produces an increase in the person's tolerance of exercise. In order to increase cardio-respiratory fitness, exercise must be taken daily to such an extent that the person becomes out of breath and the heart rate increases. With the increase in heart rate there is also an increase in the capacity of the heart so that the volume of blood pushed out on each contraction is increased. The trained heart will be able to push out a far greater volume of blood on each stroke than the untrained heart. In order to

achieve cardio-respiratory fitness the best forms of exercise are swimming, cycling, either on a normal bicycle or using a static bicycle, cross country skiing, either actual or using a cross country skiing machine, running or even *very brisk* walking. Although running and jogging are popular they do have some serious drawbacks. For most people the running will inevitably mean doing so on the pavements or on the road. This, despite the best of running shoes, produces repeated jarring and leads to problems with the back, knees, feet and ankles. It is better if the running can be carried out on grass. If not, one of the other forms of exercise is far less likely to cause injury.

Increase to Muscle Strength

Exercise is essential to strengthen the skeletal muscles in the body. Exercise in this form may be directed at certain muscle groups that the dancer or sportsman wishes particularly to strengthen or it may be a more general strengthening programme. It is important to emphasise that not only should muscle groups be strong, but they must also be balanced. It is obviously unhelpful to have a group of muscles on one side of the body much stronger than the same group on the other. There is a normal tendency for this to happen because most people have a preferred side for working and this side will therefore usually have more exercise for the muscle groups concerned.

Increase of Mobility and Joint Range

Exercises in dancers and certain sportsmen are designed to increase mobility and joint range. This is, of course, accompanied by stretching of the soft tissues. However, pure stretching does not necessarily or effectively increase the range of movements of the joints. It is equally important if not more important to exercise the muscles groups controlling the movement of a joint in order to strengthen them. Only too frequently a dancer will think that he has some restriction at a joint whereas an examination of the range of movements will show that the range is in fact full, but the dancer is unable to use the available range of movement because the controlling muscles are not strong enough. Therefore in addition to pure mobilisation exercises, attention has to be given to strengthening the groups of muscles controlling the joint so that the full range of movement can be used with complete muscle control *throughout* its range.

TYPES OF EXERCISE

Passive Exercises

These have very little place as far as sportsmen and dancers are concerned. Passive exercises are where a joint or part is moved by another person in order to maintain full mobility in a joint. This is applicable particularly where there has been paralysis of a limb. Passive exercises are undertaken in order to prevent contractures occurring around a joint. Passive exercises do nothing to strengthen the muscles concerned.

Active Exercises

Active exercises are those which are carried out by the dancer and they entail an active contraction of the groups of muscles concerned. This contraction can be either *isometric*, when the muscle is contracted hard but the actual movement is prevented due to increasing resistance being applied, or the contraction can be *isotonic*, where the resistance remains constant but the joint moves. Only active exercises can increase muscle strength. Normally, resistance in some form is required and the common method of applying this resistance is to use weights. Early in the training programme the resistance may merely be gravity, particularly following an operation. But soon the dancer will need to use some weights or other form of resistance. Occasionally the resistance may be provided by the physiotherapist who is supervising treatment if it is following an injury. The resistance can take two forms – very heavy resistance where the patient is only able to exercise the muscle against this resistance for a relatively few number of contractions. These are referred to as high resistance low repetition exercises. The alternative is to have a relatively low resistance (in using a weight this will often be somewhere between one and four kilograms) with a far greater number of contractions or movements. These are low resistance high repetition exercises. They are preferable and probably more effective at building up muscle strength than the high resistance low repetition exercises which used to be favoured a decade or two ago.

It is now generally recognised that work with *very* heavy weights can produce actual muscle damage, increase the rate of wear within the joints themselves and can predispose to the development of osteo-arthritis. It can produce an unnatural and undesirable increase in muscle bulk. It is less effective in producing muscle strength than the low resistance high repetition method.

Active Assisted Exercises

This is a form of combination exercise where, although the patient is actively contracting the muscle, he is also receiving some assistance from the physiotherapist. This can be particularly helpful in the early days following an injury or after an operation when even the resistance of gravity can be more than the muscle can contend with, yet the physiotherapist does not want an exercise with gravity totally eliminated. Similarly the faradic machine, by initiating a contraction which is reinforced by the patient's own efforts, can help to produce a far more satisfactory muscle response. Exercises for individual muscles groups and the methods by which they are carried out will be considered in detail in **Section 4**.

EXERCISE TRAINING

In the dancer, exercise training is aimed at strengthening various groups of muscles in which strength is required but which may have been neglected during ordinary classes due to the way that the classes themselves have been structured, or due to the type of dance which is predominantly filling the dancer's working day. Basically it must be realised that the muscle groups have two main functions. There is that which everybody appreciates, i.e. the muscles are required in order to move the different parts of the body and the limbs. However, equally important and frequently neither recognised or given enough attention is the requirement that the muscles must also produce stability in both trunk and limbs. Without complete stability in the supporting parts, the working parts cannot achieve their best results. This strength and stability has to be achieved throughout the whole organism, starting at the centre and working outwards. Any area that is neglected will prevent the whole from working satisfactorily. The effects of weakness in particular areas will be discussed in **Section 5**. However, a few general considerations can be dealt with here.

In the presence of muscle groups there are several different effects. Firstly, in the weak groups, if they are trying to stabilise an area which is supporting a working part, they will tend to tire rapidly. They will then go into spasm. This spasm will spill over as tension and affect other areas, including the working areas, thus impairing the performance of whatever action is taking place. Secondly, because of the weakness in the supporting area, there will be a feeling of insecurity and this insecurity will itself cause tension in the working area and prevent proper relaxation of the antagonistic muscle groups, interfering with the fluidity of the movements (see **Section 1.3** Muscle Contraction, page 19). Thirdly, the weakness will generally bring about a limitation of range of movement. This is because the weakness prevents complete control of the joints and, without this control, a full relaxation of the muscles opposing a movement cannot be achieved and hence there will be an interference with the full range of movements at the joint or joints.

Only too frequently dancers may be trying to stretch areas which they consider are tight when in reality there is no genuine tightness present and the lack of adequate range of movement is merely due to weakness of the muscle groups controlling that part. Taken overall, a dancer who appears tight in the joints is far more likely to be in need of strengthening than stretching. It is obviously vital in the initial stages to determine which actual cause is present so that the appropriate series of exercises can be worked out.

The other important aspect of exercise training is to realise and fully comprehend *the importance of balance* between the various muscle groups. Any imbalance can only lead to instability with its attendant problems. Only too often one sees dancers who have quite rightly felt that they are weak in one particular area and have been given exercises for that area without any exercises being given to the opposing groups or the synergistic groups. As a result, a pre-existing imbalance can be aggravated and the situation made worse. It is not exercise and muscle build-up as such which has been at fault but merely the programme which has been devised for that particular dancer. It is also extremely important to realise that the weakness may be in groups of muscles somewhat removed from the area where the dancer feels that there is a problem, or even where the casual observer thinks the problem lies. This is particularly seen where a dancer may be having difficulties or even injuries around the hip region and although receiving treatment and exercise around that area, the feet can be completely neglected. They may in fact have been the initial cause of the problem and be requiring a great deal of work in order to strengthen them up and give support at the bottom end of the pillar.

In doing exercises to strengthen muscles, there are a whole variety of methods that can be employed. Apparatus such as is found in professional gymnasia is far from being essential and basically the only benefit that it gives is possibly to make it a little easier from the psychological point of view to carry out the exercises. Otherwise, all exercises can be done using weights, normally in the region of two to five kilograms, which can be fixed to the part by using Velcro strapping. Frequently, no actual weights are required at all and the weight of the limbs against gravity is all that is necessary.

If weights are used, this can be done in two ways. Using a lower weight with a higher number of repetitions is felt to be the most advantageous. The muscles must be exercised to fatigue and it is this exercising to fatigue which is the essential part of the training programme to strengthen the muscles. Should a high weight, low repetition regime be used, this does not imply that the muscle has to struggle to cope with this level of weight, as this would be totally counter-productive. When exercising to strengthen muscles it is absolutely essential that the muscles are worked throughout their effective range. They must be able to exert full power through the full range of movement possible at the joint they control. In other words the exercise regime must be directed at achieving work against resistance through the arc from full extension to full flexion. If the regime is so constructed that the muscle is only exercised through a part of this range far less satisfactory results will be obtained.

We see a different picture when considering isometric and isotonic exercises as the effects of these cannot be equated with each other. Isometric exercises are those which are carried out with the muscle remaining at the same length but the resistance varying. Isotonic exercises are those carried out where the length of the muscle alters but the resistance remains constant. It has been shown by experiment that if an exercise programme is made up using isotonic exercises only, then the benefits achieved are not transferable and the person will continue to perform best at the isotonic type of exercise on which he trained. Similarly an isometric programme will not produce an equal improvement in isotonic performance. This shows that it is important therefore to build up an exercise programme of a combination of both isometric and isotonic exercises.

Concern is often expressed by girls and female dancers about the possible adverse effects of exercise programmes on their general appearance. However, they have nothing to fear. The proper strengthening of the correct muscle groups will usually produce an improvement in their overall outline and silhouette. They certainly have no reason to believe that because they are doing a lot of exercise and building up muscle that they will start to look like Miss Atlas. It is impossible for a female with normal endocrine function to achieve that type of muscle build-up. In order to do so, she has to take hormones.

FATIGUE

It is worth repeating that in order to increase muscle strength significantly the muscle has to be exercised to the point of fatigue. If a muscle is exercised well within its capabilities, it has, as it were, no incentive to become stronger. (Physiologists thoroughly disapprove of the way the last statement was framed, implying as it does that muscles or other tissues have independent thought processes or psyches of their own!). In order to strengthen a muscle it is necessary to work it to the point where it tires.

What is meant by fatigue? It has been defined as the inability to carry out the assigned task in the assigned manner under specific conditions known to the subject as a result of prior activity. However, this is a behavioural definition. Physiologically, the point of fatigue is very much more difficult to measure. It may be done by measurement of the maximum aerobic capacity after which the oxygen consumption does not increase despite an increased performance of work. This extra work is anaerobic and the onset of fatigue will quickly result in a failure to continue the work at that intensity. Alternatively, electrical activity can be measured electromyographically during a maximal isometric contraction. When the electrical activity increases at the time that the mechanical force is decreasing, this shows that despite a continuing full effort by the subject, fatigue is occurring in that muscle.

Unfortunately, both of these methods of determining fatigue can really only be carried out in the laboratory and as a result the physiotherapist has to push the dancer, or the dancer has to push himself, to continue with the programme of exercises until it is felt that genuine fatigue of the muscle is occurring.

Medical and Surgical Treatments

In dance injuries as well as sports injuries, the role of the orthopaedic surgeon or sports physician is largely one of diagnosis. Most treatment is conservative (i.e. non-operative) and will be applied by the dance physiotherapist. The orthopaedic surgeon is there to examine the patient and make an accurate diagnosis of the underlying problem and to exclude fractures or other significant injuries which might need special treatment; then, in conjunction with the physiotherapist, to devise a programme of treatment and rehabilitation, including technical correction, that is most suitable for that patient with that particular injury. Every patient and every injury is slightly different and needs to be assessed carefully. There are, however, some treatments that can only be administered by the orthopaedic surgeon.

DRUGS

Simple analgesics such as paracetamol and soluble aspirin can be very beneficial in helping the patient in the early stages after an injury but certainly should not be used merely to allow the patient to continue a performance in the face of an undiagnosed injury. The most important preliminary to any type of treatment is an accurate diagnosis.

Non-Steroidal Anti-inflammatory Drugs
These are Brufen, Naprosyn, Indocid and a multitude of others. Their action is to decrease the inflammatory response which occurs following any type of injury as well as in other disease processes. As explained in **Section 2.1**, the inflammatory response is part of the healing process and it is absolutely essential for recovery of an injured part. Interference with the inflammatory response will decrease the rate of healing and will be totally counter-productive. There is, therefore, very little indication for the use of these anti-inflammatory drugs. Occasionally, the inflammatory response as a result of the injury is excessive and in these cases an anti-inflammatory drug may be helpful and beneficial, in which case a very accurate diagnosis is essential before they are administered.

The indiscriminate use of these drugs can only be deplored. Without an accurate diagnosis, taking an anti-inflammatory drug may well mask some significant underlying problem which in the longer term could cause serious damage and disability. They are all prescription-only drugs and administration by anyone other than a registered medical practitioner is, of course, illegal. Quite apart from the undesirable effects that have already been mentioned in relation to the actual injury, all anti-inflammatory drugs have side effects of greater or lesser importance. In particular, they can all cause upsets of the gastro-intestinal tract, including gastric haemorrhage and ulceration. If they are used in the presence of a peptic ulcer they may cause an exacerbation of the condition and a possible perforation.

Hydrocortisone Acetate and Similar Preparations
These drugs, which are given by injection, certainly have a limited application in the treatment of dance and sports injuries. Their action is by abolishing the inflammatory response but, because they are suspensions of the steroid, their action is entirely local. They have no general effects elsewhere in the body and they certainly produce none of the side effects that are brought about by steroids that are administered by mouth. In any case, the dose that is given in one injection of

Hydrocortisone Acetate amounts to about one twelfth of the body's daily output of naturally occurring Hydrocortisone.

In order to be effective, Hydrocortisone Acetate, which is the insoluble form of Hydrocortisone and is the one used in the treatment of injuries, has to be placed at the exact area where the lesion to be treated lies. It may increase the pain locally for some twentyfour hours and is frequently given together with a local anaesthetic. Its main use is where an injury has become chronic, i.e. there is a very low grade inflammation still present and the healing process is incomplete. It is typically of value in conditions such as tennis elbow, chronic tenosynovitis and chronic tendonitis.

Contra-indications are as follows:
1. Hydrocortisone should *never* be used in an acute injury as it will totally stop the healing processes.
2. It should *never* be used if a fracture is suspected or possible, e.g. a stress fracture.
3. In relation to the large tendons (Achilles tendon, patellar tendon, etc.) it should be used with caution and probably only one injection given. It should never be given into the tendon itself but merely into the tissues surrounding the tendon. One of the reasons for the great caution here is that if the tendon itself is the site of damage, the presence of the Hydrocortisone may abolish the healing process which is taking place and result in a complete rupture of the tendon. Similarly, if it is injected into the tendon rather than into the peritendinous structures, it can cause damage to the tendon and subsequent rupture.
4. It should never be given if the diagnosis is uncertain or for want of anything better to advise.
5. As far as dancers and sportsmen are concerned, Hydrocortisone should never be given into a joint. The indications for intra-articular steroids are usually confined to those people who have arthritic conditions of the joints and this is not normally found in dancers or sportsmen during their active careers. It should certainly not be given when the joint is merely recovering from an injury.
6. The administration of either a local anaesthetic, or of steroids particularly, merely to enable a dancer or sportsman to perform, can only be condemned. It is asking for an exacerbation of that injury with the conversion of what is possibly a minor injury to something that is major.

Oral Steroids
In some quarters oral steroids (cortisone, prednisone, etc.) are administered for 3–4 days following an injury on the grounds that it reduces or prevents swelling.

However, it does this by suppressing the inflammatory processes in all their aspects and not just the swelling. As seen from **Section 2.1**, this will totally interfere with the early phases of the healing processes. While this may not matter if the injury is really trivial, if there is any significant tissue damage the delay in the onset of the healing processes can only be disadvantageous. Also by the suppression of these inflammatory processes the dancer may be encouraged to continue full activities with potentially serious or disastrous results.

A further complication is that by the administration of oral steroids the natural body production of its own steroids becomes suppressed, together with more widespread alterations in other hormone levels. The suppression of natural steroid production even for 4–5 days may lead to a much longer period of hormone imbalance before the body finally settles down into equilibrium again.

Use of oral steroids in dancers is unwise, unnecessary and can only be condemned.

OPERATIONS
Surgical operations should only be undertaken when there is a very specific indication, when an accurate diagnosis has been made and when conservative treatment has failed or is not indicated.

These statements may seem so obvious that they are not worth printing. However, far too many dancers are subjected to totally unnecessary surgery for a variety of reasons. On the part of the orthopaedic surgeon there may be a lack of knowledge about dance or sports injuries, leading to an inadequate or inaccurate diagnosis. The surgeon may opt for an operation because he lacks the knowledge and understanding to recommend the correct type of conservative treatment. An example of this is the totally unnecessary surgery which is so often undertaken to remove spurs or areas of calcification which may be seen on an X-ray but are irrelevant to the patient's symptoms. Before embarking on any operation there must be an absolute indication for surgery which must be understood by both the surgeon and by the patient.

Surgery sometimes appears to come about unnecessarily due to pressure from the dancer himself. Only too naturally, the dancer is anxious to get better and return to work as quickly as possible and surgery may appear to be the easiest and quickest way to achieve this end. The dancer may have been shown an X-ray which shows a spur and then, far more justifiably than the surgeon, has fallen into the trap of saying that that is something that should not be there, therefore it must be causing the symptoms, thus pressuring the surgeon, who may be a little reluctant, to carrying out an operation. Only too often, dancers are seen who have undergone surgery and in the longer run are no better as a result and often worse.

It should be realised by everybody that these little spurs and calcifications nearly always represent old minor damage to ligament and capsular attachments and they have formed merely as part of the healing process. Once they have reached that stage, they in themselves are very rarely the source of symptoms.

The other aspect which has to be remembered is that after any operation there is inevitably going to be a period where the dancer is unable to do anything other than rest while the wounds and tissues heal. During this time the muscles will weaken generally throughout the body and more so in the limb which had the surgery. He will then have a period where he gradually progresses back to work. Only too often, if the original cause for the symptoms had been treated simply, possibly with a short period of rest but certainly with progessive treatment including technical help if necessary, then resolution would have taken place without any form of surgery and usually far more quickly and completely.

Finally, it must always be remembered that any operation, however small, carries risks. The anaesthetic itself has a definite, though small, risk. Any wound that is made in the skin has a risk of infection. The post-operative complications include deep vein thromboses. Although the percentage of patients who suffer from any of these complications is fortunately very small, the complications do exist and surgery should not be undertaken lightly or unnecessarily. Ignorance on the part of the orthopaedic surgeon is no excuse for surgery.

Alternative Therapies

Much as their exponents would like to persuade people otherwise, all the alternative therapies are aimed at merely relieving symptoms. This neglects that very important aspect of proper treatment which is to so construct a programme of treatment and rehabilitation as to *prevent further injury, or recurrent injury, of the same area.*

ACUPUNCTURE AND ACUPRESSURE

This has already been mentioned following the section on Transcutaneous Nerve Stimulation. In certain people and certain conditions it can be very effective in relieving pain. It does by its very nature, however, penetrate the skin and is therefore not without potential dangers. Even sticking a needle into someone does carry a very trifling risk. The greatest danger is by visiting an acupuncturist who does not use disposable needles. In the consulting room sterilisation of re-usable needles can be difficult, viruses are mostly not destroyed by simple boiling and a higher temperature with a steam autoclave is required. Inadequately sterilised needles can commonly transmit diseases such as hepatitis or AIDS.

Many physiotherapists now use acupuncture in conjunction with the more conventional therapies.

Acupressure is a variant of acupuncture where pressure is applied to the various points instead of inserting a needle. It is, as previously stated, harmless and free from the problems of virus transmission.

OSTEOPATHY

The conventional osteopath (see note at end of this section) will maintain that most symptoms arise from spinal vertebral malalignment or possibly from some malalignment of some other joints and muscles. The osteopathic treatment consists of forcible manipulations to 'put back' the malaligned joint or to stretch soft tissues and adhesions. The manipulations may also be accompanied by some massage of the soft tissues.

CHIROPRACTIC

This is somewhat similar to the conventional osteopathic treatment although the theory relies even more on spinal manipulation. The chiropractor maintains that the cause of most symptoms is a vertebral malalignment. The manipulations tend to be even more forcible.

Most people who take themselves off to the osteopath or chiropractor will be suffering from some form of back pain, although occasionally they will take disorders of other joints. Fortunately, most back disorders arise from soft tissues, ligaments and facet joints and although they may not respond particularly well to the manipulative procedures, usually no real harm is done. Those patients who are likely to benefit most from this type of manipulative procedure are those who have developed a sudden acute neck pain, frequently with the head to one side with limitation of movement, or a sudden lumbar back pain with similar limitation of movement and often a tilt to the side. Here an early manipulation can frequently settle things satisfactorily. However, these manoeuvres are within the ambit of the properly trained physiotherapist who will usually choose to use what the physiotherapist will call mobilisations (vide supra) in order to achieve the same result. The main hazard in conventional osteopathy and chiropractic is when the neck or back pain is due to a disc prolapse. A forcible manipulation in those circumstances, although it may shift the disc prolapse away from the nerve root where it is causing symptoms, can equally well cause a further and massive disc prolapse, producing paralysis. Production of quadriplegia (paralysis from the neck down) or paraplegia (paralysis from the waist down) is by no means unknown following forcible spinal manipulative procedures.

Note: I have used the expression 'conventional osteopathy' because in the United States the whole role and position of the osteopath has altered radically. There the osteopath receives very much the same sort of training as the medical student. Once qualified as a Doctor of Osteopathy, his career amd further training from then on tends to be similar to the medical student who qualifies as an M.D., and he can proceed into any of the fields of medicine and surgery by following the same sort of training as the newly qualified Medical Doctor. At present in the United Kingdom most osteopaths still fulfil their traditional manipulative role. The British School of Osteopathy is giving a proper formal training to osteopaths so that the approach of the rising generation of osteopaths will be different from that of their relatively untrained forbears. It is therefore difficult at present for patients to know exactly where they stand if they decide to opt for some osteopathic treatment.

2.6 The Prevention of Injury

Although the methods for the prevention of injury can be deduced when reading the other Sections, the main factors in the prevention will be summarised.

The Development and Maintenance of Good Technique

As described in **Section 2.3**, the cause of dance injuries is faulty technique, therefore conversely if a good technique is developed and maintained, the chance of sustaining a dance injury is minimised. Of great help in maintaining a good technical level of dancing is regular attendance at a class run by a *competent and observant teacher*. As in all activities, whether mental or physical, it is only too easy for technique, the application of technique and mental attitudes to gradually deteriorate with the passage of time. Even serious self-appraisal and self-criticism may not be sufficient to prevent the development of errors and flaws in technique. However, by attending a really good class regularly, the chances of injury can be kept to a minimum.

The Development and Maintenance of Muscle Strength and Joint Mobility

In the prevention of injury, the importance of maintaining adequate muscle strength cannot be over-emphasised. However, it must also be stressed that this does not mean an over development of bulk such as one sees in weight lifters and in those people competing in the 'Mr Atlas' contests. Pure bulk does not necessarily equate with desirable strength. Over-bulky muscles can be a distinct disadvantage to a dancer for they not only look unsightly but also may make dance more difficult. For example, over-development around the shoulder girdle and arms, due to an excessive enthusiasm for weight lifting, can raise the centre of gravity of the body and make the dancer rather more unstable when he tries to balance. Additionally, bulky muscles can get in the way at the extremes of joint movement range.

Correct muscle balance is as important as muscle strength; firstly, between one side of the body and the other and one limb and the opposite limb and secondly, between the various groups which control the movements of a particular joint or joints. A good instance of this is the over-emphasis which is so often placed on building up the quadriceps muscles in the thigh to the neglect of the other groups in that region, i.e. the adductors, the hamstrings and the gluteals. The ill effects of muscle imbalance are mentioned elsewhere, particularly in **Sections 3** and **5**.

Joint mobility goes hand in hand with muscle strength. If the muscles controlling a joint are weak, then the joint will not be stabilised sufficiently for it to be used satisfactorily in its full range. Therefore in maintaining muscle strength and balance, joint mobility will also tend to be maintained. Also playing a very significant part in achieving the fullest possible mobility of a joint is the necessity to exercise the controlling muscle groups through the *full range* of their movement. For instance, the muscle group controlling extension of a joint must be able to act powerfully throughout the full range of movement, from full flexion to full extension and not during only part of that range. In order to achieve this it is essential that any exercise programme is directed at providing a correct exercise pattern for that muscle group throughout this range. *Only when the muscles controlling the joint are strong, can the range then be increased to the anatomically full range by gentle graduated stretching.* Stretching must go hand in hand with an exercise programme to strengthen the muscle groups. A weak muscle must *never* be stretched.

The Preservation of Cardio-respiratory Fitness

This will normally occur as a result of any exercise programme that the dancer is carrying out in order to maintain his muscle strength and joint mobility. Any form of general exercise will have its effect on the cardio-vascular and respiratory systems in helping to maintain them in the peak of condition. However, during vacation periods it can be helpful if the dancer continues to do some form of exercise, not necessarily related to dance, as a recreational activity. This can take the form of swimming, cycling or tennis, which may be more appropriate during a holiday. As previously stated, in order to maintain cardio-respiratory fitness it is essential that the exercise is vigorous enough to make the person concerned short of breath. This will ensure that during these times the cardiac output is called upon to increase. It is this regular demand on the cardio-vascular system which maintains it in a state of physiological fitness.

On a more general line, the dancer, as with any other athlete, should avoid any action which abuses his body and, in particular, the cardio-vascular and respiratory systems, as these are so essential for the maintenance of a good performance. To this end, the avoidance of smoking plays an extremely important part. Not only are there the long-term ill effects of cigarette smoking on the lungs and the coronary arteries but there is also the constant effect on the blood stream. During the smoking of cigarettes a very significant amount of carbon monoxide is inhaled and, as was described in

Section 1.8, this carbon monoxide combines with the haemoglobin in the blood, preventing it from carrying the oxygen around the blood stream, thus depriving the tissues (particularly the muscles in the case of an athletic performance) of the maximum amount of oxygen. Excessive consumption of alcohol can have a direct effect on both cardiac and skeletal muscle, producing an actual deterioration in both.

Good Nutrition

The maintenance of a satisfactory nutritional state is essential in the prevent of injury and also in the healing of injuries. (See **Section 2.7.**)

The Orthopaedic Assessment of the Dancer in the Prevention of Injury

One of the most important aspects in the prevention of dance injuries is in the assessment of students before they are accepted by professional schools. This could, with great advantage, be extended to an assessment of each dancer when they are first taken into a Company.

The purpose of this orthopaedic examination is to determine whether there are any anatomical areas which are likely to cause physical problems during a dance training or, when assessing adults, whether there is anything that is going to cause any particular problem with different types of dance. Although there are occasionally physical aspects of a person which can preclude any satisfactory participation in dance, in most instances although someone may be unsuitable physically for certain forms of dance, for example classical ballet, there are other types of dance with which they would cope perfectly satisfactorily. A careful assessment can therefore be used to guide a young dancer along the right lines. The orthopaedic assessment can be a great help when a teacher has a student who is apparently finding difficulty with some of the technical aspects of the work. Frequently there is some physical aspect of the dancer which, although not very obvious, is sufficient to make certain areas of dance technique difficult to carry out correctly.

By the time students have got through all the preliminary auditions, before attending for a final audition at a professional dance school, the auditioning panel will have rejected most of those applicants who are obviously unsuitable. Were the population to be examined orthopaedically at random with a view to their suitability for dance, then large numbers would be found to be unsuitable. However, in the professional schools the auditioning panels will have rejected most of those applicants who are physically unsuited to dance before they are actually sent for an orthopaedic assessment.

It is always important to remember that artistic talent can overcome many apparent physical problems. If a student does show great potential talent then it is usually right to give them the chance to dance by allowing them to start training. Their progress should be carefully monitored in order to determine whether they are overcoming these difficulties. In these circumstances it is very important that all the teachers and the student are fully aware of any potential physical problems that are present and which may cause technical difficulties or injury either during training or later in a professional career. The orthopaedic surgeon must, therefore, have two thoughts in his mind while doing the assessment – first, whether there is any physical problem which calls for an outright rejection, for example an established spondylolisthesis, and secondly, to note carefully those areas which are potential problem points. During the course of this assessment there may be some aspects which can be amenable to early help from the physiotherapist or teacher, usually in the form of special exercises to strengthen or mobilise a particular area or areas.

Fig. 2.6 is a reproduction of the card that we have used for many years for the orthopaedic assessment of both students and professional dancers. It is largely self-explanatory. The presence of a tight trapezius is noted because this will affect head movements, particularly if there is some limitation of rotation was well as of lateral flexion. At the shoulders a discrepancy in level can be very suggestive of an underlying abnormality such as a scoliosis or leg length discrepancy. However, the majority of cases where the shoulders are at different levels is purely postural and possibly associated to some extent with the carrying of heavy bags on one or other side. (The old-fashioned school satchel had a great deal to commend it as it did mean that the loading of the shoulders was equal.) Under 'shoulder line' we are looking for those children who have their shoulders forward, thus appearing to narrow their chests. Although the braced back shoulders of the old military stance was a very poor position, equally bad is the narrowing caused by shoulder girdles that have rotated forwards around the chest.

Winging of the scapula is very indicative of upper trunk weakness. Frequently the scapulae stand out sufficiently to slip a hand between the medial border of the scapula and the chest wall.

This is often part of a scapula rotation and due to some weakness of the latissimus dorsi, so that the slip to the inferior pole of the scapula does not act sufficiently to hold the scapula down. In improving the posture the scapula has to be held down, largely by the latissimum dorsi, and must not be braced backwards.

Under 'elevation' we are looking at the combined abduction and flexion of the shoulders. This is of great importance in the boys as if there is some restriction it means that when lifting they are unable to hold the girl up above their heads without tilting backwards in the lumbar region of the spine.

In the arms the presence of swayback elbows is looked for as well as hypermobile wrists as part of a general indication of the presence of hypermobility. Hypermobility in a dancer is a very potent cause of injury, as is mentioned elsewhere in this book. If a student or dancer is hypermobile they then have to work far harder at maintaining muscle strength in order to control the hypermobility of their joints.

In the wrists, particularly in boys, one is looking for any restriction of dorsi-flexion as this can also cause problems when lifting.

In the back, the presence of a scoliosis or kyphosis is noted. In children, this orthopaedic assessment may be the first time that they have been looked at thoroughly by any medical practitioner so occasionally a hitherto undetected scoliosis is picked up and can be referred for treatment. A very mild scoliosis is no contra-indication to dancing, but in the younger student the parents should be warned that there is a possibility that the scoliosis will progress as part of the natural history of the condition and that the child will have to remain under observation. Dance training in no way aggravates a scoliosis. In fact, the opposite occurs and the extra exercise of dancing, coupled possibly with side shift exercises and other trunk exercises, can actually be beneficial in stopping the progress of a scoliosis or in reversing the condition.

At the knees, the presence of hyperextension or swayback is observed. The heading 'patellae' refers, in fact, to the presence of tibial rotation. When the feet are pointing straight forwards if there is any tibial rotation or torsion then the patellae will point inwards (the so-called squint patellae) and the amount of rotation is measured and noted.

The presence of a tibial bow, whether it affects the whole tibia or whether it is just the lower quarter, is assessed. A lower tibial bow will produce an angle at the ankle joint so that the plane through the ankle joint is not parallel to the knee.

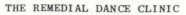

Address: .... Name:.............................

.... Christian Name: ....

.... Age: .... d.o.b. ....

Tel. No. Home:......................

          Work:...................... G.P.: ....

                                       ....

Company: .... School: ....

Referred by: ....

HEIGHT:................C.R.............. HEAD: A.P..........Lateral.......

WEIGHT:........PELVIS: A.S.I.S..........I.C........G.T......Shoulder width...

NECK: Length..... Tight Trapezius ....

    Range: Flexion.....Extensn..... Lat.Flex R....L.....Rot.R....L............

SHOULDERS: Level........Line......Winging Scap....Elevation R......L........

ARMS RANGE:Sway back elbows ....Wrists:..................

BACK: Scoliosis ....Kyphosis:..................

....

RANGE: Flexn......Extn.....Lat.Flex.R.....L....Rotation R......L..........

PELVIS: Level...................Assymetry............

KNEES: .... Sway back R......L...... Patellae R......L...........

LEGS: Length R.......L....... Tibial bow...........R.........L.........

POINTE: R.......L.....Ankle R.........L......Metatarsus R......L........

BIG TOE EXT: R.........L.....Big toe posture ....

LESSER TOES: ....

INTRINSICS:...

SUB-TALOID: R........L..... Mid-Tarsal: R........L......Navicula.......

ACHILLES TENDONS: R...................L...................

HAMSTRINGS: R..................L...............

TURNOUT FROG:..

HIP: Extension R...................L...........Flexion R............L.......

HIP ROTATION FLEXED: Right E.R.....I.R.......Left E.R........I.R........

HIP ROTATION EXTENSION: Right E.R..........I.R......Left E.R.....I.R.......

OTHER COMMENTS: ....

....

EXAMINER:..Date:...................

As a result the patient will tend to both roll and sickle with the problems that can be associated with these two factors.

Big toe extension is particularly important. In the student an early developing hallux rigidus can often be detected by noting the restriction which is already present in dorsi-flexion at the 1st metatarsophalangeal joint. If there is significant restriction this is an important contra-indication to proceeding with a dance training. All forms of dance call for demi-pointe work and as the hallux rigidus progresses it becomes more and more difficult to get up onto a reasonable demi-pointe and certainly prevents the dancer getting up onto three-quarter pointe or performing a correct relevé.

'Lesser toes' refers to the presence of any lesser toe deformities, the relative toe lengths and metatarsal lengths. In order to obtain a good support with a foot on both demi-pointe and full pointe it is far more satisfactory to have an even length of metatarsals and of toes.

In the feet, the intrinsic muscles are important as they allow the dancer to obtain a good pointed foot with straight toes when they are working strongly. If the intrinsics are weak when the dancer pointes the foot the toes claw, due to the action of the long flexors.

Achilles tendons refers to tightness in the back of the calf. Dancers always refer to tight Achilles tendons as do other sportsmen. In the calf the gastrocnemius and soleus muscles join together at their lower ends to form the Achilles tendon. It is this whole complex which makes for tightness and not the Achilles tendon alone. Any tightness in this area will, of course, prevent the dancer going down into a good plié. Similarly, an assessment of the hamstrings for any tightness is important, particularly in girls. However, if the Achilles tendons and calf muscles and the hamstrings are very loose then the height of the jump becomes impaired, so too much looseness at these sites is a disadvantage in boys.

The turn-out in the frog position and its genuine irrelevance to the dancer is discussed later in the book when dealing with turn-out. However, most dancers and teachers look upon the frog position as one of the methods of assessing turn-out. Therefore it is examined for their benefit.

The extension of the hip is important as tightness in the front of the hip causes a variety of problems. This is dealt with later in the book.

The measurement of hip rotation with the hip flexed to 90° is noted. The measurement of hip rotation with the hip in full extension is a far more important measurement and reflects the degree of turn-out which is present when the dancer is standing, which is, of course, the normal position during working.

The other items on the form which have not been mentioned are really self-explanatory.

Despite the use of a form such as this the genuine assessment of the dancer certainly calls for a lot of experience. For example, when examining an area which seems to be tight, the general feel of the tissues will give an experienced examiner a very good idea of whether the dancer will be able to stretch out the area with exercise and good training. This is something which cannot be learnt from a book but only by practise and by seeing a large number of dancers and dance students and being able to follow their progress over the years.

2.7 Nutrition

Every member of the population requires an adequate standard of nutrition. This must give sufficient but not an excess of calories, the correct balance of protein, fat and carbohydrate and all the necessary minerals, vitamins and water. Without a correctly balanced diet the physiological mechanism of the body cannot function at the utmost peak of efficiency. Dancers and athletes are no different from ordinary members of the population in this respect. However, dancers have a disproportionately high number of food fads. They labour under a whole variety of misapprehensions. They are led astray by old wives' tales which are repeated, propagated and multiplied by their elders and by their colleagues. They are ready victims for any ill-informed advice that is proffered, whether in the printed form or verbally, which claims to enable them to reach or maintain their desired level of activity or give them boundless energy at the times they need it.

Unfortunately, these misapprehensions are aggravated by the fact that many dancers are either in relatively poorly paid employment or are out of work and have to exist on a very small amount of money. This does not help them to eat a sensible and satisfactory diet. In the professional dance schools, whether they be producing dancers hoping for a stage career or dance teachers, there should certainly be an emphasis on instruction in nutrition. This would best be carried out by a sympathetic dietician who could advise them, not only on the elementary basics of nutrition and diet, but would also help them to plan their daily eating so that it would fall within their limited budgets and yet provide all the essentials for a healthy existence. So many of the good books on the subject of diet and nutrition recommend foods that are beyond the financial reach of both students and professional dancers. A sensible and well-informed choice of food and meals not only provides adequate nutrition but also helps to prevent the dancer becoming either overweight or underweight. A good diet is important in maintaining the healing processes at their peak of efficiency and also helps to prevent injury by keeping the body in the best condition.

Nutritional Requirements

PROTEINS

These are required for muscle and tissue development and repair. They also provide essential amino acids which are needed for the normal metabolism in the body. Protein is found particularly in lean meat, poultry and fish. It also occurs in variable amounts in milk and dairy products including cheese, eggs and in some vegetables. Although the human body can convert carbohydrates and fats into most proteins and amino acids (amino acids are substances which are obtained from metabolism of protein) there are what is known as essential amino acids which the body is incapable of synthesising. These, therefore, have to be obtained directly from the diet. Although these can be found in certain vegetables, they are far more abundant in animal protein. Animal protein is frequently referred to as first-class protein. If the total diet is insufficient to provide enough amino acids, the body will start to break down its own proteins, which largely means the muscular tissue, in order to provide the amino acids that it requires. This can happen in people who diet injudiciously or embark upon a badly structured diet.

CARBOHYDRATES

These are required as an energy source. This group is divided into two, the simple carbohydrates such as glucose, cane sugar and other simple sugars and the complex carbohydrates such as starch and complex sugars. The simple carbohydrates can be absorbed and metabolised very rapidly whereas the complex carbohydrates take longer to absorb and metabolise and will therefore give a slower release of energy.

FATS

These provide a high energy source. (High energy means also high calories.) They are metabolised and used very much more slowly than the complex carbohydrates so their benefit as an energy source will be much longer-term. Fats are a vital carrier for the fat soluble vitamins A and D.

VITAMINS

There is a daily minimum requirement for vitamins. While they are not a food as such, inasmuch as they do not provide energy, they are essential for the proper functioning of the body. Provided the minimum requirements are met, there is no evidence at all to show that boosting the intake by the use of vitamin supplements has any benefit. It certainly has no effect on enhancing performance or increasing endurance. An excessive intake of Vitamins A and D can be extremely harmful. The former can cause damage to the eyes and the latter upsets the calcium and phosphorous metabolism and balance. As sufficient intake is included in the diet, it is unwise to supplement these two vitamins.

At present there is no evidence that over-dosing with either the B complex vitamins or with Vitamin C has any harmful effects. Both are excreted in the urine if they are in excess. This is very obvious in the case of the B complex, as you will observe if you take a couple of Vitamin B tablets following which you will notice that your urine becomes a bright yellow. The only time when a large dose of Vitamin C *might* be helpful is at the onset of development of the common cold. Some research workers have produced possible evidence, although it is by no means conclusive, that if Vitamin C is taken at the rate of a gramme a day, starting right at the commencement of common cold symptoms, the course of the disease is significantly shortened or even aborted. Although relatively expensive to buy, the dancer might feel that the chances of deriving benefit are worth the cost and they can certainly rest assured that they will come to no harm. There is, however, no evidence whatsoever that taking Vitamin C in large doses permanently has any preventive effect at all in respect of actually catching a cold.

Vitamin B12 is sometimes considered to be an aid to performance. There are some ignorant athletic trainers who demand that their athletes have an injection of Vitamin B12 prior to a performance. Although Vitamin B12 by injection certainly gives many people a feeling of well-being, there has, despite intensive investigations, been no evidence that this extra B12 enhances either the performance of intricate tasks or increases endurance or sprint activities. Its use in these circumstances cannot be condoned and is only another example of the ill-informed pressing for the unjustified use of some or other preparation. Every injection, breaching as it does the integrity of the skin surface, carries with it a very small risk, however minimal this risk might be, and the athlete and dancer should avoid foolish advice such as this.

MINERALS

There is a very long list of essential minerals that are required in the diet. Most of these are required in very small quantities and are adequately provided in the daily food intake. The only exceptions are iron and calcium, both of which can be very deficient in dancers. Iron, particularly, can be low in the female because of menstruation. However, as most female dancers are of exceptionally low weight, many of them do not menstruate or only irregularly and occasionally, so iron depletion may not be as marked even when there is a minimal intake in their diet. If there is any doubt at all, then the dancer should consult her doctor, as a simple blood test will rapidly show whether there is any anaemia present. This can readily be corrected with an iron supplement. The requirement is 18 mg daily. If a dancer is anaemic, she will certainly not be able to perform at her best. She will tend to feel tired and listless and be a ready candidate for injury and various infections. Incidentally, research has shown that dancers who weigh less than 45 kilograms do not menstruate and as far as some research has progressed at present in America, this seems to be a fairly critical figure.

The calcium requirement is 1200 mg daily. This can be obtained by drinking 4–5 glasses of milk each day. Otherwise a supplement will be necessary.

WATER

A sufficient intake is essential for the satisfactory physiological processes of the body. The kidneys require an adequate output of water in order to be able to excrete the waste products of metabolism. If the body is short of water then the blood volume will decrease and this can interfere with the transportation of both nutrients and oxygen to the cells as well as delaying the removal of carbon dioxide and metabolites. Water is also essential for the regulation of body temperature which it does by the production of sweat. If dancers become dehydrated, fatigue of both the muscles and the body as a whole will set in much earlier and they will become very much more liable to sustain injury. The dehydration can also cause cramps and heat stroke and a genuine exhaustion of the whole being. Also, a failure to take enough fluid can make the dancer initially feel nauseated, even in the absence of the other effects of dehydration, and this nausea can itself do nothing to help performance.

When water is lost through sweating, salt is also lost. However, the salt is readily replaced with the diet, although heavy performances, particularly in hot working conditions, may call for the addition of salt. This is very adequately done by taking some extra salt at mealtimes and the use of salt tablets is unnecessary. This addition of salt is certainly a wise precaution as a lack of salt will lead to quite severe cramps. The dancer should take great care to prevent dehydration and should take plenty of water during the course of each 24 hours. Food provides a certain amount of water during its metabolism but additional fluid will be required, the volume depending upon the ambient temperature and the degree of sweating. The fluid does not need to be taken as pure water but can be consumed as fruit squash, some fizzy drinks such as fizzy orangeade, lemonade or similar flavours. However, the various cola drinks, together with tea and coffee, should not be included in fluid replacement drinks as they all contain substances which act as diuretics. A diuretic acts directly on the kidney in order to increase the excretion of water, so consumption of these three items can increase fluid loss to a greater extent than it replaces it. Alcohol comes under the same heading as it also acts as a diuretic and can produce dehydration. It certainly provides some calories but should not be looked upon as a source of energy as it has depressant and sedative effects. However, a little alcohol after a performance may help the dancer to relax and to this end a glass of wine will do no harm.

The presence of dehydration and proof of its correction can be effectively carried out by regular weighing. This is frequently done in top class athletics and sports. A deficiency of one litre of fluid will produce a weight loss of one kilogram. Weighing before and after a heavy performance or class, particularly in hot conditions, will give an accurate indication of the quantity of fluid replacement required.

The Daily Diet

In deciding what to eat each day, it is not particularly easy or helpful to think in terms of protein, carbohydrates, fats, vitamins, minerals and water. It is easier to produce a balanced set of meals by considering what are known as food groups and making certain that one has sufficient out of each of the four groups. These groups are as follows:

THE MEAT GROUP

Two portions daily (one portion is equivalent to two ounces of meat with the fat removed, or poultry or fish, or two eggs, or four ounces of cottage cheese).

THE CEREAL GROUP

Four portions daily. (One slice of bread, preferably wholemeal, or two ounces of cereals such as cornflakes, or pasta such as spaghetti makes up one portion.)

THE MILK GROUP

Three portions daily. (One portion is equivalent to about half a pint of milk or yoghurt both of which can be low fat or skimmed, or one and a half ounces of ordinary cheese.) This group provides the calcium as well as other nutrients.

THE VEGETABLE/FRUIT GROUP

Four portions daily. (One portion would be equivalent to a large helping of vegetables or one fruit such as an apple, orange, pear, etc.) The dark green leafy vegetables or orange vegetables such as carrots contain Vitamin A and one portion of these should be taken four times a week. The other vegetables, particularly citrus fruits such as oranges, contain Vitamin C.

When working out the meals for the day, try to take one portion from each group in each meal. If possible, try to eat three meals a day, rather than taking more portions of each group in fewer meals. In particular, try to avoid a large meal at the end of the day just before going to bed. The best method of cutting down on calories is to reduce the fat intake; for example, make certain that the meat is well trimmed, use skimmed milk and low fat yoghurt, and cottage cheese rather than normal cheese. Weight for weight, fat provides twice as many calories as either carbohydrate or protein, both of which provide the same amount of calories for a given weight. In planning your diet do not forget that calories equal energy and energy is required to carry out a full dance programme each day. Also, the body requires a minimum number of calories just to keep going, even if the person remains perfectly still for each 24 hours. The actual level of calories required varies from individual to individual and depends upon their own metabolic rate. The basal metabolic rate, which is that which occurs when the person is completely inactive, is greatly increased during any form of activity.

Pre-performance Intake

Although most dancers will determine for themselves what they can or cannot eat and drink before performances, there are certain guidelines which they should try to follow. First, they should make certain that they are well hydrated during the course of each day. This is best achieved by drinking small amounts fairly frequently and regularly. During a performance, particularly if it is energetic and there is a high temperature, sips of water can be taken regularly. By doing this, dehydration and excessive thirst can be avoided. Half a pint or a pint of fluid taken immediately before a performance is as likely to end up over the conductor as be satisfactorily absorbed by the body and the dancer should not have let himself get into such a situation as to need this quantity.

Avoid concentrated sweet fluids. These will be absorbed far more slowly and they do nothing to enhance the energy levels or activity. Even if carbohydrate is taken in a dilute form, such as a dilute glucose drink, the effect will be counter-productive during the course of the performance. If the glucose is taken in a dilute form it will certainly be absorbed rapidly but this will produce a peak of glucose in the blood stream, the physiological mechanisms of the body will be stimulated to deal with this peak and metabolise it and as a result there will be a sudden burst of insulin poured into the blood stream. This peak of blood sugar will then fall and there will be a trough below the normal level (Fig. 2.7). The dancer may therefore suddenly feel halfway through a performance that he is excessively tired due to this troughing effect. In order to ensure a satisfactory energy supply during the course of a performance, a small meal taken one and a half to three hours before the performance would be far more satisfactory. For energy requirements, this meal should contain complex carbohydrates such as starch. This can be readily supplied by eating a small pasta dish or a sandwich, followed by a little fruit. If taken well before the performance this will have been digested by the time the dancer wishes to start a pre-performance warm-up but the energy supply will continue throughout the performance. Following a performance a large meal is not particularly satisfactory and, as was mentioned earlier, it is far better to try to provide for your food requirements by taking several small meals a day.

Having indicated some general guidelines for dancers to plan their diet and food intake, it is strongly recommended that if dancers have any

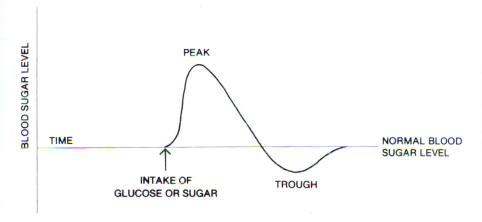

2.7 Diagrammatic representation of peaking and troughing of the blood sugar levels following an intake of glucose, sugar or other simple carbohydrate.

particular concerns about weight or problems with food or diet, they should seek the advice of their doctor or a fully qualified dietician. A dietician will be able to help them to plan an appetising and nutritious diet which comes within their budget and would also fit in to their daily work programme.

In ensuring that their dancers performed at their best, management would be well advised to consider far more carefully the way they structured their dancers' day. They would obtain better results if they ensured that in the middle of the day each dancer had sufficient time to have an adequate meal without being pressurised to attend class in the morning, then only be given time to snatch a quick snack before being rushed into rehearsals. These should be arranged to allow those who are performing that evening to get a small meal well before the performance is due. While it may be thought that these are counsels of perfection, both management and dancers would be well rewarded by paying a little more attention to the physiological demands of the bodies upon which they both depend for their livelihoods.

SECTION THREE

Specific Injuries: their Cause and Treatment

In this section we will describe the injuries commonly found in dancers, progressing systematically through the body rather than dealing with the injuries in the order in which they occur most commonly. This latter method would give a very haphazard and rather disjointed layout.

In the discussion of injuries in this section, where necessary we describe the injury, the cause or causes of the injury and follow this with a description of the treatment and any special complications which may occur that are relevant to the dancer. We have not included the various medical and surgical complications which are all covered in standard textbooks on injuries suffered by the general public and which do not pertain particularly to dancers. Similarly, we have confined ourselves to discussing only those injuries which have some aspect which is of specific interest to dancers, e.g. the cause of the injury, some aspects of its treatment, etc.

In the description of the causes we hope that the dancer, dance teacher or medical attendant may be able to determine the possible reason why the patient should have sustained the injury. This will usually be associated with some aspect of their dance technique. The cause is particularly important when the injury is recurrent and during the course of treatment it is vital to eliminate or correct all possible causes.

Although weak areas, technical faults or anatomical problems may have existed for a long time without symptoms, it may take only a very small increase in work, a variation in technique or choreography or work on a raked stage, etc. to precipitate quite severe symptoms.

The section on treatment indicates the general lines that treatment should take but the details of application of the physiotherapy methods or surgical methods have been assumed to be known and understood by the physiotherapists or surgeons concerned with the patient. For those in doubt about treatment or for dancers who wonder whether the treatment that is costing a lot of money is relevant, reference can be made to **Sections 2.4** and **2.5**. Unfortunately dancers, like other athletes, are desperate to get better and back to performance or to continue performing without having to take time off. They are therefore

particularly vulnerable to the undesirable attentions of the unscrupulous who offer the quick cure (usually ineffective, particularly in the longer term). It is essential for those who depend for a livelihood on returning to a full level of physical fitness and who usually have very little money to spare for treatment, that they obtain the *correct* treatment, that they attend for the fewest number of treatments compatible with full recovery and that they obtain proper value for the money that they have to expend. However, it is only proper to emphasise in this context that the quick twist or manipulation or the quick injection, is frequently far from being the most satisfactory method of obtaining permanent relief. It may seem a speedy or cheap answer and may give short term relief but it rarely produces a long term cure. Far more commonly it will lead to recurrent injuries and problems, each of which may be more severe than the one before, so that finally the dancer ends up with an extended period off dancing, whereas a correct diagnosis followed by the correct treatment methods applied early would have prevented all the subsequent misery.

The section on special complications tries in each case to give some indication of the problem that can accompany a particular injury, either in the short or long term. Any factors affecting return to dancing are mentioned, together with any precautions which should be taken to prevent recurrences. Reference to these little sub-sections may aid the practitioner treating the patient in avoiding the less obvious or more remote pitfalls.

3.1 Sprain of the Lateral Ligament of the Ankle

This is the commonest injury in dancers and usually affects the anterior fibres, known as the anterior talo-fibular ligament. When the patient is initially seen it is very important to exclude a fracture of the lateral malleolus (lower end of the fibula) by X-rays (Fig. 3.1). A fracture of the 5th metatarsal is a commonly associated fracture (Fig. 3.2). It is

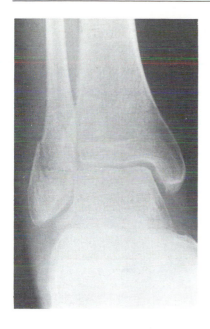

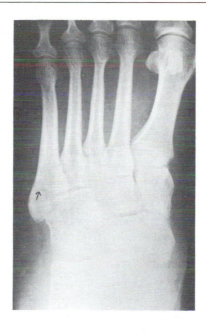

3.1 (left)   Spiral fracture of the lateral malleolus.

3.2 (right)   A fracture (arrowed) of the base of the 5th metatarsal.

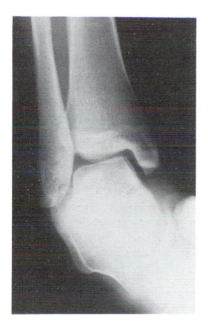

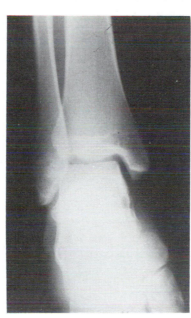

3.3A (left)   An X-ray showing tilting of the talus in the mortice of the ankle joint. This is a stress view when the foot and ankle are forcibly inverted and held in that position while the X-ray is being taken. Very frequently this procedure requires an anaesthetic as it is otherwise too painful for the patient. The talus can tilt because the ligaments restraining this movement have been torn.

3.3B (right)   This X-ray shows the same patient without passive inversion. As can be seen, there is no evidence of any instability on this standard X-ray view. If there is doubt about ligament damage then a stress X-ray must be carried out.

also equally important to exclude a complete tear of the ligament. In order to see whether the talus tilts excessively in the ankle joint mortice (Fig. 3.3) it may be necessary to carry out special X-rays under general anaesthetic, when the ankle can be forced into inversion, i.e. the foot can be turned inwards. Equally important and far more commonly missed is the situation where the damage to the ligament affects those fibres which, by their tearing, allow the talus to rotate forwards in the ankle mortice. On normal inversion X-rays the ankle will appear stable. If, however, the hindfoot is grasped firmly in one hand and the leg in the other and forward traction of the foot towards to the toes takes place, then it can be seen that the talus slides forwards in the ankle mortice and at the same time rotates slightly medially. If this type of instability is missed it leads to chronic problems for the dancer and the ankle remains permanently unstable.

CAUSES

The lateral ligament of the ankle is always damaged by acute trauma. It follows an inversion injury. This is often a rather more complex injury where there is an element of inversion, an element of rotation, an element of excessive plantar-flexion or, very rarely, dorsi-flexion. In most injuries the actual direction of displacement is not purely in one direction or another. It commonly occurs when a dancer falls off pointe, or in boys during grand allegro. In boys it is usually the middle fibres (calcaneo-fibular ligament) which are affected, in girls it is usually the anterior fibres (anterior talo-fibular ligament). It seems that, almost as commonly, the injury comes about in dancers in a manner which is totally unconnected with dancing – they may slip off a kerb, fall down stairs or suffer some other everyday mishap.

Predisposing or Contributory Causes

There are a whole variety of factors which may predispose to an injury of the lateral ligament. Probably the most important is a previous strain which has been inadequately rehabilitated. Weak feet (that is, the intrinsic muscles), weak ankle control, especially the peroneal group of muscles, and weak calf muscles producing a lack of control when landing from a jump are all common precursors of this injury. Lack of control of the turn-out allows the knee to turn in, the leg then goes out of alignment over the ankle so the weight is no longer correctly placed over the foot, resulting in a weight back situation (**Section 5.20**). As a result this makes the ankle unstable. Badly-fitting shoes aggravate the problem. An unstable pelvis, producing either a lordotic spine or tucking in, combined as it usually is with weak trunk muscles, aggravates the instability at the lower end of the leg (**Section 5.6**). A similar effect is produced by faulty head posture or faulty jumps. Working with tension interferes with control, not only in this type of injury but also in most others. Poor floor surfaces are a frequent cause of problems, particularly if they lead to a bad take-off which will, of course, produce a bad landing.

TREATMENT

Initially, the dancer should remain non-weight bearing until fractures are excluded. The associated fractures are those of the lateral malleolus and the base of the 5th metatarsal. During this initial stage ice packs should be applied and the leg elevated and rested. With very minor strains, once diagnosed and more serious injury excluded, the dancer may continue limited work using a supporting bandage. However, as in all other injuries, it is essential that

an accurate diagnosis is made before the dancer is allowed to continue. The long term ill-effects of a mis-diagnosis cannot be over-emphasised.

Definitive treatment

Icing, elevation and rest should be continued. The patient can be given ultrasound and/or interferential therapy and should start non-weight bearing exercises, particularly local exercises with the leg in elevation. The muscle contraction and relaxation with the leg elevated helps to get the swelling down more rapidly. During this time elevation of the foot of the bed at night can be very beneficial in reducing swelling. This applies to all lower limb injuries. The exercises should be carried out for all muscle groups around the ankle and should be done with the foot pointed, i.e. in full plantar-flexion, and with the foot at a right-angle, i.e. in neutral. These two different positions are necessary in order to include all the peroneal muscles in the exercise programme. From the early stages of treatment the calf muscles should be kept well stretched as there is a tendency for them to contract. (See *Complications* below.) Also faradic foot baths and intrinsic muscle exercises should be carried out as these muscles tend to waste very rapidly. During this period the patient can also spend a great deal of time doing general exercises for the rest of the lower limbs and trunk.

As the condition improves the patient passes through partial weight-bearing exercises and finally to full weight-bearing exercises. Use of the balancing board in the later stages is very important. Its use can, however, start with the patient sitting, when these exercises will be non-weight bearing with the foot on the balancing board. They help to achieve mobility and also to give the patient the feel of all the ankle movements (Fig. 3.4). In partial weight-bearing the balancing board can be used at the barre (Fig. 3.5), with the dancer facing the barre with the hands supporting the body. Once the patient is fully weight-bearing then the balancing board can be used in the normal manner (Fig. 3.6).

At the time of the actual injury there is always damage to nerves and nerve endings within the ligaments and joint capsule unless the injury is only trivial. These nerve endings are responsible for proprioception (appreciation of joint position) and loss of or interference with this enhances or is sometimes totally responsible for residual feelings of instability in the ankle. The dancer will feel insecure on the ankle, suspecting that it will give way at any moment. He will lack confidence in the joint when trying to dance or sometimes, if badly affected, even when walking. The balancing board

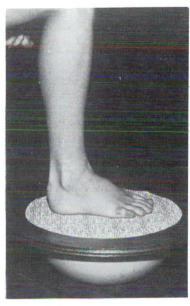

3.4   The use of the balancing board when sitting. The correct placement of the foot can be taught while sitting, in preparation for standing weight-bearing on the board.

3.5   The use of the balancing board at the barre. This is an intermediate stage between sitting and standing freely, when the dancer still requires a little help with balance.

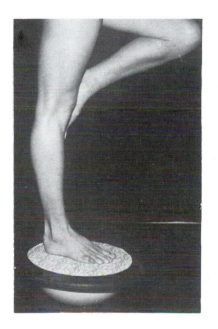

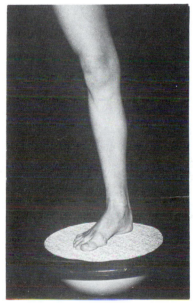

3.6A (left)   The use of the balancing board standing without support. The dancer has not yet achieved the control of her hyperextended knee and, as can be seen in the photograph, is still pushing a great deal of her weight back on her heel.

3.6B (right)   The position is correctly held. The balancing board is used to re-educate the postural reflexes which rapidly become ineffective following an injury or even a prolonged break from work.

is the most effective method in treating this and in re-educating the local postural and joint control reflexes.

Complications

Ankle sprains are probably the most inadequately treated of all dance and sports injuries. So often the dancer is dismissed with a bandage and told the injury will settle itself. Unless the injury is extremely trivial, this lack of adequate treatment will lead to chronic ankle problems with recurrent swelling, persistent pain and a feeling of instability of the ankle with lack of confidence. Adequate vigorous treatment is essential if this is to be avoided.

In almost all ankle injuries and certainly not in lateral ligament sprains only, the Achilles tendon (i.e. the calf muscles but always looked on by the dancers as the Achilles tendon alone) tightens within a few days of the injury. This tightening is almost always asymmetrical within the muscle so that later, when the dancer starts to perform a plié or a fondu, the foot is pulled into a bad position producing rolling. The tightening can be tested for by passively dorsi-flexing the foot with the patella in line with the centre of the foot and pressure equally placed beneath the metatarsals with the flat of the hand (Fig. 3.7), taking care not to extend the toes dorsally above neutral. During this

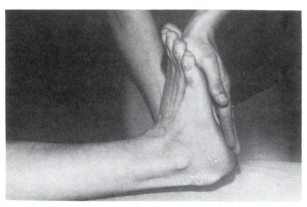

3.7   Testing for tightness of the Achilles tendon (actually the calf muscle/tendon complex). The foot must be correctly aligned with the leg and not inverted or everted. The flat of the hand is used to dorsi-flex the whole foot while keeping the toes straight.

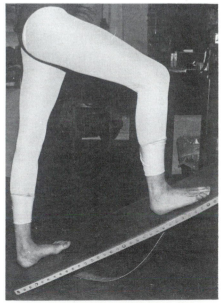

3.8   Working on a slope to stretch the Achilles tendon/calf muscle complex. The feet must be kept parallel.

manoeuvre the tendency of the foot to go to one or other side can easily be detected. Also the tightness in the calf can be felt by the free hand of the examiner. The tightness is treated by interferential therapy to the whole length of the calf muscles from the ankle to the origins of the gastrocnemius just above the back of the knee. Passive stretching is carried out by the physiotherapist. (N.B. See the comments on stretching in **Section 2.5**, page 88). Later this stretching can be continued by the patient. In the final stages of rehabilitation a slope can be used by the patient (Fig. 3.8). A watch must he kept for a contracture of the lateral ligament due to scarring. This will require very gentle, and certainly not forcible, stretching.

3.2 Rupture of the Lateral Ligament of the Ankle

The causes are the same as for a sprain of the lateral ligament. It is essential that the diagnosis is made immediately following the injury. If missed, the consequences to the dancer are extremely serious. A complete rupture of the ligament or portion of the ligament, most commonly the anterior talo-fibular portion, requires surgical repair. If in doubt the injury can be confirmed or excluded by X-rays taken under a general anaesthetic when the foot and ankle can be forcibly twisted to place the ligament under tension. The X-ray can show the degree of instability. It is very important not to miss the condition of anterior instability. This is caused by rupture of the anterior talo-fibular ligament and the anterior capsule of the ankle joint. Its presence can be demonstrated by drawing the talus forward in the ankle joint mortice. Normally, the talus should not slide anteriorly to any appreciable extent (compare with normal side). If there is instability, the talus (and whole foot below it) will move forward and probably also rotate slightly medially. The anterior drawer test (as it is known) can be confirmed to be positive if a lateral X-ray is taken at the same time, if necessary under an anaesthetic; the talus will be seen to slide forward in relation to the lower end of the tibia.

If there is any doubt about the presence or otherwise of a rupture of the ligament then it is probably wiser to explore the area rather than wait and see whether anything shows up with the · passage of time. A late repair of a rupture leads to poor results compared with those following an immediate repair. If the injury is severe enough for there to be doubt as to whether there is a rupture or not, then the operation, which basically will only be through the skin and subcutaneous tissues to inspect the ligament, will add little or nothing to the period of convalescence if the ligament is in fact found to be intact.

Rehabilitation, once the surgical treatment is completed, is the same as for a sprain of the lateral ligament of the ankle (**Section 3.1**).

3.3 Sprain of the Medial Ligament of the Ankle

This is uncommon in dancers. It is, however, very important to exclude a fracture of the medial malleolus or a complete rupture of the ligament, both of which require immediate orthopaedic treatment. Ligament rupture will certainly require surgery and a fracture of the medial malleolus, if it is more than just a crack, will probably require screwing back into place.

CAUSES

Commonly the injury occurs due to a bad landing with the weight mainly over the medial side of the foot and big toe. As a result the foot rolls and everts.

TREATMENT

This is similar to a sprain of the lateral ligament. Special attention must be paid to strengthening the invertors and evertors.

Complications
See **Section 3.1**. Additionally, tibialis posterior tendonitis can ensue due to lack of proper strengthening of the invertors. This produces a recurrent mild eversion strain by the rolling which occurs. Also as a result of this rolling, the lateral ligament can become crushed by the impingement of the lateral malleolus and the talus.

3.4 Chronic Sprains of the Lateral and Medial Ligaments of the Ankle

CAUSES

These most commonly follow an acute sprain. A chronic sprain is the result of inadequate post-injury treatment, i.e. poor physiotherapy, the failure of the dancer to carry out instructions, or returning to work too soon after the injury – a danger with the free-lance dancer. However, a chronic sprain can also be produced gradually, without an acute phase, by faulty technique which allows incorrect weight-bearing on the foot.

TREATMENT

This is similar to that for the later stages of an acute sprain. However, there may be a great deal of scarring of the ligament and this may require a lot of extra attention from the physiotherapist. Very much more effort will have to be put into the exercises for the various muscle groups. In this instance the weakness and wasting may well, and usually will, have spread to the muscles groups higher up the leg and even in the trunk. As a result of the chronic sprain, the dancer will have been working badly. The technique before the onset of symptoms may have been faulty, thus allowing a chronic sprain to occur, but even if not faulty before then, definite faults in technique will have set in as a result of the chronic sprain. This means that a great deal of time will have to be spent on correction.

3.5 Anterior Capsular Sprain of the Ankle

This injury may accompany either lateral or medial ligament sprains because of the hyperflexion element of the injuring force (plantar-flexion). It is very important to note that injuries are rarely pure and localised and nearly always involve adjacent structures. The force applied is equally rarely purely inversional, eversional, etc. The treatment and complications of anterior capsular sprain are similar to that in lateral ligament and medial ligament sprains. However, an anterior capsular sprain is additionally complicated if swayback knees (hyperextended knees) (**Section 5.13**) are present and also if the weight is too far back when working (**Section 5.20**). Both these produce an excessive strain on the front of the ankle when on pointe. This 'weight back' situation can also apply during pliés due to the tension anteriorly.

3.6 Fracture of the Lateral Malleolus

This fracture is caused by the same mechanism as a sprain of the lateral ligament. Usually, there is an inversion and rotation force, hence the actual fracture is most commonly spiral or oblique (Fig. 3.9). In most circumstances there is little displacement and complete reduction, even when displacement is severe, is usually easy and complete. If the trauma has been severe this fracture may also include a fracture of this medial malleolus and the posterior articular margin of the tibia, the degree of damage equating to the strength of the damaging force.

TREATMENT

This is standard orthopaedic care. Usually a plaster of Paris cast is applied for 6 weeks (or longer if a severe injury). Occasionally, if the fracture is minor, simple elastoplast strapping can be used but this is usually much less comfortable than a plaster cast. The strapping certainly does not imply that the dancer can continue work. Sometimes an operation to fix the fracture internally with screws may be necessary.

During the period in plaster the dancer can, as in other injuries, continue to exercise all areas not immobilised in the cast. Not only will this keep the muscles strong but by promoting a good circulation will actually increase the rate of healing of the fracture within the cast.

Once out of plaster the muscle groups that have been inactive can be started on intensive exercises. Exercise will also be required to mobilise all the joints which have been kept immobile. Ultrasound, interferential therapy, ice for swelling and other therapeutic aids can also help. From here onwards the treatment pattern is similar to that following a sprained lateral ligament of the ankle (**Section 3.1**).

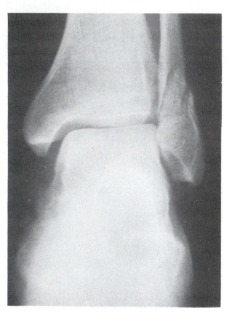

3.9   A spiral fracture of the lateral malleolus.

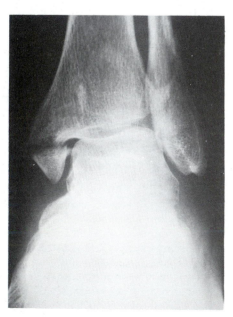

3.10   A typical transverse fracture of the medial malleolus. There is also a fracture of the lateral malleolus present.

3.7 Fracture of the Medial Malleolus

This is caused by the opposite force to that causing a lateral malleolar fracture if it has occurred as an isolated fracture. As stated in **Section 3.6** it can also be associated with the severer degrees of lateral malleolar fracture. In the former situation (isolated fracture) it is usually oblique or spiral; in the latter situation, when associated with a lateral malleolar fracture, it is a transverse fracture as the medial malleolus is pulled off by the strain on the medial ligament (Fig. 3.10).

TREATMENT

This is standard orthopaedic treatment. Usually, medial malleolar fractures require internal fixation with a screw, though even so non-union remains common. However, this non-union takes place with the medial malleolus in the correct anatomical position and the sound fibrous union is usually sufficient to give total stability and is mostly painless. In the unusual circumstances where it remains painful a small bone graft may be required.

Further treatment – exercise regimes: treatment once the fracture has united and the general rehabilitation is as described above for a fracture of the lateral malleolus (**Section 3.6**) and the later stages of rehabilitation following lateral or medial ligament damage (**Sections 3.1** and **3.3**).

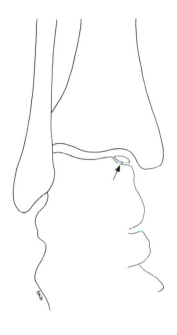

3.11A   An osteochondral fracture (arrowed) of the dome of the talus.

3.11B (below)   An X-ray of a patient demonstrating an osteochondral fracture (arrowed).

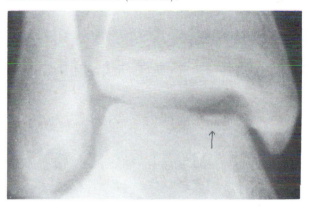

3.8 Osteochondral Fracture of the Dome of the Talus

This condition, which is a small chip fracture involving a portion of the articular cartilage and a small piece of underlying bone, occurs when the fragment is knocked out of the dome of the talus (where it forms part of the ankle joint) by a compression force (Fig. 3.11). Thus it occurs at the same time as a sprain of an ankle ligament or, more rarely, an ankle fracture. The osteochondral fracture may be difficult to demonstrate on an X-ray and as a result may not be found until very much later when, as a result of persistent ankle symptoms, further X-ray views are carried out and possibly an arthrogram. (This is an injection of air and radio-opaque dye into the joint.)

TREATMENT

If it is detected when fresh and if it has separated, then the fragment should either be removed if it is small, or else if it is larger, it should be pinned back into place. If it has not separated, then simple immobilisation may allow the fragment to heal in the correct position. Unfortunately and only too frequently the fragment, being deprived of its blood supply, separates at a later date and forms a loose body within the joint. The most important aspect of the condition is to think of the possibility if symptoms are persisting for longer than would be expected for the original injury.

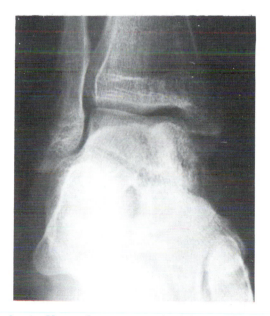

3.11C   An X-ray of a more extensive injury at the same site showing an osteochondritis of the talus supero-medially and also long-standing damage to the medial malleolus. These types of changes within a joint can follow the injudicious injection of Hydrocortisone or other steroids into the joint. In the long term these changes result in severe osteo-arthritis of the joint.

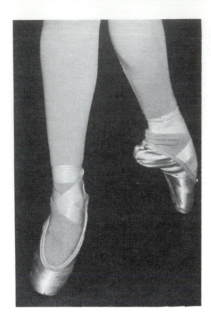

3.12A
Sickling when
on pointe.

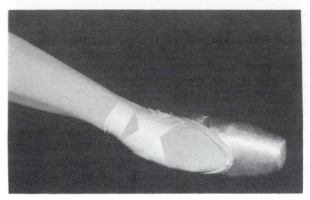

3.12B   Sickling when in the air (fishing).

3.9 Achilles Tendonitis

The Achilles tendon does not have a sheath, so
inflammatory conditions in this area affect either
the loose fibrous tissues surrounding the tendon
causing a peritendonitis, or the tendon itself causing
a tendonitis, or both. In the case of a tendonitis this
may merely be an inflammation of the tendon or
there may be small micro-tears within the substance
of the tendon or even larger partial tears.

CAUSES

Over-use due to extra work following fatigue of
muscle groups, or weakness of the feet, the
gastrocnemius, the quadriceps, the hamstrings, or
the gluteals or most or all of these. It is very much
aggravated by swayback (hyperextended) knees
(**Section 5.13**), or by working with the weight too
far back (**Section 5.20**). All these factors will cause
over-use of the gastrocnemius which has to do
much of the work which should be carried out or
aided by other muscle groups. The soleus is
under-used in this situation because it does not cross
behind the knee. The condition tends to be
precipitated by a lack of work on three-quarter
pointe in class. A muscle has to be worked
throughout its full range in order to gain adequate
strength. If sufficient work is not undertaken on
three-quarter pointe in class, it means that the
muscle will not be fully strong so when the foot has
to actually work in and through three-quarter
pointe, Achilles tendonitis will frequently result.

Three-quarter pointe is necessarily used on all
jumps and landing and on going through the foot
to rise on to pointe. If this is the only time that
three-quarter pointe is in use, then the muscle will
not gain sufficient strength to cope adequately.

Achilles tendonitis may also be caused by
tight-fitting shoes and ribbons which cut in; by
shoes which are too small, causing a curling of the
toes and pushing the weight back (**Section 5.20**);
or shoes that are too wide and give no support to
the forefoot, thus diminishing strength from the
foot during jumps. Rolling with an unstable foot
leads to the calf muscle not being worked correctly.
Pointing with a sickled foot produces over-working
of the inner (medial) side of the calf muscle and
also of the medial hamstrings. Working with a
sickled foot also tends to produce stretching of the
medial side of the front of the ankle (Fig. 3.12) and
nipping of the insertion of the Achilles tendon.
Anything which produces a tight pointe, such as an
os trigonum or enlarged posterior tubercle of the
talus, can precipitate an Achilles tendonitis. Also,
failing to get the heel down properly when working
and as a result not stretching the calf properly may
be the cause. Working on a raked stage can
aggravate the effects of all these causes.

TREATMENT

Use ice, ultrasound, interferential (to above the
knee to include the origins of the gastrocnemius;
use of interferential over this distance will also
produce a concentration at the musculo-tendinous
junction which is frequently thickened). When the
inflammatory aspects have settled, progressive
strengthening followed by stretching must be
carried out. Attention obviously has to be paid to
all possible causes of the condition with their
elimination and correction (for example,

strengthening other weak muscle groups). If treatment is prolonged or appears to fail, there will always be found a hitherto undetected cause, which is most commonly a technical fault. Very rarely, if there is a *long persisting* well localised area of tenderness and thickening, an injection of Hydrocortisone Acetate may be given *once* into the peritendinous tissues – never into the tendon itself. Repeated injections or an injection into the tendon may predispose to a total rupture of the tendon.

Complications
The tendon and calf must be stretched evenly (medial versus lateral and right versus left) otherwise as soon as work is started again, a pelvic tilt will be induced which destroys the whole balance of the dance technique.

3.10 Rupture of the Achilles Tendon

Although micro-ruptures or small partial ruptures may occur in Achilles tendonitis, we are dealing here with complete ruptures. Beware of missing a complete rupture and of labelling the condition as a partial rupture.

CAUSES

This will most commonly occur when the tendon is subjected to sudden unaccustomed stress. This may happen in the teacher who is out of training attempting to demonstrate a jump, particularly if not warmed up. In the dancer who is in a physically trained situation it is most commonly associated with an inadequate warm-up or by an unprecedented number of repetitions which call for explosive calf-muscle action.

DIAGNOSIS

Initially a gap can be felt in the tendon but, soon after the injury, local swelling may mask this and make diagnosis more difficult. Pain, swelling and an inability to stand unsupported on demi-pointe on the affected foot is an urgent indication for an orthopaedic surgical opinion.

TREATMENT

This is by early (within twenty-four hours) repair of the rupture. Immobilisation in a simple plaster of Paris cast has been shown to give less good results, though a large *partial* rupture, *if the diagnosis is certain*, may be treated successfully in plaster of Paris without surgery. If in doubt about whether the rupture is complete or partial it is better to look and see. Even with a good surgical repair this injury frequently spells the end of an active performing career. After the surgery the rehabilitation starts early with exercises for all other muscle groups. When the post-operative plaster is removed (usually at six weeks), an intensive programme of muscle strengthening will be required followed later by technical help. It may well be up to six months before full work can be resumed, although some early class work can be used as part of a carefully devised rehabilitation programme.

It is possible to manage the post-operative period without a plaster of Paris cast if the repair is carried out using braided stainless steel wire. The technique at this site is difficult as too tight a repair will cause shortening of the Achilles tendon; if the frayed tendon ends are not brought together sufficiently the tendon will be too long. A long tendon will result in poor elevation when jumping as well as other difficulties; a short one will limit the plié.

3.11 Achilles Tendon Bursitis

The Achilles tendon bursa lies between the tendon just above its insertion and the bone of the calcaneum (Fig. 3.13). It can become the site of inflammation with thickening and swelling if it is irritated.

CAUSES

It may be associated with an Achilles tendonitis, especially with the over-use aspects of that condition. It may occur alone in an over-use situation or from pressure over a prominence of the posterior part of the os calcis (calcaneus altus).

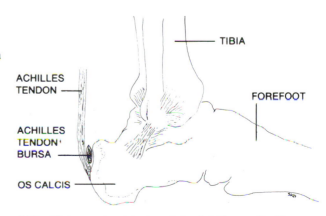

3.13 Diagram showing site of the Achilles tendon bursa, which provides a cushion between the tendon and the heel bone (os calcis).

TREATMENT

Use pulsed microwave particularly. Ice, interferential and ultrasound may prove helpful. Elimination of the cause is required. Only very rarely should a Hydrocortisone injection be contemplated as the condition will most commonly settle without it.

Complications
Nothing special.

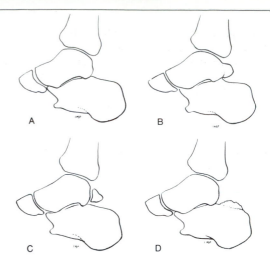

3.14   A. Normal ankle.
      B. Large posterior tubercle of the talus.
      C. Os trigonum.
      D. Exostosis on the dorsum of the os calcis.

3.12 Os Trigonum and Large Posterior Tubercle of Talus

In most, if not all, cases an os trigonum represents a stress fracture of a large posterior tubercle of the talus (Fig. 3.14). The onset of the stress fracture may be the reason for the onset of symptoms. In many instances surgery may not be required. However, once symptoms have started they frequently do not settle satisfactorily with conservative treatment. Nevertheless conservative treatment should be undertaken conscientiously. Symptoms may also be precipitated by weakness developing in a previously symptomless foot or calf due to an illness or stress, e.g. an absence with influenza if inadequate convalescence is taken. Symptoms may also be brought about by any situation which causes the dancer to work with the weight back (**Section 5.20**). The symptoms may start when the dancer returns, proceeding suddenly from immobility to full work, and this may occur particularly in a commercial dance situation. The actual weakness may be far removed from the ankle region, e.g. weak gluteals causing sitting in the hip and the weight being too far back. A differently fitting shoe may also start symptoms. In a student the symptoms may come gradually due to the slowly improving pointe.

Very occasionally similar impingement symptoms may be associated with an exostosis on the dorsum of the os calcis just behind the talo-calcaneal joint.

TREATMENT

Once symptoms have started, they may be impossible to relieve without surgery, but despite this every attempt should be made to alleviate the situation before surgery is undertaken, as often success can be obtained. The treatment is directed at strengthening the foot with faradic foot baths and intrinsic muscle exercises, strengthening the quadriceps, adductors and gluteals to eliminate any overworking by the calf muscles and technical help to correct any faulty weight transmission.

Only if conservative treatment fails should surgery be considered. In this case removal of the os trigonum or enlarged posterior tubercle of the talus will be required. The approach surgically should be through the medial side of the ankle. A lateral approach interferes with the peroneal tendons and their sheaths, greatly prolonging the convalescence. Immediately post-operatively exercises must be started to both passively and actively encourage plantar-flexion or pointing as this was the movement which was limited before the operation. A few days after the operation gentle non-weight bearing dorsi-flexion should be commenced actively or assisted actively but not using any passive forcing. When the foot and ankle can be dorsi-flexed to neutral then gradual weight bearing can be commenced. Once the wound is healed much more active weight-bearing and dorsi-flexion should be encouraged including some pliés, with the dancer supporting himself on the barre. Faradic foot baths and intrinsic exercises can be started even before removal of the sutures. As progress continues, ankle strengthening exercises, the balancing board and slope walking can be started. The more distant groups of muscles must not be neglected.

Complications
For six months or more post-operatively there will be a tendency for the scarring behind the ankle to contract. A very careful watch must be kept for this and gentle stretching must be continued for a long time. Early contractures will be shown by a decreasing depth of demi-pliés.

Inadequate post-operative physiotherapy and/or inadequate technical correction can completely destroy any early improvement in pointe following the operation as well as allowing a gradual decrease in depth of plié. The long term follow-up is too frequently neglected.

3.13 Tibialis Posterior Tendonitis and Tenosynovitis

CAUSES

This is caused by incorrect weight-bearing (**Section 5.17**). It is particularly aggravated by correcting rolling at the ankle instead of carrying out the correction higher up the leg. Correcting at the ankle produces tension aggravated by weak intrinsic muscles, especially when associated with an oblique line of the metatarsal heads (Fig. 3.15), or during pointe work with old shoes or badly-fitting shoes, or failure to hold the turn-out correctly, or a combination of these factors. The condition is made worse by working on a raked stage and on slippery floor surfaces.

TREATMENT

Ultrasound, interferential and ice are required. Faradic foot baths and intrinsic muscle exercises are always necessary. General strengthening of all groups around the ankle and of the groups higher up the leg should be carried out. A considerable amount of technical correction is necessary and the shoes must be checked.

Complications
The condition can be very slow to settle and it is difficult to treat satisfactorily. It will tend to niggle on for a long time and a great deal of supportive treatment is required. The jumping section of class work must be carefully regulated during rehabilitation.

3.14 Flexor Hallucis Longus Tendonitis and Tenosynovitis

This condition is an inflammation which can affect either the tendon or its surrounding sheath or, most commonly, both elements. Problems can occur anywhere along its length from the proximal end where the muscle fibres pass into the tendon to its insertion into the base of the distal phalanx of the great toe.

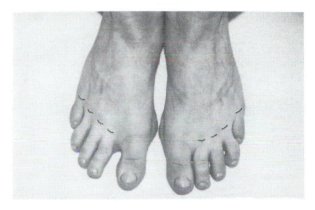

3.15   An oblique line of the lesser metatarsal heads.

There is one condition which is exclusive to the flexor hallucis longus and its tendon and this occurs at the musculo-tendinous junction. In this particular muscle the fleshy fibres extend distally as far as the level of the back of the ankle joint. The tendon sheath, which extends past the ankle and through the foot and contains the actual tendon, commences just distally to the line of the ankle joint. As a result of this anatomical arrangement, the situation sometimes arises where full dorsi-flexion of the great toe at the metatarso-phalangeal and inter-phalangeal joints pulls not only the tendon but also some of the fleshy part of the muscle, where it is joining the tendon, into the tube of the tendon sheath. If this happens recurrently it can lead to local swelling at the musculo-tendinous junction where it is being pulled in and out of the tendon sheath. Symptoms of pain may be persistent at this site in which case surgery to split open the proximal portion of the tendon sheath will relieve the symptoms.

CAUSES

This condition is caused by incorrect weight bearing on the foot (**Section 5.17**). It may also arise from a direct blow, a not infrequent cause, or by a cutting pressure from badly-fitting shoes. Weakness of the first interosseus muscle may aggravate or cause the condition.

TREATMENT

This is by ultrasound and interferential, which must include the muscle belly, together with faradic foot baths and intrinsic muscle exercises. The intrinsics in the former circumstances are usually very weak and cannot extend the interphalangeal joint of the great toe fully. At the same time the first space (between the 1st and 2nd metatarsals) opens out due to the weakness of the first interosseous. Strengthening of the intrinsics helps to

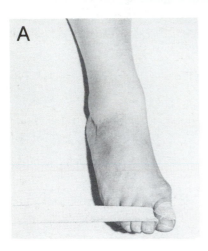
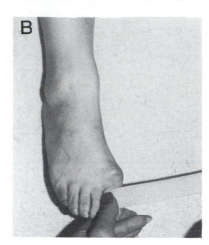
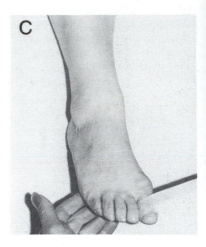

3.16   Six successive steps in strapping a great toe to help keep the interphalangeal joint straight.

close this space and allows the interphalangeal joint of the great toe to extend, permitting the weight to be brought to the correct position from having been too far back (**Section 5.20**). While the strengthening process is going on, special strapping can be applied to help keep the interphalangeal joint of the great toe straight (Fig. 3.16).

Complications
The condition is usually very slow to settle and treatment and technical correction may be required for a prolonged period.

3.15 Extensor Hallucis Longus Tendonitis

This may occur at any level of the tendon.

CAUSES
Direct blows are not uncommon. Rolling is a very potent cause as is also weight back with the toes clawed (**Section 5.20**). In this situation the extensor hallucis longus tendon tends to become shortened. Weakness of the intrinsics prevents proper extension of the great toe when working. Even when the toe is not being clawed, the weight being too far back may also cause the toes to repeatedly lift off the ground and hence tend to shorten the extensor hallucis longus. A high longitudinal arch where the plantar surface never touches the floor, tends to lift the great toe off the floor. Cutting from the block or vamp of the shoe may cause a tendonitis distally. Coming up on to pointe and working there with bent toes (knuckling) can cause the situation, particularly if it is associated with sickling.

TREATMENT
Ice, ultrasound, and interferential, faradic foot baths, intrinsic muscle exercises to strengthen the intrinsics, strapping the great toe in order to keep the interphalangeal joint straight (Fig. 3.16) and correction of the underlying cause are all required.

Complications
The condition can be difficult to get settled. Inspection of everyday shoes should be undertaken as unsuitable daily footwear can delay or prevent resolution. If it followed a direct blow, there may be other damaged tissues to treat. A developing stress fracture of the 2nd metatarsal may confuse matters by appearing to cause pain along the extensor hallucis longus tendon.

3.16 Stress Fractures of the Metatarsals

See also **Section 2.2**, page 70.
     The affected metatarsals are commonly the 2nd and 3rd. Occasionally the 4th or 5th metatarsals may be the site of the stress fracture. In dancers it is very rarely the 1st metatarsal unless the technique is very poor or the choreographic circumstances are very unusual. Fracture in the 2nd or 3rd metatarsal is usually mid shaft (Fig. 3.17), but a basal stress fracture in the 2nd metatarsal is not uncommon. Being a superficial bone, diagnosis is straightforward with local warmth, tenderness and swelling being easily detected.

CAUSES
Discrepancy of metatarsal length, for example, where there is a long 2nd metatarsal or short 1st

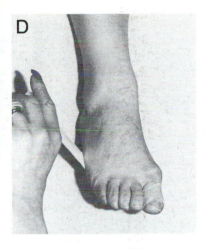

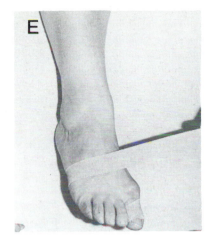

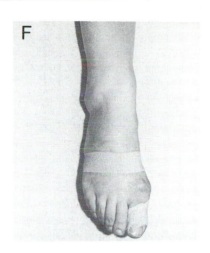

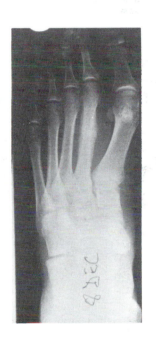

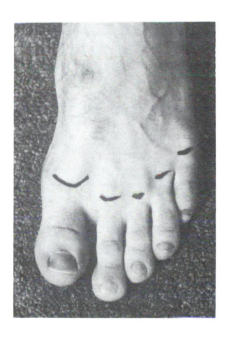

3.17 (left)   X-ray of a stress fracture of the 2nd metatarsal shaft showing healing with plentiful callus (new bone).

3.18 (right)   Short 1st metatarsal in relation to the 2nd metatarsal. In this instance the 2nd and 3rd metatarsals are of equal length.

metatarsal (Fig. 3.18) or occasionally a long 3rd metatarsal. Long toes and weak forefeet predispose to a basal fracture of the 2nd metatarsal. A predisposition anatomically is greatly aggravated by weak intrinsic muscles. Dancing on concrete or solid wood floors and other surfaces without any elasticity or spring may fairly rapidly produce a crop of stress fractures in a class or company. A sudden increase in heavy workload, especially if a lot of pointe work or jumps are required, may produce a stress fracture. This is often seen where there is a sudden move from corps de ballet to principal or possibly, more commonly, the transition from part-time student with three or four classes a week to that of full-time student with classes all day. Badly-fitting shoes or worn-out shoes with soft blocks can also be a predisposing factor. Frequently when the discomfort starts, the dancer will move to wider-fitting shoes, assuming that the shoe itself is causing the pain. This means that the forefoot will have even less support and the situation will be aggravated.

Weak intrinsic muscles leading to dropping of the lesser metatarsal heads can cause a stress fracture because of the additional load placed on the metatarsal. The presence of even a moderate degree of hallux rigidus (degenerative arthritis of the great toe joint, see **Section 3.22**) will cause incorrect weight placement (**Section 5.20**), because the dancer cannot rise correctly through the foot as a result of the limited movements in the 1st metatarso-phalangeal joint. The 5th metatarsal is a special case, and a stress fracture often starts here as a complication of a severe sprain of the lateral ligament because the secondary weakness of ankle control, particularly laterally, i.e. from the peronei, places extra weight transmission through the 5th metatarsal. This tends to be brought about by a too early return to dancing following a lateral ligament sprain. There are also technical causes of which incorrect weight transmission is the commonest - rolling, sickling, over turning or failing to hold the turn-out, working with clawed toes and working with the weight too far back, which aggravates weak intrinsics (incorrect weight placement; **Section 5.20**).

TREATMENT

Rest is required to allow the fracture to unite. During this period, give exercises to strengthen all deficient groups and particularly faradic foot baths and intrinsic muscle exercises. Correct the cause where possible (anatomical aberrations may not be correctable but a strong forefoot will lessen the stress on the bone).

Complications
The most commonly seen complication is an interference with healing due to an ill-advised injection of Hydrocortisone by someone who has failed to make the initial diagnosis and thinks that he is merely dealing with a soft tissue lesion. Oral anti-inflammatories in full dose will also very markedly slow healing by their suppression of the inflammatory response which is a vital part of the healing process (see **Section 2.1**). It is extremely important to note that X-ray evidence of a stress fracture will not appear for at least ten to fourteen days after the onset of symptoms. Although a bone scan would show a developing stress fracture, it should be perfectly possible to make the diagnosis with a fair degree of certainty on clinical grounds. The metatarsal bones are extremely superficial and the presence of local warmth, swelling and tenderness which is very well localised to the bone should cause little difficulty in enabling the examiner to come to the correct diagnosis.

3.17 Osteochondritis of the Head of the 2nd or 3rd Metatarsal

This is a condition which occurs in childhood. It is probably caused by trauma to the metatarsal head. As a result of this, changes occur in the head of the

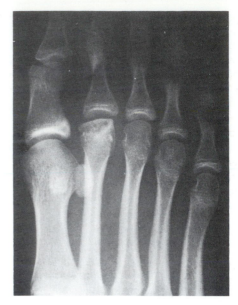

3.19   Osteochondritis of the 2nd metatarsal head (X-ray).

metatarsal and the articular surface begins to collapse. It is seen not only in dancers but also in sprinters and other athletic children. The diagnosis can be made clinically because of localised thickening and tenderness at the metatarso-phalangeal joint. The diagnosis is confirmed by X-ray, which shows an alteration in structure of the metatarsal head and early or even late collapse of the articular surface (Fig. 3.19).

TREATMENT

If the condition is seen early when collapse of the articular surface is still only minor, then surgery should be undertaken. The neck of the metatarsal can be opened and the articular surface elevated to its proper position and the head packed with bone chips, which can be obtained from the metatarsal shaft. This is followed by protected weight bearing until consolidation takes place. Rehabilitation will necessitate faradic foot baths and intrinsic muscle exercises to strengthen the forefoot which will have weakened during the period of convalescence. However, during convalescence the dancer must spend a considerable amount of time exercising all other groups.

Unfortunately, cases usually present very late. When the patient is first seen with pain it may be found that not only is there marked thickening and tenderness around the metatarsal head and metatarso-phalangeal joint but that there is marked restriction of movement in the affected joint, particularly shown by a greatly decreased range of dorsi-flexion. This will be causing problems on demi-pointe work. At this stage X-rays will show that the articular surface has been completely flattened and the metatarsal head broadened, sometimes with some osteophytic formation. Treatment is again surgical but it is impossible to restore the normal anatomy. Instead, the proximal half of the proximal phalanx of the toe is excised in order to produce a pseudarthrosis and restore the range of dorsi-flexion of the toe. At the same time it may be necessary to trim any large osteophytes from the metatarsal head as occasionally they are sufficiently prominent to cause local pressure. If, however, there is no evidence that they are going to cause any local pressure, then they should be left alone. Treatment in the form of faradic foot baths, intrinsic muscle exercises, together with active and passive exercises for the toes, can start as soon as the wound is healed. The results are usually very satisfactory. The shortening of the affected toe does not hamper the dance performance in any way.

3.18 Plantar Fascial Strain

The plantar fascia lies in the sole of the foot, covered only by fat and skin. It is a very strong inelastic band of tissue which is attached to the heel bone at the back and runs forward to divide into little slips which end up in the various tendon sheaths associated with the toes.

CAUSES

This condition can arise with weak feet, particularly when associated with a high longitudinal arch. It is aggravated by wearing shoes that are too short. It occasionally arises when a female dancer wears unaccustomed very high heels and then stands in these shoes for a very long period.

TREATMENT

In the initial stages, ice and faradic foot baths and exercises are most effective. If the condition is chronic with thickening, then pulsed microwave, interferential and ultrasound combined with faradic foot baths and intrinsic muscle exercises will be required and the condition will take somewhat longer to settle down than if it is more acute and of brief duration.

3.19 Capsular Strains of 1st Metatarso-phalangeal Joint

CAUSES

Direct violence, e.g. stubbing the toe, or landing badly. The condition tends to be commoner in boys. Another prime cause of symptoms is repeated

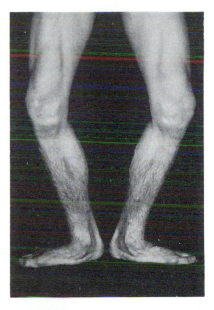

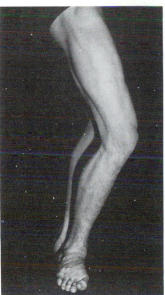

3.20A (above) Rolling with a twist of the great toe. From the front.

3.20B (left)   From the side.

technical faults, particularly if they give a twist to the toe, for example rolling (Fig. 3.20) and all its causes (see **Section 5.17**) and, of course, sickling. The condition tends to be very much worse if there is a short 1st metatarsal, or conversely, a long 2nd metatarsal which produces a similar overall mechanical effect. Shoes that are too short cause the great toe to claw up. The presence of a hallux valgus will cause joint strain because, in rises, as the weight comes over the toes, there is a further valgus strain placed on the great toe and on the medial aspect of the joint. In the presence of a weak first interosseous muscle with a palpable gap between

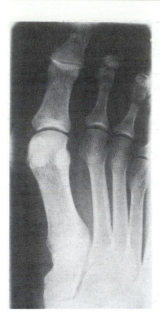

3.21A (left)   The sesamoid bones lying beneath the 1st metatarsal head. The X-ray is taken from above looking through the foot.

3.21B (below)   Here the X-ray is taken looking along the sole of the foot.

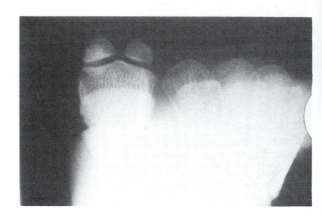

the 1st and 2nd metatarsal heads, even in a case where there is not a congenital metatarsus primus varus, the situation would be greatly aggravated, as would also be the case where there is general weakness of the intrinsics.

In both situations, most of the weight is going through the great toe joint rather than correctly down through the centre of the foot. Shoes that are too wide give no support at all. There is certainly a general inclination, when there is any sort of toe discomfort, for the dancer to go into a wider fitting and this, of course, makes matters worse. Worn-out pointe shoes will also stress the great toe joint greatly. A painful toe, for example an ingrowing toenail, painful corns or verrucae will all cause a weight shift. In many instances the strain may be isolated to the medial ligament and capsule of the metatarso-phalangeal joint. When symptoms at this joint are troublesome there will often be restriction of movements and the clinical appearance of a hallux rigidus. However, mobility will return when the capsular strain has been treated adequately.

TREATMENT

Ice, ultrasound in water, interferential, faradic foot baths and intrinsic muscle exercises are all helpful. Strapping of the great toe to help to maintain alignment can help while treatment is in progress. The dancer can also carry out hot and cold contrast baths himself because frequently this condition tends to be rather more resistant to treatment if circulation is not particularly good in the toes and feet. The shoes should be checked carefully,

including outdoor shoes. Frequently traction on the great toe, to ensure the correct alignment and to gently stretch any tightness, accompanied by passive movements, can be very beneficial.

Complications

Poor circulation makes the condition slower to settle and much more difficult to treat. Usually there is a technical fault associated with this condition and this will lead to other injuries if the technical aspects are not very carefully checked. Any underlying tendency to hallux rigidus will be greatly aggravated. The condition may also cause a sesamoiditis if it persists or is not fully treated, or if it is of long standing. It is often not at all easy to obtain full resolution of the condition because it so frequently follows bad working habits which can be very difficult to eradicate adequately. An example of this is working with the weight back (**Section 5.20**).

3.20 Sesamoiditis

Beneath the head of the 1st metatarsal lie two small bones within the tendons to the great toe (Fig. 3.21). They are known as the medial and lateral sesamoids. They are exactly like a small version of the patella or knee cap, which is a sesamoid bone lying within the tendon formed from the quadriceps muscle on its way down to be inserted into the tibia. The patella is so large that it has a name of its own, whereas the two sesamoids under the 1st metatarsal head are small, each being the

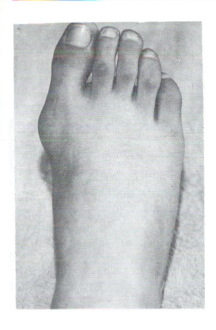

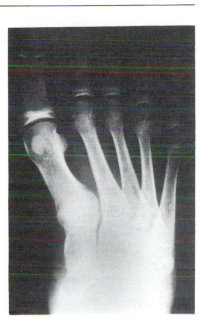

3.22A (left)   A metatarsus primus varus with a mild secondary hallux valgus developing.

3.22B (right)   An X-ray of the same foot.

size of a small bean. In normal walking and running they take the load and pressure beneath the metatarsal head and help to distribute it and also protect the tendons which would otherwise be subjected to direct crushing pressure on each pace.

They are surprisingly free of trouble considering the great forces transmitted through them and their vulnerable position.

Occasionally one or both can become inflamed and painful so that weight bearing is extremely uncomfortable, this condition being known as sesamoiditis. Very rarely a sesamoid can be fractured as a result of direct violence. A fracture must be differentiated from a bipartite or tripartite sesamoid, which is a congenital condition when a sesamoid is in two or three separate parts from birth. A similar condition can occur in the patella. Sesamoiditis presents with local pain and sometimes swelling. Tenderness is localised to beneath the head of the 1st metatarsal. Passive dorsi-flexion of the toe with pressure applied beneath the 1st metatarsal head makes the tenderness worse.

CAUSES

Sesamoiditis is precipitated by direct trauma usually brought about by a bad landing. Sometimes prolonged work on a hard surface will cause the condition.

TREATMENT

Sesamoiditis is frequently extremely slow to settle. Patience on the part of the dancer and the medical attendant is the most important factor.

For local treatment ice, ultrasound, pulsed microwave and interferential can all be used. Felt padding to temporarily relieve pressure from beneath the 1st metatarsal head can be helpful.

Only too frequently none of these physical modalities makes any difference. If the condition is of long-standing then an injection of Hydrocortisone Acetate sometimes improves the symptoms though the results are often disappointing.

Only too often it is just the passage of time, frequently very many months, which allows the symptoms to subside.

Surgery has nothing to offer. Excision of the sesamoid more often than not leaves permanent residual tenderness. To risk surgery on the small chance of gaining relief is unwise. With patience the symptoms will always settle.

3.21 Hallux Valgus and Bunions

CAUSES

Probably the commonest cause seen in dancers is where there is a congenital metatarsus primus varus which produces a secondary hallux valgus (Fig. 3.22). Later in life a hallux valgus (Fig. 3.23) can appear following the use of very poor footwear or if the dancer as a child is put on pointe far too early when the feet are not strong enough. It can also be caused by very prolonged rolling or by weak forefeet (i.e. when the intrinsics are very weak).

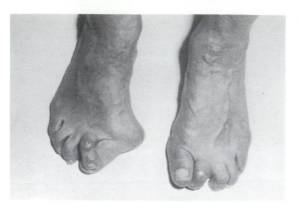

3.23   A severe hallux valgus in the right foot. Note the over-riding 2nd toe. Sometimes the great toe comes over the top of the 2nd toe. The left foot has been improved in appearance by a Keller's operation. This shortens the great toe moderately. There is a marked decrease in power of movement so the operation is not suitable for the dancer who is still working.

There must, however, be an underlying mild hallux valgus deformity before these other latter causes will produce ill-effects and an aggravation of the already slight valgus posture. Overall it is surprising how frequently a very severe valgus deformity is seen which causes little or no symptoms.

TREATMENT

In the situation where there is a congenital metatarsus primus varus a Hohmann's osteotomy of the 1st metatarsal produces a very satisfactory result (Fig. 3.24). This corrective operation does not interfere at all with the capsule or ligaments of the 1st metatarso-phalangeal joint and therefore does not lead to any stiffness if it is carried out correctly. It should ideally be undertaken in the mid teens. If the deformity is fairly marked, then it should

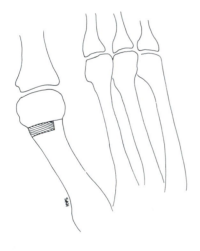

3.24   Hohmann's operation. The shaded section in the first diagram shows the area of bone removed. The second shows the displacement of the 1st metatarsal head towards the 2nd metatarsal and the positioning head securely on the bone peg formed at the end of the shaft. This is the subject of the X-ray.

   The projecting corner of bone at the medial end of the metatarsal shaft becomes absorbed and remodelled during union of the osteotomy and subsequent consolidation.

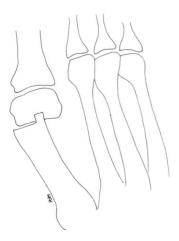

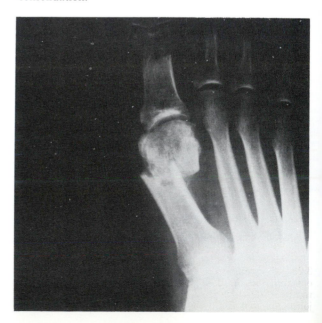

almost certainly be carried out even in the absence of symptoms at that time. This also applies if there is a strong family history of bunions. After about the mid to late twenties or possibly the early thirties, a Hohmann's operation is usually contra-indicated, because the alteration in mechanics of the foot are not accommodated well by a foot of greater age and it may leave a painful foot with tenderness, particularly under the lesser metatarsal heads.

In the case of a hallux valgus without a metatarsus primus varus, operation in active professional dancers is contra-indicated and no radical surgery should be undertaken before they have retired from performing. However, in a teacher, they will usually cope perfectly satisfactorily following the standard Keller's operation (Fig. 3.25). If the bunion area becomes repeatedly infected, then it is possible to carry out a subcapsular excision of the bony osteophyte with a careful reconstruction of the medial capsule. The operation, however, may occasionally lead to some restriction of movements and it should not be carried out unless there is very definite indication for surgery. This indication is largely repeated episodes of inflammation or infection and a risk of underlying bony involvement. The operation must be done open so that the soft tissues can be identified clearly and preserved. One of the most important aspects of this operation is the accurate reconstruction of the medial capsule. If this is not done then a rapidly increasing valgus deformity

will follow this type of procedure. To carry out the operation through a very small incision and blindly grind off the prominent bone is totally irresponsible and can only be condemned. Only too frequently the capsule is severely damaged and there is certainly no opportunity for its reconstruction.

Conservative treatment in hallux valgus and bunions is directed at care of the bunion area. Use of a felt ring pad can relieve local pressure over the bunion. Sometimes a wedge between the first and second toes can be helpful to support the great toe. However, this occasionally has the disadvantage that the pressure is transmitted to the lesser toes which causes them to start to drift into valgus. Faradic foot baths and intrinsic muscle exercises can also help by strengthening the control of the toes.

Complications
Recurrent blistering. This can lead to inflammation and infection of the actual bunions which in occasional cases can progress to bony involvement.

3.22 Hallux Rigidus

This is a condition where osteoarthritis (degenerative arthritis) occurs in the metatarso-phalangeal joint of the great toe. It derives its name because as the condition progresses the toe joint becomes stiffer and eventually fixed or rigid. The condition starts in childhood and is first evidenced by limitation of movement at the great toe joint. At that stage there are rarely any X-ray changes, although there may be some sclerosis of the epiphysis at the base of the proximal phalanx of the great toe. Even later, when movements have become markedly restricted, the changes seen on an X-ray are often relatively mild and advanced radiological changes are only apparent when the toe joint is severely affected and very stiff.

CAUSES

The cause is probably genetic because the condition is not usually associated with trauma and is bilateral. However, like any other joint, if there has been some significant damage to the joint, arthritis may follow. This latter type of hallux rigidus can start at any time in life depending upon when the episode of trauma occurred. The condition, whatever the cause, is unfortunately progressive. The range of movement slowly decreases and because of the limitation of dorsi-flexion, it causes various technical problems. These are largely associated with the difficulty or impossibility in achieving correct weight placement (**Section 5.20**).

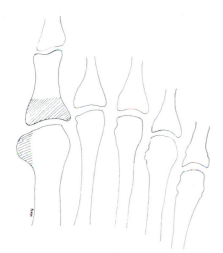

3.25   Diagram of a Keller's operation which is carried out either for a hallux valgus and bunions or for a hallux rigidus (osteo-arthritis of the 1st metatarso-phalangeal joint).

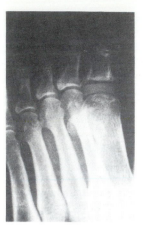

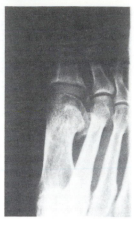

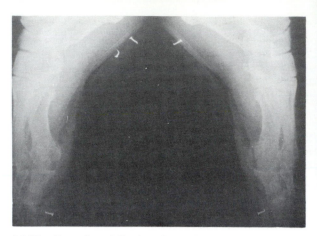

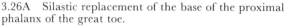

3.26A   Silastic replacement of the base of the proximal phalanx of the great toe.

3.26B   On pointe following the replacements.

TREATMENT

Progress can be slowed and symptoms alleviated by gentle traction on the great toe joint to decrease the amount of stiffness and shortening in the soft tissues, by gentle active and passive exercises and, of course, by strengthening the intrinsic muscles in the forefoot. It is advisable to tell the dancer not to force three-quarter pointe as trying to get up too high tends to make the condition worse rather than better. The dancer should be guided on how high to go by the degree of pain experienced. Some pain is inevitable in the very nature of the condition but it should not be extreme. If symptoms persist despite conservative treatment and particularly if the stiffening of the great toe is causing other technical problems and other injuries, then surgery should be considered. For a dancer this can only be in the form of a silastic replacement of the base of the proximal phalanx of the great toe (Fig. 3.26).

However, this should not be undertaken in a student. The life of the silastic replacement is limited, though variable. It is probably wrong to allow students to embark upon what will become a very brief professional career at an age when they would be better channelling their energies into some other job for the future. When the silastic joint fails it can be removed. This leaves the toe somewhat shortened and greatly decreased in power in jumps, relevés, etc. This latter state is, however, a situation which is perfectly satisfactory for normal life and probably for most dance teachers. In a professional dancer the extra working years which the silastic replacement will have allowed will be greatly welcomed. It is impossible to forecast pre-operatively how long the prosthesis might last but certainly dancers should be warned

that it is not going to last them the rest of their anticipated stage career unless they are already of somewhat mature years.

But *beware*! The diagnosis of hallux rigidus may be made when there is only an *apparent* stiffness of the great toe joint. A stiff great toe needs careful assessment as, when the patient is first seen, there may appear to be a very genuine restriction of movement in the great toe joint but often the stiffness is only temporary. This is not a genuine hallux rigidus. The situation can be brought about by working badly and repeatedly traumatising the first metatarso-phalangeal joint. This is seen particularly in rolling when the weight is repeatedly transmitted at an angle through the metatarso-phalangeal joint. The joint itself can become swollen, painful and stiff as a result. However, with adequate local treatment and correction of the technical fault, the range of movement can be satisfactorily restored. Obviously, X-rays of the toe will show that there is no bony abnormality present and no evidence of any degenerative arthritis.

Complications

The complications arise from the technical faults which result from the alteration of weight bearing line due to the dancer working away from or off the painful great toe(s). Usually one side is more severely affected by the symptoms of pain and stiffness than the other.

3.23 Ingrowing Toenail

CAUSES

This occasionally appears to be congenital. The child is seen with very curved great toenails with the sides tending to go vertically down into the flesh. This type of nail is certainly predisposed to ingrowing. However, in the main, ingrowing toenails are brought about by over-tight or unsuitable footwear. The shoes should be checked and this check must include everyday footwear.

TREATMENT

In the early stages lifting the corner of the nail and putting a little animal wool (not cotton wool) under the corners may be sufficient to stop the nail ingrowing. Also the nail should be cut straight across and the corner should not be removed. If at the same time the cause of the condition is removed, then usually no further treatment is necessary. If, however, the ingrowing persists then a wedge resection of the border of the nail is usually sufficient, provided great care is taken to remove the corner of the nailbed. A radical operation with total obliteration of the nailbed is rarely necessary. Occasionally after wedge resection a small spike of nail will regrow but this is easily trimmed and is normally painless.

3.24 Corns and Callosities

CAUSES

These are really an occupational hazard in dancers. However, they may be greatly aggravated by 'knuckling' when on pointe and by badly-fitting pointe shoes.

TREATMENT

Corns and callosities must certainly be treated with respect and care in order to avoid infection. Good quality professional chiropody is required rather than self-trimming with razor blades or similar implements, when the likelihood of infection would be very much greater. All causes must be eliminated as much as possible.

3.25 Sundry Spurs, Areas of Calcification, etc.

CAUSES

These spurs etc. usually represent areas of previous injury. They are part of the healing process during which time the damaged tissue undergoes partial repair by ossification or calcification. They frequently occur when the soft tissue damage has taken place at a bony junction. For example, if a portion of ligament or capsule is pulled away from the bone this exposes underlying raw bone, bone

cells spill out so, as healing takes place, it is accompanied by a little spike of new bone. These spurs are normally coincidental X-ray findings, in other words an X-ray is taken because of a complaint of pain and on the films one, or frequently more, of these little spurs are seen. However, it cannot be over-emphasised that their presence does not mean that they are the cause of the patient's symptoms. In fact they very rarely indeed cause symptoms themselves and removal of spurs, scraping of calcification on tendons and other miscellaneous and dubious procedures are totally unnecessary. This type of surgery is usually carried out because the true cause of the symptoms has not been determined or investigated or because conservative treatment has been inadequate or incompetent.

As a result, the dancer has an unnecessary anaesthetic and operation. The subsequent enforced period of rest may sometimes be a curative factor, giving the illusion that the surgery was the correct procedure. However, only too often, after the convalescence and when the dancer returns to work, the symptoms of which he was complaining before the operation recur because the underlying cause has not been corrected. In these circumstances the symptoms are very often worse because the dancer is weaker, further injuries then occur elsewhere, possibly leading to even more surgery with the underlying causes still uncorrected.

TREATMENT

Only very rarely indeed, a spur may impinge during joint movements and justify excision. This is unusual but even in these circumstances it is vital to correct any underlying faults.

3.26 Stress Fractures of the Fibula

These commonly occur some 8 to 12 cm above the tip of the lateral malleolus. There is well localised warmth, tenderness and thickening. There should be no real difficulty in making a clinical diagnosis (Fig. 3.27).

CAUSES

The main cause of fibula stress fractures is sickling. This is frequently associated with weak feet. It is certainly aggravated by lower tibial bowing, which seems to be common in oriental dancers. This makes it particularly difficult to strengthen the inner sides of the thighs and the lateral part of the foot (see **Section 5.15**). Failing to hold the turn-out

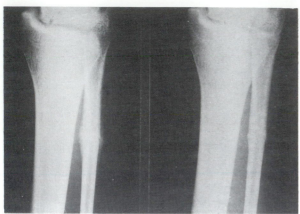

3.27   X-ray of a healing stress fracture of the fibula with callus (new bone) formation.

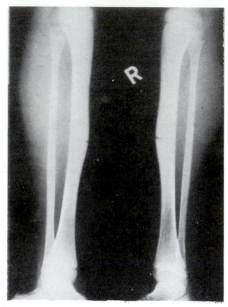

3.28   Stress fractures of the tibiae. These are nearly symmetrical. In the tibia very little new bone is seen on the X-rays during the healing process.

at the hips causes stress in the lower leg. Wrong blocks in pointe shoes can cause faulty weight alignment. Untreated ankle sprains can be followed by the development of a stress fracture and, as a corollary of this, the stress fracture may accompany the development of a chronic sprain.

TREATMENT

Work should be reduced until the patient can do this altered programme totally pain-free. If this cannot be achieved then the dancer will have to be off for a short period. Locally, interferential therapy should be given. At the same time as the reduced dancing a great deal of effort should be made to strengthen all weak muscle groups. Particularly important is the re-education of technique as this condition is basically an injury due to faulty technique. If there is an underlying anatomical variation such as a lower tibial bow, then the technique should be improved to the greatest possible extent and time given to helping the dancer to work within it.

Complications
Untreated, the stress fracture may rarely progress to a complete fracture.

3.27 Stress Fractures of the Tibia

These are commonly at the junction of the upper two-thirds and lower third on the medial border of the tibia and about mid-shaft on the anterior border (Fig. 3.28). They may occasionally occur high at the junction of the upper third and lower

two-thirds. Stress fractures may occur as a result of the tibial shape, for example – bowing and the level of a bow (Fig 3.29).

CAUSES

Probably the most important cause is when the dancer is working with the weight back (**Section 5.20**). This means that it is in part associated with uncontrolled swayback knees. This is in essence a situation where the weight is being pushed back and it is the weight back rather than the swayback knees *per se* which can lead to the stress fracture. Weak forefeet have the same effect of altering the weight alignment as does a failure to hold the turn-out. A weak trunk and a lordotic posture and extraneously, a raked stage, can induce a weight back position, particularly if the dancer is not accustomed to working in that situation, or is not particularly strong. Dancing on hard floors causes the forefeet to overtire. The muscles cease to work and the weight then moves back. At the same time the tiring muscles cause the dancer to crash through plié, landing heavily and jarring the tibia (see **Section 5** for various technical faults which may cause stress fractures).

DIAGNOSIS

This must initially be on clinical grounds. Careful examination will show a very definite well localised area of thickening, warmth and tenderness. This

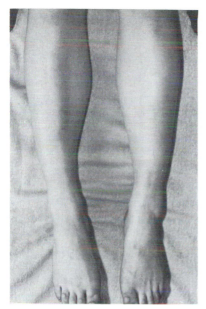

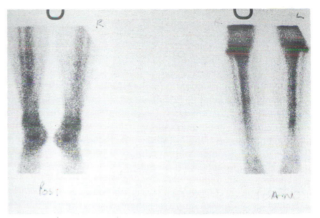

3.30 An isotope bone scan showing a 'hot spot' where a stress fracture is developing at the junction of the middle and lower third of the tibia.

3.29 Lower tibial bows.

certainly indicates the presence of a developing stress fracture. This can be detected four to six weeks, or even more, before X-ray changes are present. A bone scan will show a 'hot spot' of increased vascular activity at the site of the developing stress fracture long before any X-ray changes occur (Fig. 3.30). Poor nutritional habits may play their part in the cause of stress fractures and certainly can cause delay in healing.

TREATMENT

This must start as soon as the clinical diagnosis is made and long before X-ray changes appear. It is essential that the dancer is off work, both performance and class. Delay in treatment may more than quadruple the length of time that the dancer is finally off. Conversely if he is off early this will allow a fairly rapid healing of the stress fracture. Locally interferential can be given to the tender area and this may speed union. Although this is at present not proven, it is certainly harmless. Exercises should be given for all muscle groups. Technical correction is essential and without this, complete recovery and non-recurrence is less likely. Attention should also be paid to the general nutrition and eating habits of the dancer.

Complications
A stress fracture may be mis-diagnosed as anterior compartment syndrome but the localised nature of the clinical findings should prevent this. However,

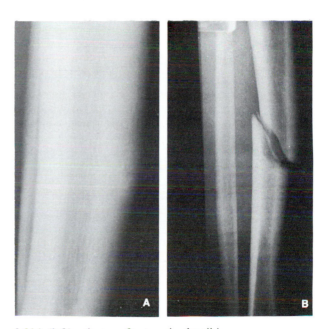

3.31A (left)   A stress fracture in the tibia.

3.31B (right)   The stress fracture has become an acute complete fracture. In this case it was caused when the patient jumped down the last few steps when hurrying to catch a train. A not dissimilar type of jump could have occurred during a performance.

if the stress fractures are multiple confusion is more likely but in these circumstances at least some of the fractures should be visible on an X-ray. If allowed to progress the stress fracture may gradually develop into a complete fracture of the tibia (Fig. 3.31). In this case union is desperately

slow and may take a year or more. The only
exception to this would be the case when a dancer
was undertaking a big jump which produced a
sudden acute fracture at the level of the stress
fracture. In these circumstances, if the stress
fracture had not passed through too great a
proportion of the shaft diameter, union could be
expected to be at the same rate as a 'normal' type
of fracture occurring as the result of a sudden acute
injury, i.e. some three to four months to achieve
complete union.

3.28 Anterior Compartment Syndrome

The anterior compartment of the shin is bounded
by the two bones, the tibia and fibula; by the
interosseous membrane which is a very strong
fibrous sheet of tissue lying between these two
bones, joining them together; and then superficially
by the deep fascia (Fig. 3.32). None of these
structures are stretchable and it is this
non-stretchability which accounts for the problems
which occur in anterior compartment syndrome. If
there is any swelling (which can arise from injury
or other causes) within the anterior compartment,
there will necessarily be a rise in pressure because
of the non-stretchability of the structures encasing
the anterior compartment. This rise in pressure will
cause increasing pain, often known as shin splints.
If the swelling becomes excessive, the rise in
pressure within the tissue can become sufficient to
interfere with or completely obstruct the blood
flow, in which event the tissues within the
compartment will then die from lack of oxygen.
This situation, where there is greatly increased
pressure, is a surgical emergency and urgent
decompression of the anterior compartment
syndrome is required before necrosis (death) of the
tissues takes place. Fortunately, an anterior
compartment of this degree of severity is rare and
the condition does not usually progress beyond the
milder, early stages.

CAUSES

The commonest cause is unaccustomed exercise or
extra exercise of the muscle groups within the
anterior compartment (anterior tibial muscle and
extensors to the toes). The extra exercise produces
swelling of the muscle bellies (as will happen with
any sudden extra excessive use of muscles) and this
causes the symptoms of shin splints. The weight
back situation will also cause extra tension in these
muscle groups (**Section 5.20**). Weak feet produce a
similar over-work of the muscles. Over-tight

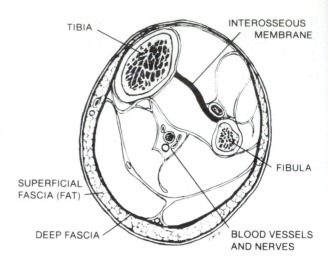

3.32   Cross-section of a leg in the upper third showing
the fascial compartments.

ribbons, by constricting the lower leg, may interfere
with circulation superficially and restrict
movement. This can produce an irritation of the
tendons of the tibialis anterior and of the toe
extensors, producing a mild degree of anterior
compartment syndrome. Short shoes, by causing
clawing of the toes, have a similar effect. Rolling
will cause over-work of the anterior compartment
muscles. If the dancer is observed in class, the great
prominence of the tendons can be seen (Fig. 3.33).
A similar effect can be brought about by a tight
Achilles tendon restricting the plié. Anterior
compartment syndrome, usually very mild, is
common in first year full-time students and also
during a growth spurt. Often during periods of
stress, muscle tension causes the dancer to grip the
floor unnecessarily with the toes.

TREATMENT

Provided the condition is not severe enough to
place the circulation in jeopardy, conservative
treatment is effective. Treatment should be carried
out with the leg in elevation, using ice and
interferential from the ankle to the groin to
stimulate the circulation and venous return. (Make
sure the knee is supported at the back as should be
the situation in all treatments of any lower limb
condition). Exercises are given to strengthen all the
other groups including the feet, calf, quadriceps,
hamstrings, adductors and gluteals, all of which are
more likely to be relatively weak in a dancer who
has shin splints. The strengthening of these other
groups will facilitate the technical correction which
will be required. Also advise the dancer to sleep

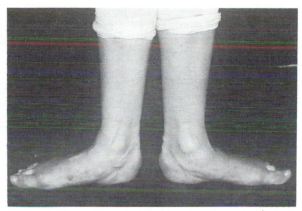

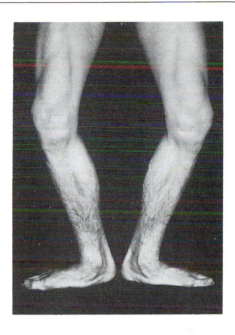

3.33   Both photographs illustrate rolling at the feet and ankles. Also shown is the beginning of the tension which develops in the front of the ankle.

with the foot of the bed elevated by about 25 cm. It is sensible to elevate the legs between classes and without shoes if the condition is not severe enough to warrant total rest from work. Massage can be helpful, although it is time-consuming. Faradism under pressure in elevation can be effective in more severe cases, although it is very painful. Tight Achilles tendons, if temporary, should not be neglected in the treatment programme. (See **Section 5.14**.)

Complications
Muscle necrosis may occur if the condition is severe and remains undiagnosed, thereby not giving the patient the benefit of surgical decompression. A diagnosis of a stress fracture in the tibia may be missed as it can also arise from the same cause as the shin splints or, alternatively, a stress fracture may be mis-diagnosed as an anterior compartment syndrome. It is incorrect to call a developing stress fracture 'shin splints'.

3.29 Calf Muscle Tears

TREATMENT
The treatment is described in the general section on the treatment of muscle tears. (**Section 2.2** Muscle Tears, page 72).

Complications
Calf muscle tears are particularly prone to contracture. This is in part from the scarring but also in part from the inherent tendency of the calf muscle and Achilles tendon complex to tighten up

far more rapidly than might be expected. Calf muscle strains may present as pain behind the knee and may be mis-diagnosed as a hamstring problem or a knee injury. Remember that the two heads of the gastrocnemius are inserted in the lower end of the femur and therefore pass behind the knee joint.

3.30 Anterior Knee Pain

This is a blanket term which covers conditions in patients whose actual pathology and precise cause of the pain is not exactly known, even after extensive investigations, although the general expression anterior knee pain does also include definite conditions which can be diagnosed. Treatment is by a combination and variation of the modalities outlined below. When trying to make an accurate diagnosis and before concluding that the actual cause cannot be determined, it is most important to consider all the possible definite diagnoses and eliminate them in succession.

Tight Tensor Fasciae Latae

CAUSES
This is usually brought about by muscle imbalance in the thigh when the medial side muscles are weak (less strong – it can happen in strong legs and it is the imbalance which is the vital clue). In these circumstances the lateral side, including the tensor fasciae latae, is over-used. In extreme cases the over-use is readily visible, with bulging outer sides

of the thighs and apparently very little muscle on the inner side, including a very underdeveloped vastus medialis. The overall appearance is reminiscent of someone wearing a pair of jodhpurs. However, it can still occur with little obvious outward developmental difference. In these cases the difference in muscle tension can be felt on palpation. During examination, close observation of the patella will show that it moves laterally as well as proximally during an isometric quadriceps contraction. This is diagnostic of lateral/medial muscle imbalance, provided the patient does not have knock knees.

TREATMENT

The soft tissue and capsular contraction laterally which is much beloved by proponents of lateral release operations, *only* occurs after there has been lateral/medial muscle imbalance and *never* occurs *de novo* as an entity in its own right. Lateral release procedures, even if indicated because the soft tissue tightness has developed beyond the point of being stretchable, are useless unless the cause of the imbalance is diagnosed and fully corrected by post-operative physiotherapy *correctly* carried out. If this is not achieved the operation will make the patient worse.

These remarks have been particularly emphasised because unfortunately only too often dancers and dance students are seen who have been the subjects of a lateral release operation which has not been followed up by adequate physiotherapy. Certainly in many of these cases it is apparent that the operation was never indicated in the first place.

Tightness of the tensor fasciae latae certainly prevents proper adjustment of the pelvis or transference of the weight. This can therefore cause excessive corrections to take place in the lumbar spine with injuries occurring there.

Patellar Tendonitis

This usually occurs at the patello-tendinous junction. It is an imflammatory reaction due to strain at this junction between the bone of the patella and the tendon.

CAUSES

The commonest cause of patellar tendonitis is imbalance of the quadriceps between the medial and lateral components, giving rise to an unequal pull on the patellar tendon. It is often associated with rolling (**Section 5.17**) or with over-turning (**Section 5.7**) or with having the body weight too far back (**Section 5.20**). It is also frequently

associated with an over-development of the lateral side of the thigh. In the presence of tight Achilles tendons and/or weak feet, when the dancer lands he cannot absorb the shock at the feet and the patellar tendon has to take the strain. Sticky surfaces can also cause strain in this area on any sort of twisting due to the increased friction between the foot and the floor.

A period of rapid growth may produce temporary inadequacy of the quadriceps and this can induce a tendonitis. Inadequacy of the quadriceps can also be produced by pushing back on a swayback knee. In this instance it may be coupled with lateral/medial imbalance, both of these contributing to the patellar tendonitis. In the weight back situation (**Section 5.20**), the extensor reflex is not stimulated because the main weight is on the back of the heel pad and not towards the front of the heel pad. Pressure at the latter point will stimulate a much more effective quadriceps contraction. Tightness at the front of the hip (**Section 5.9**) prevents a satisfactory quadriceps pull up. Tight hamstrings (**Section 5.12**) – often associated with growth – may precipitate a patellar tendonitis because of inhibition of the quadriceps action by the tight hamstrings. Finally, kneeling routines may produce a tendonitis and this is often associated with an infra-patellar bursitis.

TREATMENT

Local treatment starts with ice, particularly if there is any swelling, and then proceeds to ultrasound and interferential therapy. There then has to be a correction of any muscle imbalance. This is often helped by faradic stimulation to the vastus medialis to reinforce active contraction. As the condition settles, add a small weight, either 1 or 2 kilograms at most. If the fascia lata area is tight, benefit cannot be achieved by attempts to strengthen or correct imbalance of muscles without first giving interferential to the fascia lata followed by stretching. Then, during each treatment session, follow this with active exercises. There is also a need for careful examination for any of the causes outlined above and their elimination. Without this taking place local treatment will either be ineffective or only very temporarily effective.

Complications

Inadequate treatment at any of these stages leads to the development of a chronic lesion. Inadequate treatment is also a precursor of other injuries around the knee and in particular of the development of chondromalacia patellae. Later, spurs may develop at the lower pole of the patella, particularly if early treatment is inadequate and the condition is allowed to become chronic. The spur itself is very rarely the source of any symptoms and does not normally require excision. The symptoms will clear when the tendonitis is treated correctly.

Osgood Schlatter's Disease

This is an apophysitis of the tibial tubercle in adolescence, which is an inflammation of the growing portion of the bone at the upper end of the tibia to which the patellar tendon is attached. Usually there is a separate growth portion, sometimes it is attached to the epiphysis. An apophysis is similar to an epiphysis inasmuch as it is a separate growing portion of the bone and does not become attached to the main part of the bone until growth ceases. However, unlike the epiphysis, the apophysis does not take part in increasing the length of the bone. There are many of these little apophyseal areas of growth throughout the body and they are usually the site of attachment of a large tendon.

CAUSES

Osgood Schlatter's disease is probably most commonly produced by relative weakness of the quadriceps muscle, often associated with a period of rapid growth. This weakness results in a jerking pull on the lower tendon attachment rather than an even controlled pull. On initial examination, frequently the quadriceps do not appear to be weak, hence the term relative weakness. This relative weakness takes into account the level of activity which is being carried out by the person suffering from Osgood Schlatter's disease. It is most common in children who are keen on games, sports and other activities. However, during adolescence the strength of the quadriceps may not be quite up to the effort which is being demanded of them and this then results in the uneven pulling on the tendon and subsequent apophysitis.

TREATMENT

The dancer should rest off activity if the condition is very painful and there is marked tenderness over the tibial tubercle. This area may be swollen and warm. During this time the dancer should concentrate on exercises and build up the quadriceps muscles as well as the adductors, gluteals and hamstrings. Correct any imbalance and also any tendency to push back on the knee. Technical correction may also be of value here. As the acute pain settles, the student can return gradually to class and dancing.

Complications
The actual bony tibial tubercle can become permanently enlarged if a lot of strenuous activity is continued despite the warnings of pain. This enlargement is not in itself of great significance. However, girls find it very unsightly. In boys, should they be called upon to kneel much, it can produce a local painful area later in life purely because of the mechanical prominence. The treatment of Osgood Schlatter's disease can be difficult, as continued rapid growth may prevent the patient catching up sufficiently with his strengthening routines to match the growth rate.

Chondromalacia Patellae

This name is often loosely applied to non specific anterior knee pain. Chondromalacia patellae is, however, a very definite entity and the term should, if possible, only be applied when there are actual changes in the articular cartilage on the retro-patellar surface. This cartilage becomes yellowed in patches, it softens, frays and then wears away. A true, well established chondromalacia patellae can be a precursor of patello-femoral osteoarthritis.

CAUSES

Most commonly this is incorrect tracking of the patella (i.e. muscle imbalance) especially when associated with overall weakness of the quadriceps muscles. It is therefore common after a growth spurt which will have caused relative weakness of the muscles, hence its frequency during adolescence and the teens. Tightness in the fronts of the hips can cause tight quadriceps. In the presence of tight Achilles tendons, the knee tends to be the main shock absorber and this aggravates the condition. Chondromalacia patellae is more commonly seen in runners, gymnasts and dancers than other types of athlete. These three groups all have a very high repetition of particular movements. It is also more common in the presence of swayback knees. It may occasionally be precipitated by a direct blow on the patella. However, in this situation it should not be confused with an osteo-chondral fracture. This is an acute fracture occurring in the bone just beneath the articular cartilage and will often break out a small fragment of bone together with the over-lying cartilage. Chondromalacia patellae is of more gradual onset and, following a blow on the patella, bruising of the retro-patellar cartilage can take place and this can then lead to the chondromalacia.

TREATMENT

Local treatment comprises pulsed microwave, which is very soothing, plus interferential therapy, not only from the mid leg to the mid thigh, but also in a more localised form from just below the patella to just above. Ultrasound also may be helpful. Exercises should be directed towards re-balancing muscles, quadriceps strengthening and also strengthening of any other weak muscle groups, particularly hamstrings, adductors, gluteals and calves, stretching any tightness in the front of the hips and also the quadriceps themselves and the calf if they are tight. A small heel (three-quarters of an inch – 2 cm) can prevent the weight being pushed back too far in the presence of swayback knees and similarly a lift inside a ballet shoe. This, using orthopaedic felt temporarily placed there until the muscle strengthens, can be very helpful. Once the symptoms have improved these aids should be discarded. Checking technical faults is, as always, of the greatest importance.

Complications

True chondromalacia patellae is very persistent and can be difficult to treat if it is long established, although if caught early, treatment is very much easier. An arthroscopy may be required, if only to confirm the genuine diagnosis. Surgery, for example shaving the retro-patellar surface, is disastrous and makes matters worse. A lateral release operation merely aggravates muscle weakness and hence the imbalance is increased, even if there is some faulty patella tracking. A lateral release should only follow a muscle strengthening programme when it has been demonstrated that there is a true tightness in the lateral capsule which cannot be stretched out.

3.31 Capsular Strains of the Knee

These may occur anywhere around the knee but are rather more common posteriorly.

CAUSES

Forced hyperextension of the knee is probably the commonest cause and in these cases it may also be associated with a strain of one or both heads of the gastrocnemius. This can occur in many dance steps; for example, landing from cabriole with the weight on the heel, snapping the knee backwards. Frequently there is a significant amount of bruising and swelling associated with this injury.

TREATMENT

Locally ice, ultrasound and interferential are used

to decrease the swelling. The dancer should definitely be off until settled. During this stage strengthening exercises should be undertaken as wasting will rapidly occur. Pay particular attention to the hamstrings which are usually neglected in knee conditions of all types.

3.32 Injury of the Medial Ligament of the Knee

CAUSES

Tears are usually caused by a faulty landing or collision or a fall, which may be precipitated by sticky floors. *Sprains* are caused by faulty landings and bad floor surfaces, i.e. much the same as events and conditions that can cause a tear but when the force is less.

They are also seen in unusual choreography with which the dancer is not familiar and in jumping off various stage props. Sickled feet greatly increase the possibilities of a bad landing and injuries of various types to the inner side of the knee. Anything which produces tiredness in the dancer, e.g. over-rehearsal, particularly on solid floors, can make the injury more likely to occur.
injury more likely to occur.

TREATMENT

Tears are an urgent orthopaedic problem and will require surgery if complete. In lesser cases, plaster of Paris is required unless the damage is very minor. The later stages of the rehabilitation, when surgery is complete and the tear has healed, are the same as for a sprain, as follows.

For *sprains*, local use of ice, ultrasound and interferential are indicated. The dancer will probably have to be off dancing unless the injury is very minor. Exercises are particularly important during the rehabilitation period with special attention to the quadriceps medialis and the adductors. Correct action of the foot, with a build-up of intrinsic muscles and correct weight distribution to prevent sickling, is particularly important. Care should be taken to eliminate any tendency to overturn the feet, which always puts an excessive strain on the medial side of the knee. As in any knee injury, the muscle build-up will have to extend up to the gluteals and trunk and technical correction will also have to look at these areas. Any pre-existing fault which may not have caused symptoms or injuries before this ligament sprain, will certainly aggravate the medial side of the knee once it has been the site of an injury of any sort.

3.33 Injury of the Lateral Ligament of the Knee

Injuries here are uncommon in dancers and usually only occur as a result of direct violence, e.g. collisions and falls. If the rupture is complete, the lateral popliteal nerve may also be severely and permanently damaged. The injury is one requiring urgent orthopaedic care. The rehabilitation is similar to that given to the medial ligament sprains.

3.34 Injuries of the Cruciate Ligaments of the Knee

These injuries, similarly to those affecting the collateral ligaments, commonly arise from direct violence and are frequently associated with tearing of a collateral ligament and meniscal damage. Cruciate ligament injuries are also urgent orthopaedic problems. Rehabilitation, if recovery ever reaches the stage where the dancer can contemplate a return to dancing, is long drawn out because of the extensive damage. It is similar to that pertaining to the damaged collateral ligaments. Unfortunately, when there is a cruciate ligament injury, the damage is usually sufficient to end a dancer's career. Occasionally, a dancer or other athlete can sustain serious damage to a cruciate ligament, most commonly the anterior, without leaving a serious disability. This is, however, the exception.

3.35 Damage to the Medial Meniscus of the Knee

The meniscus may be torn to a varying extent ranging from a minor tag to a full length tear or a total avulsion of the meniscus from its peripheral attachment. The problems arise in the longer term (after the initial symptoms of the original tear have subsided) because the torn fragment can catch in the joint, causing giving way or locking of the knee.

CAUSES

The tear takes place because the meniscus becomes trapped between the femoral condyle and the tibial plateau during rotation on a bent knee. There is no doubt that, by repeated malfunctions of the knee, tears can occur gradually and without immediate symptoms. This has been shown by the observation of a meniscal tear on arthroscopic examination when there has been no history of an acute episode. Frequently the symptoms can be relatively minor some long time before a final acute episode, the

latter of which is probably caused by the tearing of the last portion of an already developing tear. The situation is aggravated or caused by over-turning the feet, by weakness of the adductors and the vastus medialis, together with their associated postural muscles, and finally by a muscular imbalance causing lack of control of the knee. Weak adductors will not hold the leg correctly under the body when on one leg, thus increasing the strain on the medial side of the knee. In addition, the weak adductors will not control the turn-out at the hip, aggravating any overturning at the foot. When carrying the working leg through from front to side and especially also to the back, the pelvis will not be controlled in relation to the supporting leg and will also swing round, causing a rotation at the knee and a secondary overturning at the supporting foot, as the leg above the foot rotates inwards (Fig. 3.34). Isolated technical faults such as rolling may contribute to meniscal tears. Ligament laxity can also be a contributory factor, hence swayback knees can be prone to cartilage tears, especially as they are so often associated with weak thigh muscles.

TREATMENT

A tear *per se* does not necessarily require surgery unless it is causing symptoms, i.e. locking or giving way or restriction of movements. If symptoms are present, removal of the torn portion is required and the current practice is to leave as much as possible of the normal meniscus behind. However, correction of the causes outlined above coupled with a muscle strengthening programme and a gradual return to full work, will frequently remove the need for surgery at that stage. If surgery is undertaken, the same programme of rehabilitation will be required with even more strengthening work because of the increased muscle weakness following even an arthroscopic procedure. In all cases, thorough technical investigation and correction is required. In post-operative care, plaster of Paris should be avoided as it prevents an early and effective muscle build-up programme, particularly in the vastus medialis. Persistent or recurrent swelling can be a great enemy of progress and needs treatment with ice, elevation of the foot of the bed and an increase in controlled exercises. Exercise programmes for knee rehabilitation are probably the most misconceived of any form of recovery programme for any part of the body.

Pre-operatively, time spent on a regime of exercises to strengthen all relevant groups and rehearsals of the post-operative exercises can pay great dividends in very significantly reducing the convalescent and rehabilitation period.

3.34   Over turning on one leg with the working leg at the back. The pelvis is
not supported because of weak adductors. Frequently the pelvis is much more
tilted than in this dancer. However, it is very important to detect minor
degrees of tilt because it produces an apparent discrepancy in leg length. It
can be easily seen in the first photograph that the dancer here would
experience great difficulty in closing to any position without further distortion
of the trunk.

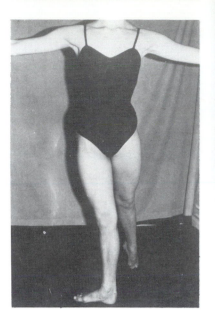

3.36 Damage to the Lateral Meniscus of the Knee

This type of damage is the same as that which
affects the medial meniscus. Lateral meniscus tears
are relatively more common in dancing than in
other types of sport, although the medial meniscus
is, even in dancers, more often damaged than the
lateral.

CAUSES

In dancers the lateral meniscus tear is commonly of
gradual onset from repeated minor trauma rather
than presenting as an acute tear, as happens in
medial meniscus damage where the chronic type
injury is less common. The tear of the lateral
meniscus can be brought about by a failure to hold
the turn-out equally so that the affected side is
back, the foot is rolled and the fascia lata is tight.
If the dancer is looked at carefully when he is
standing turned out in 1st position it can be seen

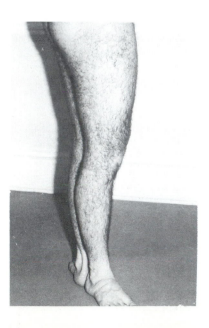

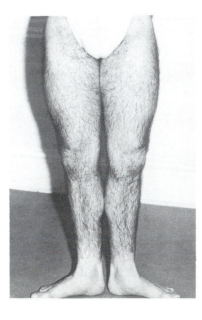

3.35A (far left)   In over turning
the feet the patella faces more
anteriorly and is out of line with the
foot. This photograph illustrates the
lack of pull up in the hamstrings.

3.35B (left)   Shows the lack of pull
up in the quadriceps, especially the
medialis which, though visible here,
is not contracting to provide full
extension of the knees. The more the
dancer over turns the bigger the gap
between the knees, reducing the
ability to pull up with the thigh
muscles. Additionally, the dancer
becomes increasingly prone to injury
at the knee the more he over turns.

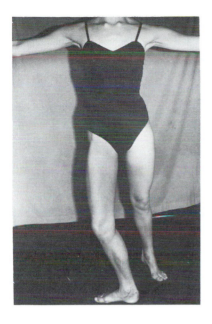
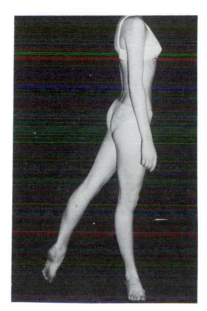
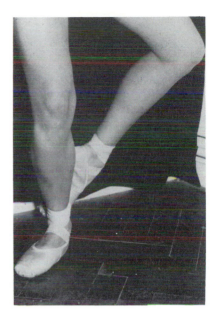

that the knees are not quite fully extended (Fig. 3.35). From the side the hamstrings can be seen to be failing to pull up fully, while from the front the failure of the quadriceps and particularly the vastus medialis to pull up and contract correctly can be observed. This failure will also include the adductors. The more the dancer overturns, the wider the gap between the knees and the more the knee will be slightly flexed. Working thus on a slightly flexed knee with the tibia twisted outwards in relation to the femur is a prime cause of injuries to the menisci inside the knee as well as ligament and capsular damage. In this situation the rotation of the tibia can produce tightening of the capsule and other soft tissues postero-laterally despite the slight flexion of the knee which would otherwise tend to relax them, whereas the same rotation can tend to slacken the soft tissues postero-medially. As a result, the lateral meniscus is chronically compressed and gradually becomes the site of a tear which may be somewhat degenerative in nature.

TREATMENT

This is similar to that for the medial meniscus, calling for arthroscopic examination to confirm the diagnosis or possibly an arthrogram. Once the tear has been confirmed it should be treated in the recognised surgical manner, preserving as much of the lateral meniscus as possible, i.e. by partial menisectomy. However, with lateral meniscus damage the technical faults are often somewhat different from those occurring in medial meniscus injury but they need just as careful assessment and correction.

3.37 Ruptures of the Quadriceps Tendon or the Patellar Tendon or Fracture of the Patella

These injuries can be considered together because the causes are the same. In each case there is a disruption of the extensor mechanism occurring between the lower part of the muscle bellies of the quadriceps muscle and the insertion into the tibial tubercle. The three levels at which this disruption can take place are at the quadriceps tendon just above the patella, through the patella itself producing a transverse fracture of the patella, or through the patellar tendon between the patella and the tibial tuberosity. Ruptures of the patellar tendon or transverse fractures of the patella occur in a younger age group, whereas ruptures of the quadriceps tendon usually occur slightly later in life.

CAUSES

All these injuries occur because of a sudden explosive contraction of the quadriceps muscle, particularly in someone who is not at the peak of training, although a technical mistake or faulty jump can produce a similar effect. The extremely strong and uncontrolled muscle contraction causes the rupture by pulling the fibres of the tendon apart. In the case of the patella fracture this pull also produces a snap back of the patella onto the femoral condyles, breaking the patella transversely across. In all three injuries the contraction of the muscle will continue to pull the proximal part up the thigh, producing a gap at the site of the rupture. Each injury is followed by an immediate and very great swelling due to an extensive haemorrhage. If examined shortly after the injury the blood is still liquid and it is usually possible to feel the actual gap. However, if some time has elapsed the blood may have started to clot and certainly if it is a day or two later the gap may be difficult to palpate.

When examined immediately after the accident the dancer can be asked to lift the leg up straight. If he cannot do so, then a rupture should be strongly suspected. In other conditions affecting the knee, even though fairly serious, the dancer is usually able with an effort to lift the leg up straight because, in the early stage, inhibition of quadriceps muscle may not yet have taken place. If some time has elapsed this inhibition does occur even though there is no disruption of the extensor mechanism and the patient will be unable to lift his leg. These tendon ruptures or patellar fractures are all acute orthopaedic emergencies requiring immediate surgical repair. Failure to recognise the injury or to suspect it and refer for an orthopaedic opinion can make the difference between the dancer being able eventually to return to a full dancing career or otherwise. If there is a delay this will usually spell the end of any return to dancing or any sort of active sport at a competitive level.

TREATMENT

This is by surgical repair. During the post-operative phase an exercise programme can be devised to keep the rest of the body in as good a condition as possible. Even while the patient is still in plaster some isometric contractions for the muscle groups on the affected leg can be commenced. Once the plaster has been finally removed intensive exercises should be instituted in order to build up the muscle groups and to mobilise the knee. It is of value in speeding up recovery if the complete plaster is removed as early as possible in order to allow the patient to come out for exercises but then, after the exercise programme, the leg can be immobilised again in a plaster back splint.

It is this early treatment with a carefully devised programme of exercise that is as important in allowing the patient to achieve their utmost recovery as is the quality of the surgery. In competent surgical hands repair using braided stainless steel wire can practically eliminate the need for a complete plaster cylinder. (Beware of the local heating effect of shortwave diathermy or microwave with buried wire – both are contra-indicated. The dancer must be told always to warn the physiotherapist about the buried wire when going for any type of treatment at a later date. However, the gain by having early access for treatment outweighs this inconvenience for the patient in having to remember to inform future physiotherapists.)

3.38 Quadriceps Muscle Strains and Tears

These have been dealt with in general in the section on muscle injuries. (**Section 2.2** Muscle Tears, page 72). However, it is particularly important in injuries at this site to ensure that the correct medial/lateral balance between the parts of the quadriceps muscles is restored during the treatment period.

Complications
These are associated with a failure to restore this medial/lateral balance with its associated problems, which have been described under various earlier headings.

3.39 Adductor Muscle Strains and Tears

The adductor muscles are probably the commonest site of muscle damage. Usually the tears occur in the proximal (upper) part of the adductor complex and are brought about by a sudden over-stretching such as may happen in forcing splits sitting in 2nd position. If the tenderness is very high and close to the bone of the pelvis an X-ray should be taken as sometimes the bony origin is avulsed together with a small piece of bone. The importance of this is that if early stretching is carried out then the injured area will be irritated and further bone cells will be shed into the haematoma (collection of blood) in the damaged area. At the time of the initial avulsion, as the bone has been exposed, there will already have been some spillage of bone-forming cells. Extra irritation will only encourage the conversion of the haematoma into a mass of bone instead of allowing the desirable absorption of the blood and repair with the minimum of scar tissue. This bone formation is sometimes seen in excess in horse riding injuries, when most of the adductors can be replaced with bone – the so-called rider's bone. This comes about because of repeated injuries and damage to the adductor muscles.

CAUSES

As mentioned, the splits in 2nd position or any forcible abduction strain can cause the damage. As in any muscle injury it is far more common in the (physically) under-trained dancer or in the (technically) badly trained dancer. The injury can range from a mild strain to large muscle tears.

TREATMENT

Locally – ice and rest are required in the early stages together with ultrasound and interferential. Strengthening exercises should commence as soon as the initial swelling has started to settle (not earlier than 48 hours because it can take this long for the bleeding to stop). The exercises should start gently and, if the damage is extensive, assisted active exercises may be required before progressing to exercises against gravity. The early use of weights is contra-indicated as in all muscle tears.

The treatment is initially aimed at:
1. absorption of the blood;
2. healing with minimum of scar tissue;
3. strengthening the muscle;
4. finally, stretching out the scar tissue.

Stretching should not start until good muscle tone is restored (this is part of a protective mechanism and can help to prevent re-tearing). Stretching is aimed at preventing the scar tissue shortening. It should only be carried out at the end of the session of local treatment and exercise and when the patient is warm. The dancer should be taught how to stretch himself as this will be required for some months after he returns to dancing, as there will continue to be a tendency for the scar tissue to contract until it is fully mature. This may not take place for some six to twelve months. If this gentle controlled stretching is omitted, even in apparently minor cases, a state can be arrived at where the adductors have tightened and contracted so that chronic and recurrent problems ensue and become almost untreatable.

3.40 Groin Strains

These can affect several muscles in the groin area. It is more important to isolate the cause of the injury rather than to worry about which particular muscle has been strained. The commonest site is the origin of the rectus femoris and the sartorius.

CAUSES

Groin strains are usually brought about by faulty technique aggravated by any weakness. There may, in fact, be no actual muscle weakness but the faulty technique encourages the use of the wrong muscles and hence their strain, especially if a high number of repetitions are carried out. Occasionally the damage can be caused by over-stretching, as in the splits. Weakness or failure of adequate function of the adductors on the supporting side will inhibit the function of the adductors on the working side, leading to over-use of the muscles crossing the front of the groin. Failure of use of the supporting adductors may arise from causes outside this area; for example, trunk faults or foot faults. In an exercise sense one or other (right or left) group of adductors can be isolated but once the dancer is standing there is considerable stimulatory overflow functionally from one side to the other, hence the lack of correct use in one adductor group will affect the opposite group. It follows therefore that a great deal of attention must be paid to the side opposite to that which has been the site of injury. The weight back situation, however caused, also leads to groin strains.

Examine the state of the hamstrings, the adductors and the fascia lata.

In the hamstrings look for tightness and imbalance medial versus lateral and particularly ask about any past history of hamstring tears. In the case of an old hamstring injury the muscle may have been left scarred and shortened because of inadequate treatment of the original injury, possibly only by rest alone. If this condition has occurred it will then give an unequal pull on the pelvis, in which case the dancer will lean over the affected leg, shortening the front of the hip and causing the groin strain.

In the adductors it is often found that they are tightened on the injured groin side. It is doubtful whether this tightness preceded the groin injury or whether it came on following the onset of the symptoms from the groin. In any case the tightness of the adductors will require active treatment.

The fascia lata is often tight when there is a groin strain and like the adductors it is questionable whether the tightness was present before the injury and therefore a contributing factor or whether it followed the injury. Tightness of the tensor fasciae latae and of the fascia lata certainly prevents proper adjustment of the pelvis on transference of the weight. This can therefore cause excessive corrections to take place in the lumbar spine with injuries occurring there as well as at the groin.

Treatment must include stretching these areas where relevant by hold/relax techniques or by static stretching (not by forced stretching). (See **Section 2.5** Stretching, page 88.) In addition, the dancer must stretch out the quadriceps muscle.

If any groin pain is persistent check that this is not a referred pain from a back injury. In teenagers, look out for glandular fever developing, in which case they may also be complaining of some tiredness and lassitude without anything more definite to indicate the presence of a virus infection.

An unusual cause of groin pain may occur when the leg is elevated to the front or side above 90°. This is probably brought about by a minor anatomical abnormality. In normal individuals there are some fibres from the rectus femoris inserted into the front of the hip joint capsule. On hip flexion they are responsible for pulling the capsule away from the joint so that it does not get nipped. Sometimes these fibres are absent and it is probable that it is in these circumstances that pain is felt in the groin because the capsule is caught between the femoral neck and the pelvis.

TREATMENT

Usually the local damage is not severe and swelling only occasionally occurs. Locally, ultrasound (which is usually best applied with the area on stretch) and interferential therapy are normally all that is required. The exercise programme is the most important part of treatment and must embrace technical correction. In this condition, the planning of the exercise regime and the technical correction must be very closely allied. One cannot be followed later by the other but must proceed in parallel from the beginning of treatment. (Unlike many other conditions when the technical correction can start towards the end of the treatment programme.)

3.41 Hamstring Strains and Tears

These may be anything from mild strains to large tears and can occur at any level. As in the adductors, damage can occur at the origin avulsing the bony attachment and sometimes pulling off a piece of bone. If the tenderness is high up in the hamstrings, then an X-ray should be taken in order to show whether there has been some bony avulsion or not. The potential complications of bony avulsion are those which have already been described for the same event occurring in the adductors.

CAUSES

The injury commonly occurs during unwise stretching, particularly when the dancer is cold. Faulty technique frequently causes the damage, particularly when the weight is back and the

dancer is sitting in the hip while the working leg is raised, as in a grand battement, penché arabesque, or even with the leg raised in 2nd position. In these circumstances the upper part of the hamstring tends to be injured. This basically comes about because when the dancer is sitting in the hip with the weight back, all the other muscle groups around the hip fail to work correctly so that the upper hamstring remains unprotected. Added to this, when the weight is back the hamstrings are themselves not being worked correctly and are therefore not in a state to tolerate stretch well. Over turning causes the medial hamstrings to over-work and this also produces under-use of the lateral hamstrings, which are then unfit for sudden stretch. A false sense of warmth can be encouraged by the use of plastic trousers or other impermeable dance wear. These make the skin feel falsely warm and commonly this is not reflected by an increased blood supply more deeply. Therefore working in the plastic covering, particularly if any stretching is being undertaken, can produce damaging results. Additionally, these types of garments produce a marked increase in the sweating which is unable to evaporate through the plastic. When the garment is removed for class or performance, the sudden increase in evaporation produces a marked local fall in temperature and this chilling makes the muscle more prone to injury.

TREATMENT

Locally, ice should be applied if there is swelling or evidence of bleeding. Ultrasound and interferential are used to reduce both swelling and pain. Once the pain and swelling are settling, an exercise programme should be commenced and this programme should also embrace the allied muscle groups such as the adductors, gluteals and quadriceps, as well as ensuring that the hamstring muscle complex is itself functioning correctly. Stretching should start gently and proceed in a manner similar to that described for the adductors. Treatment of injuries at the upper end of the hamstrings can be difficult and prolonged. Extensive technical help is required if the injury is chronic, recurrent or of long-standing.

Hamstring, adductor and groin strains are all conditions that only too frequently are treated by ill-advised injections of steroids. This is in part due to a failure to persist with conservative treatment and in part, especially in long-standing cases, due to the failure to identify the cause and to remedy that adequately. These injections will usually result in a treatable condition becoming more difficult to treat. The whole treatment period is prolonged, encouraging relapses following the apparent initial improvement from the injection.

3.42 Clicking Hip

CAUSES

This is, as in other joints, usually of no significance and harmless. It is commonly caused by the ilio-femoral ligament sliding across the femoral head or by a tight band of fascia lata slipping backwards and forwards over the greater trochanter. Its greatest problem results when the dancer, usually a student, repeatedly reproduces the click deliberately to see if it is still happening or as a party piece. This can lead to local swelling in the soft tissues around the ligament and the onset of symptoms. These rapidly settle with reassurance and avoidance as much as possible of movements producing the click, when the local deep (not visible) swelling will rapidly disappear.
Alternatively, the click may be caused by the fascia lata slipping across the greater trochanter. This can be easily felt and, if the person is thin, also seen. It may be associated with tight fascia lata which will require stretching out. Very rarely indeed local treatment is ineffective and surgery may be necessary for this latter cause of clicking.

3.43 Gluteal Bursitis

CAUSES

This condition is commonly caused by pulling too hard with the gluteal muscles when working on the turn-out, especially if the dancer also 'tucks' the buttocks and sacrum under at the same time. It may also be precipitated by sitting in the hip, particularly if many jumps are undertaken without the dancer 'pulling up' properly. In this case, the tensor fasciae latae muscle and the fascia lata itself will increase the pressure on the distal part of the gluteal tendon and insertion. It is sometimes associated with a clicking hip when the tendon of the fascia lata is clicked recurrently over the greater trochanter.

TREATMENT

Local treatment is by interferential and ultrasound. Usually the dancer will benefit from 48 hours or so of rest and then a gradual return with any technical correction that may be required.

Complications
The bursitis can become very painful if it is not treated and particularly if any underlying technical

problem is not detected and eliminated. If there has been tightness of the fascia lata there will usually be some accompanying quadriceps and adductor weakness which will need special attention to build them up.

3.44 Buttock Pain

CAUSES

Buttock pain may be produced by sciatic nerve root irritation in which case the pain may radiate lower down the thigh or leg or it may be merely localised to the buttock, producing muscle spasm at that site. Locally within the buttock the pain can be produced by tension in the small hip rotators, although even in these circumstances, the sciatic nerve as it passes by these small rotators may be irritated, producing some radiation of pain to the thigh. Thus the picture may be confused as to whether the primary origin of the pain is within the buttock or whether it is a referred pain down the sciatic nerve due to nerve root pressure in the back. Back injuries themselves will frequently produce buttock pain with a very well localised tenderness within the buttock due to secondary muscle spasm. Technical faults frequently lead to buttock pain, either because of misuse of the lower back or by a failure to hold the turn-out, particularly when jumping. The reason for failure to hold the turn-out may not be particularly obvious and may be far removed from the hip area.

TREATMENT

It is particularly important to determine the cause before starting treatment so that the cause itself and not merely the effect can be treated. If the pain is due to tension in the small rotators, i.e. a genuine local cause, the local treatment should be directed at release of the muscle spasm.

Complications
These are largely due to diagnosis failure, in particular a mis-diagnosis of a significant problem in the lumbar spine, e.g. a disc prolapse or a stress fracture.

3.45 Sacroiliac Strains and Displacements

These conditions do not exist in the dancer or sportsman. Sacroiliac pain (apart from in inflammatory disease) is referred pain from the lower lumbar spine. The sacroiliac joint is immensely strong with several very large ligaments crossing the joint binding the two parts together.

Any sort of displacement is not possible in dance type injuries. Even in severe accidents the bone adjacent to the sacroiliac joint is more commonly fractured rather than the sacroiliac joint itself being disrupted. Only in pregnancy, when all the ligaments around the pelvis soften and stretch to allow delivery, is the sacroiliac joint in a condition where it can suffer strain. The often stated diagnosis of chiropracters and others alleging that the sacroiliac joint is 'out' is absolute nonsense and even more so their assertion that they have 'put it back' by manipulation.

3.46 Pain in the Sacroiliac Area

This does not arise from within the sacroiliac joint although there is frequently tenderness over and around the joint. The pain is either referred from the lumbar spine or else it arises from the insertions of the long back muscles which are frequently in a protective spasm when there is any under-lying back injury or lumbar disc lesion. Therefore in these cases a thorough investigation of the lumbar region of the back is required. Tenderness just above the sacroiliac joint is usually due to a lesion associated with the 5th lumbar vertebra. This may be a facet joint strain or a developing stress fracture.

TREATMENT

Is of the underlying cause.

3.47 Strain of the Muscles inserted into the Iliac Crest

These will produce local tenderness and there is no real difficulty in the diagnosis. Treatment is usually straightforward but the strain can be due to a technical fault when one side of the pelvis is dropped, due to inadequate and imbalanced trunk musculature. Therefore a possible technical cause should be investigated and eliminated during treatment. Sometimes pain, tenderness and bruising occur in this area due to clumsy handling by the boys, particularly when the boys are not strong enough to cope adequately with double lifting work. It can also occur with boys who have small hands and find difficulty in handling their partner.

3.48 Interspinous Ligament Damage

These are the ligaments that lie between each spinous process in the posterior part of the individual vertebra.

CAUSES

Hyper-flexion may sprain an interspinous ligament and even produce tearing if very forceful. Hyper-extension can cause an impingement of adjacent spinous processes with a crushing of the interspinous ligament. This is particularly likely to occur in the dancer who fails to pull up the legs and trunk properly before starting a back bend and as a result will produce a localised hyper-extension at one level (Fig. 3.36). Weakness of the back muscles may fail to control flexion, particularly when the flexion movement is rapid and this carried out repeatedly may cause a sprain of the interspinous ligament.

TREATMENT

Locally, ultrasound and interferential are required and these are more effective when applied with the spine slightly flexed so as to open up the interspinous area. It is best done with the patient on the side as they seem to move around less during treatment in this position than when lying on their face slightly flexed over a pillow. The condition is often slow to settle due to the poor blood supply to the ligament. A considerable amount of work must be done on strengthening the trunk muscles in order to control movements properly and to prevent flexion and extension occurring principally at one or two levels alone.

The so called 'kissing spine' is an impingement of the spinous processes at one level. It produces a crushing of the interspinous ligament as mentioned above, with localised pain and tenderness. It is mentioned here merely because it has been described as a specific condition which requires treatment by surgery. The proposed surgical treatment is to excise the adjacent portion of the spinous process together with the interspinous ligament thus preventing the bony processes touching during hyper-extension at this particular level. As the impingement arises because of a technical fault and a failure to pull up and spread the extension movement over the whole lumbar area, surgery is certainly not indicated and can only be condemned. Removal of the interspinous ligament can cause a gradually increasing loss of stability of the spine at that level with potentially serious long term results. Proper trunk

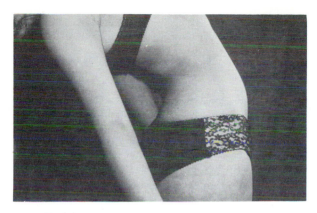

3.36   Kinking in the lumbar region on a back bend. This is due to the dancer failing to pull up the legs and the trunk (i.e. she does not have the feeling of lengthening both areas) before starting to bend backwards. This photograph also shows the presence of a stiff lower lumbar segment.

strengthening exercises and technical correction will relieve the symptoms without any recourse to surgery.

3.49 Facet Joint Strains

These joints are small synovial joints in the posterior bony complex of each vertebra and like similar joints elsewhere can be subject to sprains and strains. The injury is produced by uncontrolled movements, particularly when these become asymmetrical. It occurs most commonly during jumping.

DIAGNOSIS

Deep tenderness at the side of a lumbar vertebra or on both sides if the condition is bilateral, and pain on hyper-extension with a tilt to one side as well as backwards, is very suggestive of a facet joint problem. Similarly, pain may be caused on flexion if there is also combined with this a tilt to one or other side. This will tend to stretch the synovium and capsule of the facet joint.

TREATMENT

Local treatment to relieve pain and muscle spasm is required and this should be accompanied by a period of rest from dancing. As the initial pain settles, an exercise programme can be commenced. This should be directed at strengthening the trunk muscles, correction of any asymmetrical working and also, and very importantly, at strengthening the control of the turn-out, particularly when the dancer is in the air. In these cirumstances the

turn-out can only be held by the muscles working correctly. Those dancers who depend upon friction of their feet on the floor to hold the turn-out are particularly prone to this type of injury, as well as many other injuries at other levels.

If the condition is long-standing, it is occasionally necessary to inject the facet joint with Hydrocortisone. This should, however, only be necessary occasionally as most patients will have settled with normal conservative treatment. If an injection is to be carried out, then ideally it should be done using an X-ray image intensifer so that the exact location of the point of the needle can be visualised prior to injecting the Hydrocortisone.

Complications

A facet joint inflamed by injury can produce a referred sciatic-type pain because the sciatic nerve roots run closely past the facet joints at each level. This condition can to a certain extent mimic a lumbar disc lesion from which it must be differentiated. If there is doubt about the differential diagnosis, then infiltration of the facet joint with a local anaesthetic under visual control, using an X-ray image intensifer, will clarify the diagnosis, because the local anaesthetic will temporarily relieve symptoms from a facet joint but not from a genuine lumbar disc prolapse, provided the local anaesthetic injection is accurately placed into the facet joint.

3.50 Lumbar Disc Prolapse

A lumbar disc prolapse or so-called slipped disc is not particularly common in dancers, despite the movements which involve the back and the heavy lifting for the boys. In the acute stages, especially when there is sciatic nerve root involvement, the treatment is a routine orthopaedic problem. However, once the dancer is in the recovery phase, considerable attention is paid to strengthening the trunk, gluteal and lower limb muscles with particular emphasis on the correction of any technical faults.

3.51 Stress Fractures of the Lumbar Vertebrae

These occur in the pars interarticularis, most commonly at the L.4 and L.5 levels. Although the fracture may be unilateral, it is more commonly

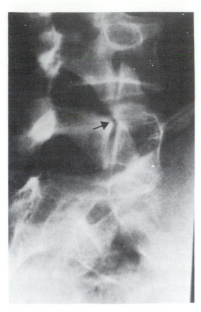

3.37 A stress fracture (arrowed) in the pars interarticularis of the 5th lumbar vertebra.

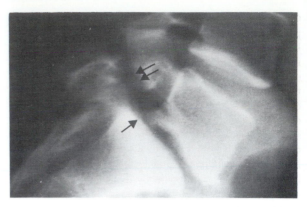

3.38 An X-ray of a spondylolisthesis. The 4th lumbar vertebra has slipped forwards on the body of the 5th lumbar vertebra. The single arrow indicates the mal-alignment of the posterior margins of the two vertebral bodies. In this instance there is a forward slip of about 1 cm. The double arrow shows the defect in the bone which started as a stress fracture (vide Fig. 3.37).

bilateral, affecting both partes interarticulares at that particular level (Fig. 3.37). The condition can occur at any age from early student days through to mature adult life. If the stress fracture is not detected early, the fracture can gradually widen and separate so that the vertebral body and the whole spine above will slowly slip forward, leaving the posterior bony ring with the spinous process and inferior articular facet behind. Once this has started to occur, there is no chance of the fracture uniting. This condition with a forward slip is known as a spondylolisthesis (Fig. 3.38).

CAUSES

The most important single cause of stress fractures is a failure to pull up at the trunk and is associated with weak trunk muscles, particularly the abdominals. The two major precipitating factors are a lordotic posture in order to try to give more external rotation (turn-out) at the hips and over turning. (**Sections 5.6** and **5.7**).

In particular these faults produce an excessive amount of movement (flexion, extension, lateral flexion and rotation) at one single level instead of having the movement evenly distributed throughout the lumbar spine. The greatest stress occurs at the point where the lumbar spine is attached to the solidly rigid pelvis at the lumbo-sacral junction.

DIAGNOSIS

Clinically the dancer will present with low back pain associated with muscle spasm and tenderness at the sides of the affected vertebra, about a centimetre or two from the mid line. These signs are very suggestive of stressing at this level, or the next stage of deterioration when there is an actual stress fracture present. As early diagnosis is extremely important. The presence of a fracture should be strongly suspected when local treatment and trunk exercises do not rapidly abolish the muscle spasm. The diagnosis can be confirmed by oblique X-rays of the lumbar spine, *but* X-ray changes will not usually be present for some one to two months, or even longer, from the time of onset of symptoms. Hence if a fracture is suspected and if X-rays appear normal, a bone scan should be undertaken. This will show a 'hot spot' at the fracture site in the early days of its development. If necessary, due to persistence of symptoms, there should be no hesitation in repeating the scan a few weeks later.

TREATMENT

A patient with a stress fracture requires a plaster of Paris jacket for four months. During this time the patient should be encouraged to exercise all limb muscles. When pain-free in the plaster, the dancer may return to some limited barre work, keeping the legs low. When the plaster cast is finally removed, a temporary corset should be fitted. The dancer then embarks upon an intensive course of trunk muscle strengthening exercises. When control of the trunk is regained, the corset can be gradually discarded.

On starting class work, although the back will be protected by the temporary corset, the legs must be kept low and port de bras limited and trunk movements kept from extreme flexion and extension, although the corset will tend to prevent this happening. When the corset is discarded for class, care must still be exercised to limit the range of flexion and extension until strength builds up satisfactorily. From the time class is commenced a careful watch must be kept for *the original technical fault which precipitated the injury*. The muscular build-up and rehabilitation will take at least two months before the dancer can gradually increase work towards a full and normal class. A plaster of Paris cast is required as the initial treatment in order to prevent the dancer from moving the spine excessively. It must not be considered to completely immobilise the spine, which would be impossible. Hence the need for a supervised programme of limb exercises and careful and limited barre work. The plaster may require changing once or twice during the four months because loss of trunk bulk will take place and the plaster jacket will become loose.

As an alternative, and only to be considered in dancers who can be relied upon 100% to obey instructions, the plaster can be omitted and a lightweight corset used instead. During the four month period, during which it is hoped that union of the stress fracture will take place, trunk muscle exercises can be carried out. These should be almost isometric. The corset can be removed for these supervised exercise sessions but must be re-applied immediately after the end of treatment. By almost isometric exercises we mean exercises that use only a small range of movement, not genuine isometric exercises which, by definition, should have no actual movement taking place. It is essential that during this four month healing period the dancer does nothing that puts the spine through excessive movement or under stress. If there is any suggestion that the dancer is not complying, then a plaster cast should be applied. After the first few weeks the dancer can do limited barre work in the corset under very close supervision. At the end of the four month period, the further rehabilitation follows that which would take place when a plaster of Paris cast has been removed. However, the dancer will be much further advanced with his muscle build-up because of the exercise programme he has been able to follow in the absence of a plaster. This shortens the rehabilitation period very significantly and to a well worthwhile extent. However, it must be emphasised that the method is only applicable in really well disciplined dancers who are going to be

under very close supervision from conscientious and aware staff. If there is any doubt, a plaster of Paris cast should be used. We have found the method without plaster very effective, although the number of dancers for which it is suitable is very limited.

3.52 Dorsal and Upper Spinal Pain

This can occur at various levels from the mid dorsal region upwards. It is frequently acutely painful and often produces girdle pain, i.e. pain radiating around the chest wall, sometimes as far as the sternum. Even more frequently, the pain radiates to the scapula area of the back. In the upper spine, especially the cervical region, it can be accompanied by head pain and shoulder and arm pain.

CAUSES

It is usually brought on by working with tension in the upper trunk, shoulder girdle or neck and is often associated with weakness of the muscles, not only in these areas but also in the lower back and in the muscle groups controlling turn-out. The two latter areas – lower back and turn-out – when weak, not only make dancers feel insecure while working and thus increase tension higher, but will also encourage rotation of one or other side of the upper trunk in relation to the lower trunk and pelvis. In these dancers the upper body weight is in the wrong place. It may also be associated with swayback knees or anything else giving rise to wrong weight placement.

In boys it can also be associated with incorrect lifting. Over-development of the shoulder girdle in boys due to ill-advised weight training can produce similar effects because of the relatively weaker and often neglected lower trunk. The mass of muscle at the top of the trunk makes balance more difficult and, when jumping, the upper trunk can frequently be observed from the side to be back behind an imaginary line passing through the centre of gravity and down through the greater trochanters. Another cause is brought about by dancers who are told to flatten their scapulae to the chest wall and do so by rotating their shoulder joints too far forward. This tends to make the pectoral muscles contract vigorously and gradually tighten. It also makes for a great deal of tension around the shoulder girdle. Flattening the shoulder blades will take place naturally as the trunk muscles are generally strengthened. The latissimus dorsi plays an important part in the control of the scapulae.

TREATMENT

Acute dorsal pain can usually be relieved by Maitland mobilisations but it is vital to remember that this method of pain relief is only the beginning of treatment and not an end in itself. Once the acute pain has been relieved, either by the mobilisations or by ultrasound, interferential or other methods, the cause will have to be investigated – usually a technical fault – and eliminated and any necessary strengthening exercises at various levels will have to be instituted. Among commonly neglected technical faults are incorrect arm movements related to dance. Unfortunately, arm movements are only too often ignored as a potential cause of problems.

3.53 Acute Torticollis

This is a condition where because of pain the head is tilted to one side. It is also known as acute wry neck and is often referred to by patients as a crick in the neck.

CAUSES

It is quite common in adolescence and is not necessarily associated with dance. In dancers, whether students or professionals, it is often precipitated by trunk instability and by a tendency to sit in one or other hip, because young dancers are usually very predominantly right or left sided (right or left handed). With training, this predominance of one side or another is decreased when dancing though it often remains to a greater or lesser extent. Most dancers never achieve a complete equalisation. They nearly all have a preferred side on which to work.

TREATMENT

Local treatment in the form of ultrasound and interferential can help. Massage is particularly useful in this condition and often some neck traction will help to give initial relief. As it is often associated with a fault elsewhere, this requires elimination and correction to prevent recurrences.

3.54 Shoulder and Arm Problems

These are not particularly common in dancers. A supraspinatus tendonitis or sub acromial bursitis can occur in boys, following a lot of lifting. Frequently, as in general members of the population, a local injection of steroid will relieve these two conditions.

Recurrent dislocations of a shoulder initially follow a fall, as in the case of non-dancers. The important aspect in dancers is that, if surgical repair is necessary, then the method used must be one which does not limit shoulder movements. To this end, the coracoid transfer operation (Bristow or Bonnin operation) is the best choice, producing as it does complete stability without any limitation of external rotation as always occurs in the Putti-Platt or Bankart procedures.

Other upper limb injuries usually follow a fall or similar trauma and are not really dance injuries but merely injuries which happen to occur in a dancer. They are all treated by standard orthopaedic measures. The only important point worth making is that during treatment (plaster of Paris, etc.) the dancer can work out or have worked out for him a programme of general exercise to keep the rest of the body as fit as possible.

Strengthening Exercises

In this Section we describe a variety of straightforward exercises which can be performed by any dancer or student (or anyone else) who wishes to strengthen up various portions of the body. The photographs should be studied in conjunction with the captions before embarking upon each exercise. In some cases there are several exercises which are graduated according to difficulty and strength required, so start with the easiest. It is important to carry out each exercise accurately. They all need to be performed slowly with the body or limb under full control the whole time. The various groups of muscles being exercised must be kept firmly tightened throughout the exercise, e.g. in a lifting exercise the muscles can be made to work just as hard during the controlled lowering phase as when lifting, thus utilising the time taken to best advantage. There should be complete relaxation between each cycle of an exercise, e.g. tighten, lift, hold, lower, relax and then repeat. If this relaxation is omitted then the muscle may go into cramp. A good routine is to count five slowly for each phase of the cycle – tighten (5), lift slowly (5), hold (5), lower (5), relax (5).

The dancer and student can with benefit take a comprehensive selection of exercises and put them into a regular daily routine. The strengthening achieved will go a long way toward helping in injury prevention.

These exercises are not designed to improve cardio-respiratory fitness, although they will have a slight beneficial effect. A different type of exercise programme will be required additionally for this, e.g. swimming, cycling, etc. Exercises are specific in their end result. 'Taking exercise' as such will not produce all-round fitness and strength of all areas. A specific programme needs to be devised to meet the requirements of the individual. These exercises are mainly devised to be an adjunct to class (or other forms of exercise for non-dancers) and are not an alternative.

We have tried to select a cross-section of exercises which should be readily understood and correctly performed without confusion as to purpose or method of performance. They are obviously only a very small number of the possible variations but may provide some help to the dancer who wishes to avoid the time and expense of visiting a physiotherapist to be taught exercises. However, if in doubt as to whether you are in fact doing the exercise correctly then some competent professional help would be advisable. If an exercise seems particularly easy and effortless you may be doing it incorrectly.

The exercises have been demonstrated by a male dancer only because the muscles are usually more visible than in a girl.

Remember:

1. All the exercises must be carried out slowly and under full control. Do not bounce.
2. Always try to tighten the muscles being exercised that little bit more especially during a 'hold phase'.
3. Repeat the exercise with the other side of the body or the other limb. A weaker group may require more repetitions than its counterpart but even so do not neglect the 'good side'.

4.1   4.2

4.1   4.2   4.3   4.4
Abdominal exercises for the straight muscle fibres (rectus abdominis). These are carried out by means of sit-ups. The knees are flexed to prevent the lumbar spine from becoming lordotic. The shoulder girdle must not do the main bulk of the work. The abdominal muscles must be used as hard on the way down as on the way up.

4.5   4.6   4.7
This is the *incorrect* way to do abdominal exercises. Lifting legs straight produces a lumbar hyperextension (lordosis) and can lead to lumbar back strains. The figures clearly show the marked lordosis that can be produced. In Fig. 4.7 the hand under the lumbar spine is merely to demonstrate the large gap between the spine and the floor.

4.5

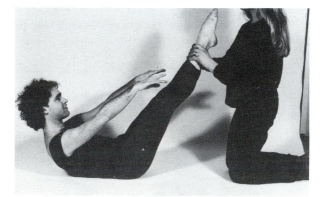

4.8   4.9

4.8   4.9
Abdominal exercises for the straight fibres requiring more control and a more powerful use of the muscles.

4.3

4.4

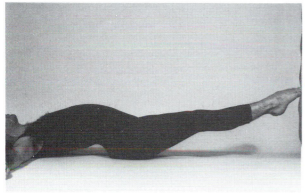

4.6

4.7

4.10

4.11

4.10 4.11
Abdominal exercises for the cross fibres (external and internal oblique muscles). The basic starting position is as for sit-ups. The twisting motion begins as soon as the movement is initiated. Do alternate sides, working first one and then the other.

4.12   4.13

4.12   4.13   4.14   4.15
Exercises for the back extensor muscles. Start lying with the shoulder blades pulled down and the buttocks held firmly. Then, while the arms are kept in contact with the floor, the head and shoulders are lifted by the back extensors. They are not pushed up by the arms. The waist is pulled in during the exercise.

4.16   4.17   4.18
Exercises for the back extensor muscles – a progression from the previous exercise. The shoulder blades are pulled down to prevent neck tension. The waist is pulled in. The buttocks are held tightly.

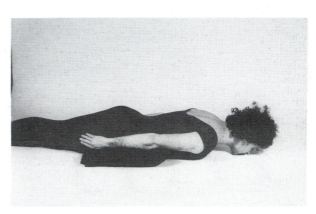

4.16

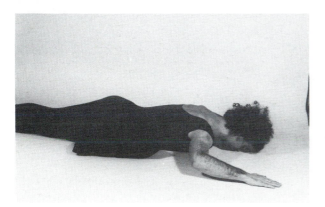

4.19   4.20

4.19   4.20   4.21   4.22
Exercises for the back extensor muscles – a progression from the previous exercise. The same rules apply. The exercise requires more powerful use of the muscles.

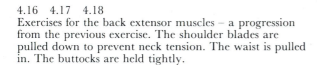

4.14

4.15

4.17

4.18

4.21

4.22

4.23   4.24   4.25
Exercises for the back extensor muscles – very much
more advanced. The same rules apply. Repeat the
exercise using alternate arms.

4.23

4.28

4.26   4.27

4.26   4.27   4.28
Exercises for the back extensor muscles with some rotation. Repeat on the other side. The same rules apply as for
previous extensor exercises. Fig. 4.28 shows a side view of the exercise.

4.24

4.25

4.29
Exercises for the back extensor muscles with some rotation, more advanced with the arm out. Repeat on the other side. The same rules apply as before.

There are many other exercises for the extensor muscles of the back but these particular exercises have been devised for people without equipment.

4.29

4.30

4.31

4.32

4.30   4.31   4.32
Simple side exercises standing. Care must be taken not to twist the pelvis and the waist. The waist must be pulled in during the exercises and must be pulled in harder on the way up. Do the exercise on alternate sides. Do not bounce.

4.33   4.34   4.35   4.36

Exercises for strengthening the lateral trunk muscles (lateral flexors). Start with the right arm above the head, waist pulled in. Bend over to the left. Bring the left arm up until nearly parallel to the right arm. Slowly stand up straight with both arms above the head. Lower the right arm. Repeat exercise bending over to the right. Keep waist well pulled in throughout the exercise, pulled in harder when coming up. Also pull shoulder blades down when coming up otherwise shoulders will tend to become elevated.

4.33

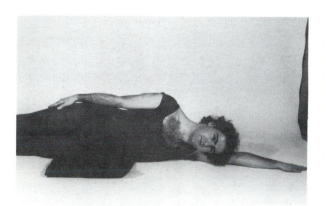

4.37

4.38

4.37   4.38

Exercises for strengthening lateral trunk muscles. A progression from the previous exercise. The lower elbow and forearm are used for balance only and not for total support. Pull waist in well. The legs and trunk must be kept lined up. Repeat the exercise the same number of times on the other side.

4.34 4.35 4.36

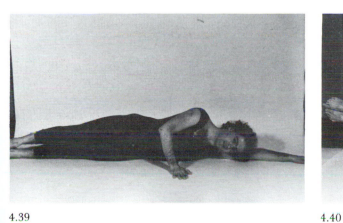

4.39 4.40

4.39   4.40

Exercises for strengthening the lateral trunk muscles. A further progression from the previous exercises. The legs must be kept lined up with the trunk and pressed together. They should also have the feeling of being 'lengthened', that is, pushed distally away from the trunk to avoid bunching up of the lateral flexor muscles. Keep the waist (the abdominal muscles) well pulled in during the exercise.

4.41 4.42 4.43 4.44 4.45 4.46 4.47 4.48 4.49
Quadriceps exercises. The same exercise seen from the side and from the front in two different dancers. Fig. 4.49 shows well that the vastus medialis is contracting very firmly. The hip, knee-cap and the centre of the foot must be kept lined up. The pelvis is kept square with the weight equally on both buttocks. The knee is allowed to flex slightly over a pillow during the relaxation phase. The trunk must lean back away from the leg because it leaves the hip more free. Repeat with the other leg.

4.41

4.42

4.43

4.44

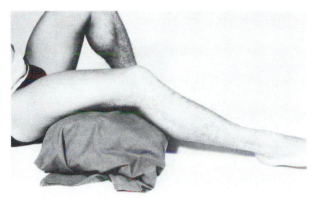

4.45

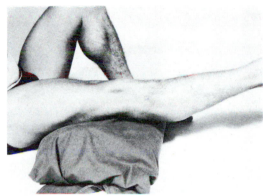

4.46

4.48

4.47

4.49

4.50   4.51

4.50   4.51   4.52   4.53
Exercises for strengthening the adductor muscles in the thigh. The upper leg is flexed at the hip to a right-angle (90°) in order to allow the lower leg which is being exercised freedom to move. The upper leg must be supported in order to keep the pelvis square with the floor – it must not rotate either forwards or backwards. This support may be a folded pillow as in Figs 4.50 and 4.51 or stool as in Figs 4.52 and 4.53, or even a low bed. Support the head on the elbow. The exercising leg must be kept with the knee-cap pointing forwards throughout the exercise. Do not pull the leg into the hip when lifting it; feel that the leg is lengthened. Pull in the abdominal muscles. Repeat with the other leg.

4.56

4.56   4.57   4.58   4.59
Adductor muscle exercises. Slightly more difficult exercises than the foregoing. The leg is carried forward and lifted.

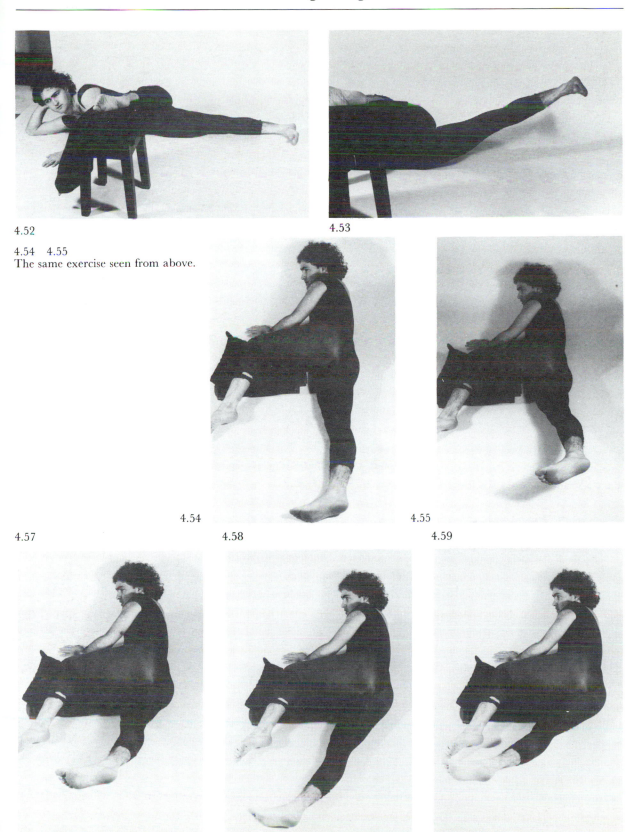

4.52

4.53

4.54   4.55
The same exercise seen from above.

4.54

4.55

4.57

4.58

4.59

4.60   4.61   4.62
Adductor muscle
exercises. Similar to the
last exercise but the leg
is carried backwards and
then lifted.

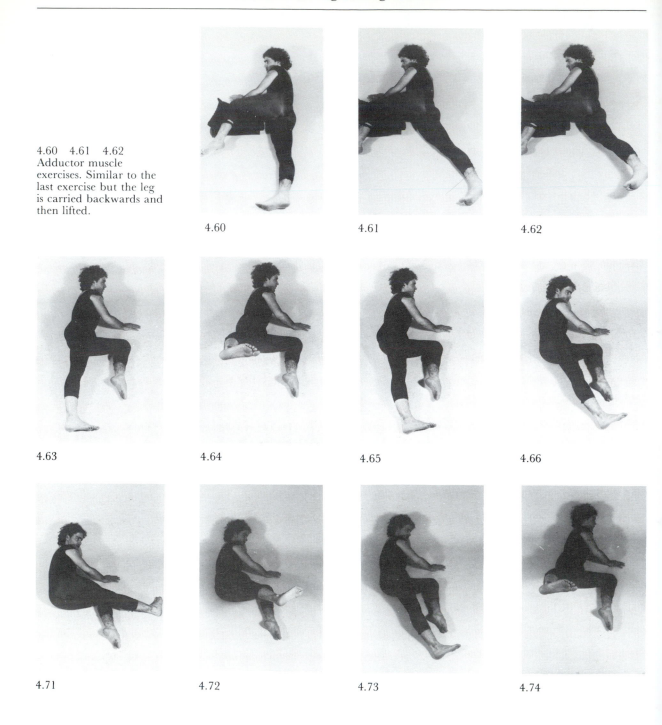

4.60   4.61   4.62

4.63   4.64   4.65   4.66

4.71   4.72   4.73   4.74

4.63   4.64   4.65   4.66   4.67   4.68   4.69   4.70   4.71   4.72   4.73   4.74   4.75   4.76   4.77   4.78   4.79
Exercises for the gluteal muscles (abductors). This exercise is carried out lying on the side with the underneath leg
bent at hip and knee. The back is kept straight. The top leg must be kept lined up with the trunk. The knee-cap must
face forwards. Lift the leg stretching it downwards, i.e. a feeling of lengthening the leg. Carry out the exercise slowly.
Control the lowering of the leg as well as the lifting.

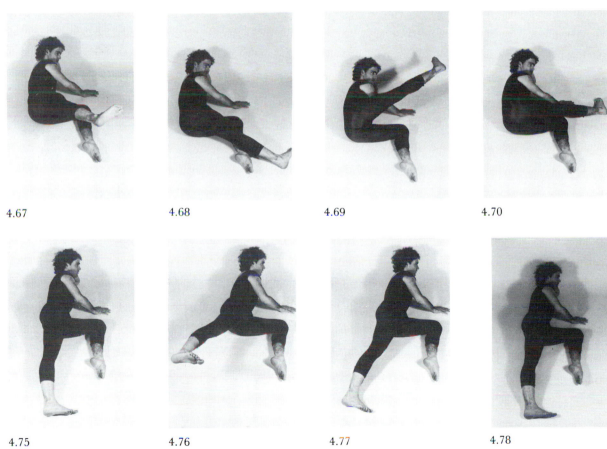

4.67

4.68

4.69

4.70

4.75

4.76

4.77

4.78

4.79

4.80   4.81   4.82
Exercises for hip extensors (gluteus maximus). Straight leg. The leg must be lined up with the trunk. Pelvis must not be twisted or move. This is purely a leg movement. The pillow is to keep the lumbar spine as flat as possible. Carry out with alternate legs.

4.83

4.83   4.84   4.85   4.86
Hip extensor exercises. Progression from the previous exercise. Start straight. When the leg is elevated take it out to the side in abduction and then across the other leg into adduction and then back to the mid-line. Pelvis *must* be kept flat and *must not twist*.

4.87   4.88   4.89
Hamstring exercises. Start lying flat. The legs must be lined up with the trunk. Flex the knee without any rotation of the thigh. The heel lines up with the centre of the buttocks on the same side.

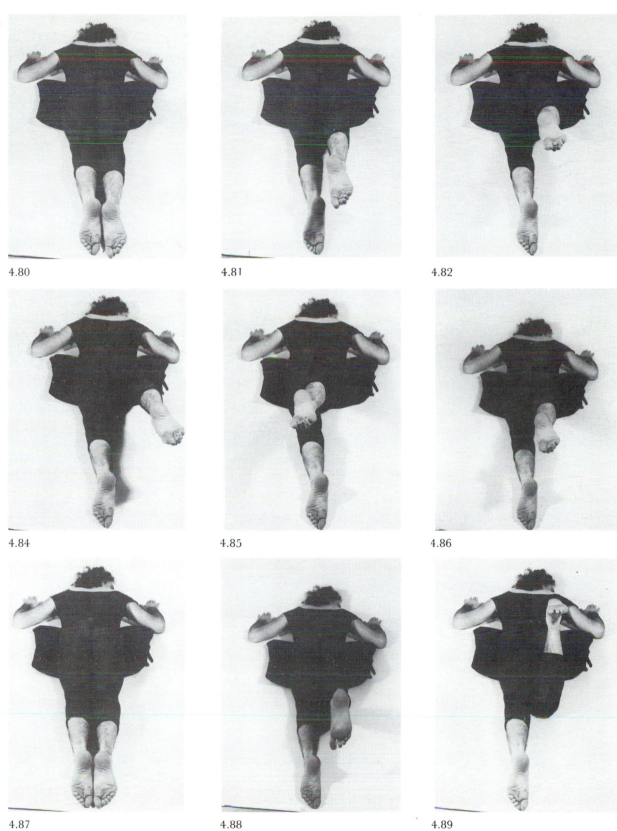

4.80

4.81

4.82

4.84

4.85

4.86

4.87

4.88

4.89

4.90 4.91 4.92
Hamstring exercises. Side view. Keep the gluteal
(buttock) muscles held tightly during the exercises in
order to prevent the hip flexing.

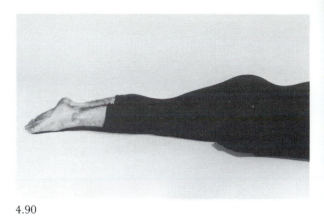

4.90

4.93

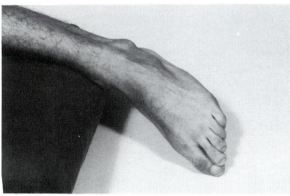

4.94

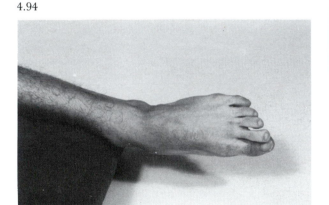

4.93 4.94 4.95 4.96
Peroneal muscle exercises. These are better done with the knee extended. Carry out the exercise first in some degree of
plantar-flexion (not full plantar-flexion, i.e. not with the foot fully pointed) and repeat with the foot and ankle at a
right-angle.

4.97

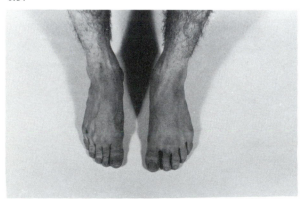

4.98

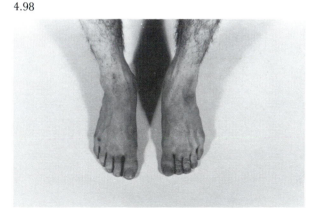

4.97 4.98 4.99
Intrinsic muscle exercises. Fig. 4.97 shows the dancer's right foot working. Fig. 4.98 shows the left foot working. Fig.
4.99 shows both feet working.

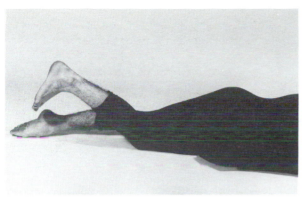

4.91

4.92

4.95

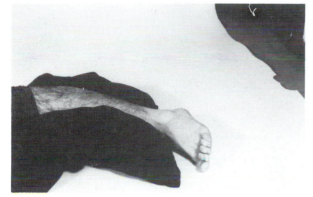

4.96

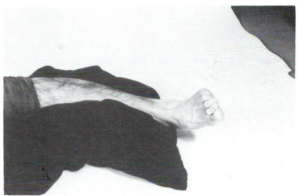

4.99

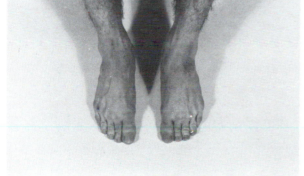

4.100

4.100
Calf muscle and Achilles tendon stretch. Keep the foot flat on the floor, the heel down and the knee straight. Stretch gently.

Further exercise for the abdominal muscles.

These are stabilization exercises for the trunk. The spine and pelvis are held still and the lower limbs are used to challenge the abdominal obliques, transversus abdominis and the back muscles in their role as stabilizers.

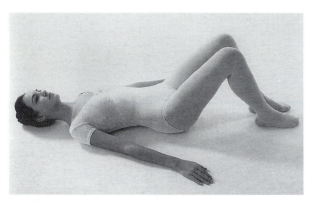

4.101

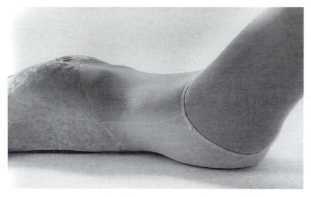

4.102

4.101   4.102
The initial position is assumed with abdominal muscles engaged and the abdomen held flat. The lumbar spine is held in its normal alignment, neither arched nor tucked under. The shoulders are held down with no tension in the neck. (Breathing is from a sideways movement of the ribs with no lifting of the chest.)

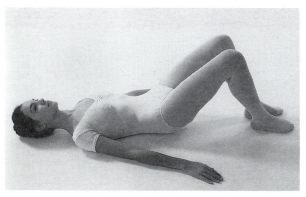

4.103
Incorrect. The pelvis here is overly tucked under.

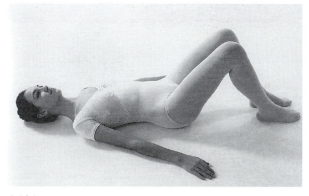

4.104
Incorrect. The abdominals are not sufficiently activated with transversus not pulling the abdomen flat.

4.105

4.106

4.105 4.106
From the initial position each knee is allowed to fall out to the side by about 45", and returned without rocking of the pelvis towards the working side. The abdomen is held flat throughout.

4.107
From the initial position the thigh is lifted to a 90° angle at the hip. If the thigh is lifted less than 90°, control of the pelvis, abdominal muscles and lumbar spine is significantly challenged. Lifting further than 90° is easier and the exercise must be carefully graded to ability. This exercise alone, lifting and returning alternate legs, is the preliminary exercise to prepare for the following sequences.

4.108
The second leg joins the first.

4.109
Abdominal control is reinforced.

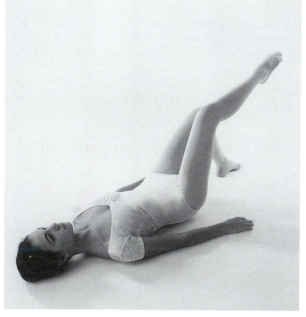

4.110
Either leg is lowered to the floor and then joined by the next. The exercise is repeated starting with alternate legs.

More advanced exercises.

4.111
Starting position. Arms and legs at 90° to the trunk. The shoulders are held down strongly by latissimus dorsi muscles and the abdominal muscles must be well activated.

4.112
The right leg extends while the left arm is raised. The lower the extending leg, the more the pelvis and abdominals are challenged. The lumbar spine must not arch.

4.113
The right leg and left arm return to the starting position to reinforce abdominals and latissimus dorsi before the opposite limbs move.

4.114
Starting position. This must be correctly placed. The spine must be held in its normal curves with the lumbar spine neither rounded nor arched. The abdominals must be fully engaged and the shoulders held down with scapulae held flat.

4.114

4.115
The knee is brought forwards to the chest but the spine is held still. The trunk remains square.

4.116
The knee is swept through towards a parallel arabesque line.

4.117
The leg is extended in line with the trunk and behind the hip.

4.118
Releasing the opposite arm further challenges trunk control but the initial exercises must be mastered first.

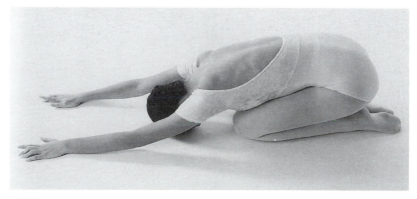

4.119
Follow these with a good stretch for the spinal sensors.

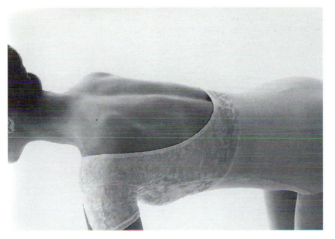

4.120
Incorrect. Weight bearing through arms is an effective way to feel scapular stabilization. Here the shoulder blades are winging out in a weak position. Make sure they are held down against the chest wall with a good neckline as in photograph 4.121

4.121
Correct. Better positioning of the spine and shoulder blade.

4.122
This exercise encourages control of extension in thoracic spine with good use of latissimus dorsi holding the shoulders down.

4.123
The use of the arm makes this exercise more difficult to control.

4.124
Follow these exercises with a stretch for the thoracic spine extensors.

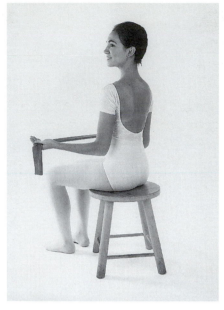

4.125
In this exercise a lightweight rubber exercise band is used. The elbows are held to the waist. The chest is held open and the shoulders are held down. As the hands move apart the band is stretched. The shoulder joints rotate outwards and the muscles around the scapulae are strongly activated.

4.126
The view from the back should show good scapular control. The exercise should be practised without the band initially as the band significantly increases resistance.

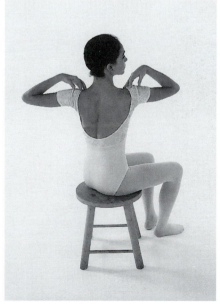

4.127

4.128

4.127   4.128
Simple rotation exercises for the thoracic spine should be practised regularly to reduce tightness and promote awareness of the part of the spine used in épaulement.

4.129

4.130

4.129   4.130
This exercise for latissimus dorsi uses the exercise band attached to the barre. From an initial good posture the band is pulled downwards and just behind the body. The shoulder girdle and pelvis remain square with the chest open and no tension is taken in the neck.

4.131
Follow this with a stretch for those muscles.

4.132
A good breathing pattern is important for all exercises. While the abdominals are pulled in, breathing must be from a sideways excursion of the lower ribs. Reinforce this by feeling the use of the ribs in the supine position. No lifting of the sternum must be involved.

4.133
In the sitting position the exercise band can be tensioned about the rib cage. On the breath in feel the lower ribs expand sideways and backwards into the band, again with no lifting of the chest in front.

4.134
The initial position involves side lying with a well aligned spine and head resting on the arm. The knees are bent at 90° with feet in line with the spine.

4.135

4.136

4.135   4.136
The top knee lifts gently with little effort. The large seat muscle, gluteus maximus is not used but instead the underlying gluteal muscles can be felt. These help with control of turnout and should accompany exercises for the adductors.

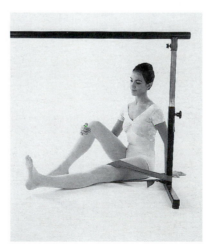

4.137
This is an adductor exercise using the exercise band for resistance. The legs are placed apart from each other. The working leg pulls across the midline in parallel towards the other leg which is bent up stabilizing the position. The trunk should remain square.

4.138
The same exercise is executed with a turned out leg. The ankle and foot can be pointed or flexed. Do not allow knees to fully hyper extend and make sure the band is above the knee to avoid strain.

4.139

4.140

4.139   4.140
This simple inside thigh exercise encourages coordinated use of the adductor, gluteal and lower abdominal muscles.

4.141
Follow this by an adductor stretch.

4.142
This shows an effective stretch for the right gluteal muscles.

4.143

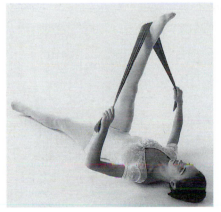

4.144

4.143   4.144
Controlled hamstring stretches.

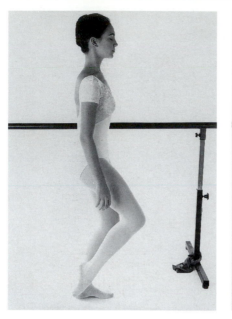

4.145   4.146

4.145   4.146
Proprioception exercises improve all the balance mechanisms. Simply practising different positions with the eyes closed improves the coordination required to balance and increases reflex reactions, especially in the foot and ankle.

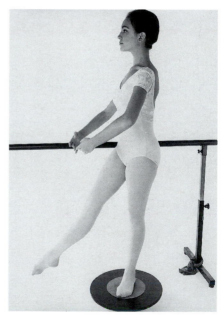

4.147   4.148

4.147   4.148
Working on the wobble board performing simple movements in parallel and turnout improves not only control of the foot and ankle, but all the postural muscles. In turnout the external rotators are vigorously exercised.

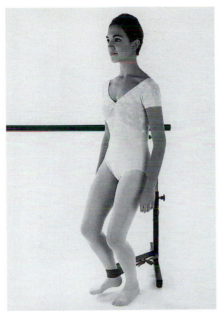

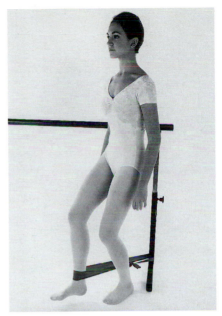

4.149
This is an exercise for stability of the left leg and foot. The exercise band is looped around the right ankle. The left knee must be held over the foot and the alignment of the foot perfectly maintained.

4.150
The right foot stretches the band forwards while the left foot retains its stability with all muscles of the ankle working. Increase repetitions as the weight bearing leg becomes accustomed to the exercise.

4.151

4.152

4.151   4.152
This exercise can be executed in different directions including stretching the band away from the standing leg and towards it. It is important to relax and stretch the calf in between exercises.

4.153
The exercise band can be used to exercise the calf and encourage a lengthened use of the foot and toes.

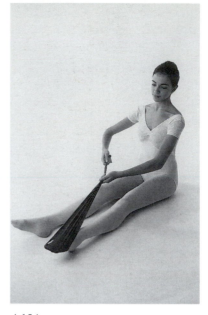

4.154
When held to the opposite side of the body the band will bias the contraction of the outer calf muscles.

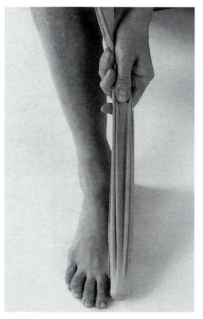

4.155
A lightweight band can be used to encourage strength in the first toe as it pulls down without curling.

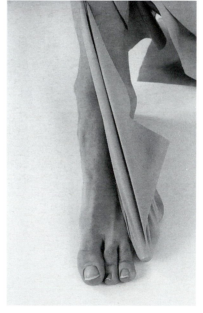

4.156
The same band can be used to encourage good use of the outer toes and outer foot. The outer toes too must be lengthened as they point downwards against the band.

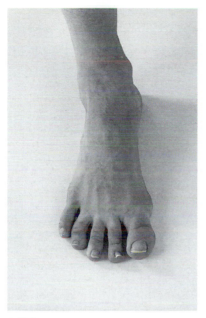

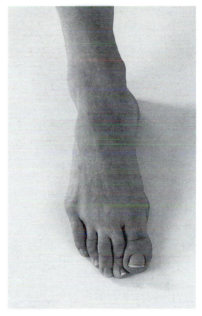

4.157   4.158

4.157   4.158
The foot requires added exercises to encourage fine control. This exercise –
attempting to spread the toes and squeeze them together – can be added to those in
photographs 4.97–4.99.

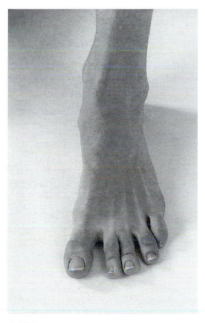

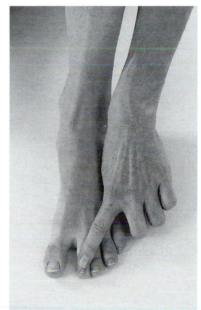

4.159   4.160

4.159   4.160
Exercise to improve abduction strength of the first toe will further protect against
the forced valgus position imposed by ballet shoes.

All intrinsic exercises for the foot are readily managed by young students
and prepare the immature foot for the rigours ahead.

Technical Faults and Anatomical Variations: Their Causes, Consequences and Treatment

> *All forms of treatment are relatively pointless without complete correction of any fault in technique*

Technical faults may arise for various reasons. They can occur as a result of the anatomical structure of the body, for example, restriction of turn-out being limited by the bony and soft tissue configuration around the hips. They may arise because of bad teaching or equally because of inattention or laziness of the student. Once faulty technique has been learned it becomes extremely difficult to correct and eradicate. Therefore poor teaching in the early days of a student's life may continue its effects throughout his professional career. Unfortunately, these faults will tend to increase with the passage of time, particularly if the dancer is working in the situation where there is no continued teaching or correction from a ballet master or ballet mistress.

> *All dance injuries arise from technical faults*

Injuries from mishaps outside the dancer's control, for example, falls downstairs or being dropped by a partner, etc. cannot really be classed as dance injuries. It should also be understood that, in general, the technical faults are frequently relatively minor but despite that they can produce major problems for the dancer, either in the actual treatment of the injury itself or more often in the prevention of recurrences of the same injury. In general also, a major fault is unlikely to pass uncorrected except in the most inadequate of teaching situations. Certainly the most important difference between the good teacher and the indifferent teacher is the ability of the former to detect small flaws in technique and to bring about an accurate and complete correction in the student. A good teacher will not allow a student to progress to more difficult and demanding work until he has mastered the details of the basic techniques. It is impossible to overstress the importance of technical

faults in their relation to both primary and recurrent injuries in dancers.

It must also be pointed out that even in the case of a non-dancing injury, when the dancer starts to return to class he may as a result of this injury start to develop technical faults, particularly if he has returned to class before the injury has settled fully and before the rehabilitation is properly completed.

Very frequently technical faults are very closely allied one with another, although their location may be widely separated anatomically. Only too commonly technical faults do not occur in isolation and this calls for a very careful assessment of the dancer. The detection of one technical fault which might have caused an injury certainly does not rule out the presence of others which could be equally or jointly responsible.

Coaching classes involving technical correction are an essential part of the rehabilitation of an injured dancer, even if the injury is only minor. A dancer presenting with an injury gives an ideal opportunity for a careful assessment of any technical faults. Referral to a coaching session should usually form part of the treatment process. These coaching classes are best carried out on a one-to-one or one-to-two or at most three basis. It is impossible to carry out an adequate technical correction class after injuries with more than that number of individuals. There is no doubt that regular individual assessments of all students with a particular eye for correct technique, would play an important part in the prevention of injuries.

The teaching of something such as dance and certainly the technical correction aspects, calls for a great deal of attention being paid to the really accurate repetition of movements and movement patterns. The more complicated these patterns of movement become, the more important it is to take time to ensure that they are learned correctly from the beginning. Short cuts will never lead to satisfactory results. Dance teaching is a form of co-ordination training which develops pre-programmed automatic multi-muscular patterns. The pre-programming is developed within the brain. It is automatic because much of it does not in the end require conscious thought. It is multi-muscular because many different muscle groups are used in order to produce the desired series of movements. These pre-programmed automatic multi-muscular patterns are known as engrams. (**Section 1.3** Neuro-muscular Co-ordination and Engrams, page 19.)

It requires constant *exact* repetitions in order to produce an engram so that conscious thought is not given to individual muscles or movements. Proprioceptive feedback gives both sub-conscious and conscious monitoring of the movement and it is this which gives the conscious mind the knowledge of whether the movement was carried out successfully or not. These automatic engrams can only be developed by voluntary repetition of the precise programme *without any variation at all from one repetition to the next.* This must be done *extremely accurately*, otherwise the input of information will vary on each occasion and the engram cannot be developed. *It follows therefore that initially the pattern must be slow enough to be accurate.* An engram allows a complicated movement to be performed far more rapidly than would be possible if conscious thought of each part of the pattern of movement were required. It is important also to realise that at the same time as the movements are occurring, the engram will also produce an inhibition of *unwanted* movements. This inhibition is an essential part of the regulation of co-ordination. Inhibition cannot be produced directly and consciously. It is only achieved by regular, active repetition of the pattern of desired movements. Co-ordination of the most

rapid, complex and skilful actions is automated by engrams rather than by a voluntary controlled series of movements.

The activation of the engram(s) is voluntary and under conscious control. In learning exercise patterns and in learning dance technique, or any other movement technique, accuracy is absolutely vital in order to develop the correct engram. If inaccuracies are allowed during the development of technique, this will produce 'bad habits' and these inaccuracies or 'bad habits' will themselves become an engram. Once this has taken place the modification of the engram will be extremely difficult and will usually call for that portion of the technique to be learned again from scratch. Hence the importance of learning any complex series of movements accurately from the start. As previously stated, in order to achieve accuracy the pattern will have to be learned slowly, and the number of repetitions required to produce a really well developed engram is almost innumerable. However, this is not as bad as it sounds because an action is usually made up of a series of engrams. It is the sum of the engrams which produces the final result. The initiation of an engram is under voluntary and conscious control, although the constituent parts of the engram are themselves not by that stage under direct voluntary control. What the mind does is to select the stored engrams and put them together in order to produce the desired result.

Individual Technical Faults

5.1 Discrepancy in Shoulder Level

This is often brought about by weakness of one side. As a result of this weakness there can be an over-compensation so that the weaker shoulder is held higher or, conversely, without this compensation the shoulder that is weaker may be lower (Fig. 5.1). Only careful examination will demonstrate which pertains in a particular individual. Elevation of one side may also be brought about by unequal muscle tension caused by unbalanced weight distribution in the lower part of the body.

The presence of a scoliosis will usually cause elevation of a shoulder, particularly if the scoliosis is in the mid or upper dorsal region. The presence of a scoliosis should be eliminated as a cause of the shoulder elevation at the initial medical examination.

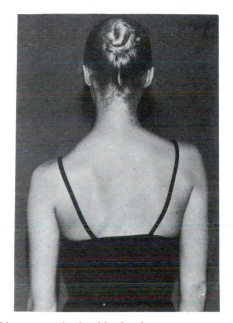

5.1 Discrepancy in shoulder level.

There are also some uncommon local anatomical variants which cause shoulder elevation. These usually prevent a correction of the shoulder level discrepancy by postural adjustment alone.

Leg length inequality may be reflected in differing shoulder heights as well as in a pelvic tilt.

Inequality of turn-out produces a swinging back of one side of the pelvis, a one-sided trunk weakness and frequently alteration in shoulder height on one side. Sitting in one hip will cause a similar picture.

The uneven shoulder level may follow an injury which has caused the dancer to take the weight off the painful side. This alteration can rapidly develop into a habit, so that even when the injury is cured and the pain has disappeared, the postural alteration remains.

One general cause of elevation of one shoulder is the habitual carrying on that side of heavy bags, only too frequently starting in students at a very early age. In many schools the children have to take all the school books for the day backwards and forwards morning and evening. Dance students may additionally be carrying several changes of clothing as well as school books. Use of the old-fashioned school satchel or a rucksack worn correctly, taking the weight evenly on both shoulders, would prevent the development of this shoulder level inequality.

Probably equally frequently the condition develops as a postural bad habit which is not helped by the total lack of postural correction and postural awareness that seems to be general in all schools today. There was a great deal to be said for the old-fashioned school teacher who insisted that the children sat up straight at their desks.

TREATMENT

An exercise programme is compiled to achieve the correction of any associated faults and this must be accompanied by constant postural correction. Underlying structural abnormalities may well call for referral for an orthopaedic opinion. If the shoulder level discrepancy is an isolated fault, it should be realised that its presence will have produced an alteration in the weight-bearing line and hence a weakness and imbalance at the level of the lower trunk, the gluteals, the hamstrings, adductors, quadriceps and even in the lower leg. Therefore, the exercise regime should be directed at strengthening and balancing all these areas.

5.2 Tension around the Neck and Shoulders

This should be considered in two sections, (a) tension in the upper fibres of the trapezius and (b) tension in the pectoralis muscles. Both are caused by inaccurate placement of arms and/or inaccurate fixation of the scapulae. The former usually comes about because the arms are held too far back with the elbows behind the line of the shoulders. It can also occur even if the arms are held forward in the correct position, but this being achieved by drawing the scapulae around the chest wall. Although this has the effect of flattening the scapulae against the chest wall, it does it by creating a great deal of tension in the pectoralis muscles as well as spasm in the trapezii.

The mechanism by which the arms are taken too far back is (a) by leading with the elbow rather than with the hand (Fig. 5.2) or (b) by over turning the feet, which causes the upper part of the trunk to sway backwards so that in obtaining a comfortable balance, the arms are taken backwards even more than the upper trunk (Fig. 5.3).

Weakness and instability of the lower trunk produces tension in the shoulder girdle because the feeling of insecurity produces an attempt at stability by tensing the upper trunk muscles.

Swayback knees which are pushed back cause the pelvis to tilt forward, the lumbar spine to become lordotic and in compensation the upper trunk goes backwards and this in turn alters the scapular fixation and scapular movements, producing increasing trapezius spasm.

A scoliosis, when present, always produces some tension to a variable degree during working. This is brought about because the compensatory curve above the scoliosis engenders some postural correction also, which then induces the tension. This postural compensation is often exaggerated as an attempt is made to put the centre of gravity over the base (i.e. the feet). In order to minimise or obviate the tension, corrective measures to obtain the best possible posture in the circumstances of the scoliosis must be instituted. These corrections must start at the feet and legs and work upwards. Unless the base is correct it is impossible to get the back in the best position. The situation is often complicated by a pelvic tilt associated with the scoliosis, giving an apparent and sometimes a true leg length inequality. Likewise, a leg length inequality occurring in the absence of a scoliosis will, by producing a compensatory pelvic tilt, frequently lead to the development of tension higher in the back.

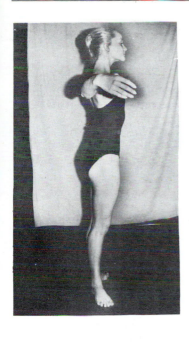 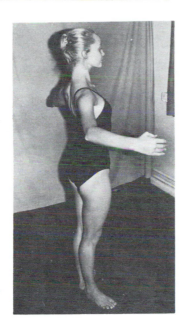

5.2 (far left)   Leading with the elbows and arms too far back. She is also failing to hold her turn-out correctly. The tension in the neck muscle can be seen.

5.3 (left)   Failing to hold the turn-out correctly. There is a compensatory tilt backwards of the trunk with the result that the arms are taken even further back and lie well behind the line of the hip joint.

A kyphosis, or in its lesser degree, a rather more rounded dorsal spine than normal, can also lead to tension around the neck and shoulders. Its presence is really a contra-indication to a performing career in dance because there are no satisfactory corrective measures. If at all marked, it is rarely if ever totally postural, although a bad posture can exaggerate the kyphotic appearance. The commonest underlying cause is Scheuermann's disease in adolescence. This is an osteochondritis of the growth plates at the upper and lower parts of each vertebral body. When the Scheuermann's disease finally settles with the cessation of growth, it may have left each of the vertebral bodies slightly wedge-shaped, narrower anteriorly, thus producing a forward curve of the spine (see **Section 5.5**).

Sometimes, and particularly during growth spurts, a child can apparently become mildly kyphotic but this is correctable with suitable exercises and attention to posture and is, in any case, usually self-correcting.

TREATMENT

Treatment of the tension is by correction of the underlying fault. Often pain is present in the muscles concerned and frequently there is chest pain caused by spasm of the pectorals in particular, as well as being referred from the origins of the trapezius at the spinous processes and interspinous ligaments. Where there is muscle pain, initial treatment may be directed at relief of the muscle spasm and pain by the physiotherapist using interferential, ultrasound or massage. This will

facilitate the identification and correction of the underlying technical faults producing the spasm.

In most causes of tension and especially in those with a scoliosis, breathing exercises should be taught. Upper chest breathers need education to use the whole chest and the diaphragm. Scoliotics need instruction to encourage the equal expansion of both sides of the chest as there is always a tendency for someone with a scoliosis to use the side of the chest on the convex aspect of the curve more than the other side of the chest. As a result, there is a gradual further collapse of the chest on the concave side and an increase in the postural component of the scoliosis. Also, in aiding correction as far as possible of the scoliosis, very significant benefit can be obtained by a suitable exercise programme to strengthen the muscles. In this context attention should be paid to the muscle groups in the legs. Frequently there is weakness of more than one group, resulting in an incorrect weight placement down at that level. Without correction here, a less satisfactory result will be obtained in the back and the chest.

5.3 Discrepancy in the Length of the Clavicles

This will produce a difference in breadth between the two shoulder girdles. As a result there will be a tendency to work with the weight placed more towards the broader side. Therefore muscle development becomes unequal in the trunk and neck. Frequently the narrow side will become tighter generally, mainly around the shoulder affecting in particular the pectorals and also slightly restricting elevation of that arm. This discrepancy in clavicular length is often merely an aberration during growth and the difference in width is not necessarily permanent.

TREATMENT

Ensure that muscle strength and build-up is equalised on the two sides of the body and also ensure that any tight areas are stretched out equally. Nothing can be done to alter the actual structural difference if it does not correct itself spontaneously.

5.4 Scoliosis

This is a lateral curvature of a segment of the spine. This curvature is accompanied by a marked rotational element (Fig. 5.4). If it is very marked then aesthetically it will be unacceptable in a professional dancer. Therefore in the assessment of dancers the examiner is looking for relatively mild degrees of scoliosis which may not be immediately apparent on initial observation. The area affected by the curvature in the scoliosis is very much stiffer than normal. As most scolioses are in the dorsal spine, this in itself is frequently not of major importance if the scoliosis is only mild and does not constitute a cosmetic disability. However, in the lumbar region, the accompanying stiffness can make the back as a whole too stiff to allow the movements required for ballet. Below the neck level, most of the movements of flexion and extension and lateral flexion and rotation take place in the lumbar region.

In the majority of cases the cause of a scoliosis is totally unknown. This is called an idiopathic scoliosis. Rarely nowadays a scoliosis is due to paralysis of a group or groups of muscles. This used to be relatively common when poliomyelitis epidemics occurred at regular intervals. There are some very rare conditions of the nerves and nervous system which can also lead to a scoliosis.

If the presence of a scoliosis is suspected, the student should be referred to an orthopaedic surgeon for an opinion. There are many different forms of treatment which can help the condition and may well be indicated in the individual case. If the scoliosis is mild, great benefit can frequently be obtained by suitable exercises. Sometimes the use of an electrical muscle stimulator worn at night can bring about very marked improvement in the

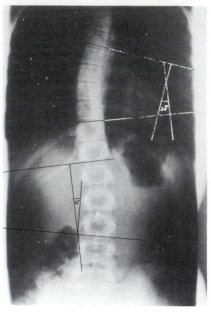

5.4   An X-ray of a scoliosis with the measurement lines drawn in. Here there is a 20° dorsal scoliosis and a 12° lumbar scoliosis. A scoliosis at a single level is more common. It is usually in the dorsal region of the spine.

degree of curvature. In more severe cases, mechanical bracing or surgery may be required. Osteopathic or spinal manipulations will not cure a scoliosis and are not indicated as a method of treatment. Forcible manipulations may produce actual damage to the bones and joints and aggravate the situation.

The presence of even a marked scoliosis is not a contra-indication in itself to the child undertaking ballet classes. Dancing can even be helpful in exercising the scoliotic areas and in strengthening up the muscles. The exercise from the ballet classes will be in addition to side shift and other exercises which may have been prescribed by the orthopaedic surgeon looking after the child as a patient. However, it should be made clear to the child and to the parents that the classes are for fun only and are not a prelude to a possible professional career. Even if the young dancer can manage the technical aspects of ballet, the presence of an obvious scoliosis will be unappealing when they come to audition for places in companies and dance groups and attempts at a professional career are sure to end with great disappointment.

Even in mild scolioses, difficulty can be experienced in centralising the line of weight-bearing and usually the weight is to one side, i.e. towards the apparently shorter side. As a result, groin, adductor and low back strains are common.

Frequently the hamstrings on one side are very much tighter than the other and this can lead to hamstring injuries. The tightness arises because of the frequent presence of a pelvic tilt associated with a scoliosis but, once established, the tight hamstrings will themselves repeatedly exert a rotational pull on the pelvis (**Section 5.20**). Very often, on the looser hamstring side a swayback knee may develop, causing its own particular difficulties (see **Section 5.13**).

Because of the rotational element of the scoliosis, difficulties may be experienced with arm positions, causing muscle tension and strains around the shoulder girdle in attempting to achieve correct arm placements. In addition, in a dorsal scoliosis, the rib cage on the two sides is different, that on the concave side being compressed and with a decrease in volume.

The presence of a mild scoliosis which is not obvious cosmetically, may be suspected if the student appears to have difficulty achieving correct head positions; if there is one shoulder higher than the other; if there is a pelvic tilt or prominence of one side of the pelvis; a forward rotation of the pelvis on one side; or if there is a leg length discrepancy. Any of these factors calls for a careful examination of the spine.

It should be emphasised again that if a scoliosis is suspected, the child should be referred for an orthopaedic opinion. Delay in seeking specialist advice should be avoided as an early scoliosis may well be correctable if treated properly initially.

TREATMENT

Treatment of the actual scoliosis is an orthopaedic problem. Exercises can certainly be beneficial in strengthening the muscle groups to decrease as much as possible the postural elements of the curve. Side shift exercises are helpful. The use of an electrical muscle stimulator at night really falls within the sphere of the treatment which will be ordered by the orthopaedic surgeon under whose care the child is.

The rehabilitation programme should start by strengthening the feet and leg muscles and by ensuring that the position is correct. If the legs and feet are not correct then all attempts to strengthen and align the pelvis and trunk will be unavailing.

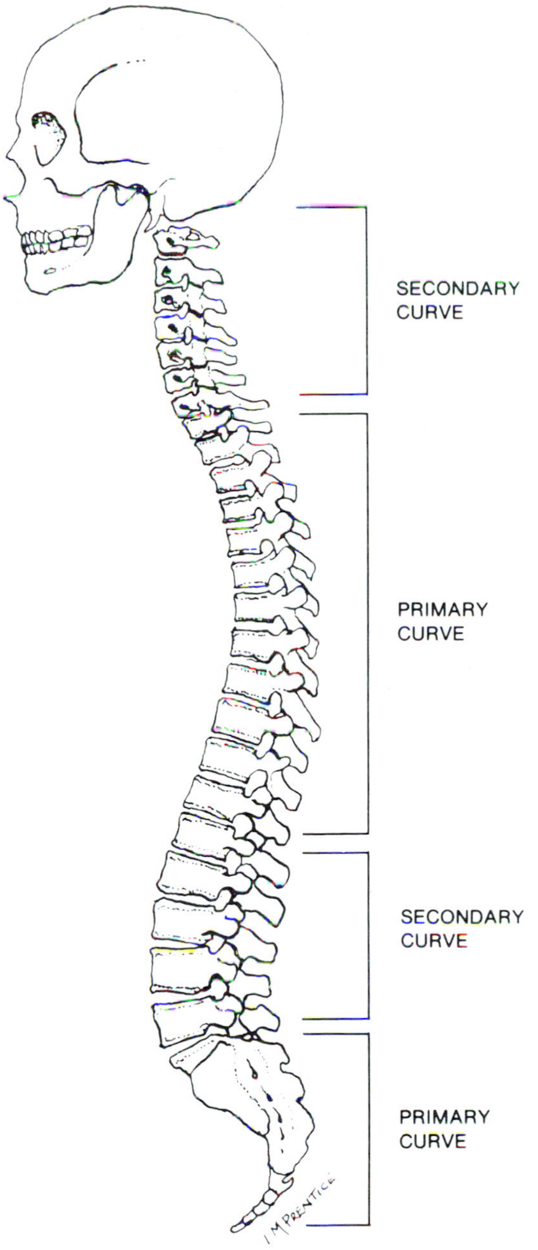

SECONDARY CURVE

PRIMARY CURVE

SECONDARY CURVE

PRIMARY CURVE

5.5 Diagram showing the primary and secondary curves. In foetal life, the whole spine is curved forwards in the direction of the primary curve. The secondary curves in the neck and lumbar regions gradually develop after birth and are in the opposite direction to the primary curve.

5.5 Kyphosis

This is a forward flexion of the spine occurring most commonly in the dorsal region. There is already a primary curve at this level (Fig. 5.5) and

5.6A   Line drawing showing a
kyphosis in the dorsal region with a
compensatory lumbar lordosis below
it.

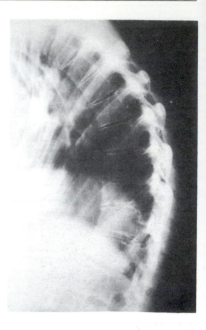

5.6B   An X-ray of
a severe kyphosis.

a kyphosis is an increase in the curve beyond the normal limit (Fig. 5.6). It may arise as a result of Scheuermann's disease in childhood when, due to the osteochondritis affecting the end plates at the top and bottom of each vertebral body, these become somewhat wedge-shaped, narrower anteriorly, thus resulting in a curve. Frequently, however, there is no apparent cause for the kyphosis.

The presence of a kyphosis is aesthetically displeasing, but functionally, any damage or injury is produced in the lumbar region. As a result of the forward curve in the dorsal region, a compensatory lordosis is inevitable (see **Section 5.6** for the associated problems). Additionally, the head and neck have to be extended more than normally in order to allow the person to look forward horizontally.

With the presence of either a scoliosis or a kyphosis the resulting loss in mobility in these regions decreases the shock absorption of the spine as a whole. As a result, injuries of all types in the lumbar region become much more frequent and the lumbar spine is constantly at risk. In the presence of a kyphosis, which inevitably leads to a compensatory lordosis, very much more additional strain is placed on the lumbar spine as the dancer attempts to assume the correct position required by dance technique.

TREATMENT

There is no specific treatment for a structural kyphosis. However, the posture can be helped by strengthening exercises for all the trunk muscles to decrease as much as possible any postural component of the curve. During treatment, the weight position must be corrected as far as possible. With the compensatory lordosis the pelvis will be tilted forward and as a result of this the weight will be pushed back. As the kyphosis is fixed, and therefore the lordosis in this case cannot be completely eliminated, full correction of the weight position will not be possible.

Due to the frequency of lumbar spine injuries associated with kyphoses, much attention must be given to trunk strengthening exercises to try to provide the maximum possible protection for the lumbar region of the back (see **Section 5.6** Treatment, page 173).

The rehabilitation programme should start by strengthening the feet and leg muscles and ensuring that the position is correct. If the legs and feet are incorrect, all attempts to strengthen and align the pelvis and trunk will be unavailing.

5.6 Lordosis

This is the name given to the posture when the lumbar spine is hyper-extended or, in other words, very much hollowed. There is normally a lumbar curve but in a lordosis this normal curve is greatly exaggerated (Fig. 5.7). It is a postural condition and can be corrected, i.e. it is not a fixed curve as is the case with the scoliosis and kyphosis described earlier. However, in the presence of a kyphosis in the dorsal spine, correction will produce such a forward tilt of the upper half of the trunk that it

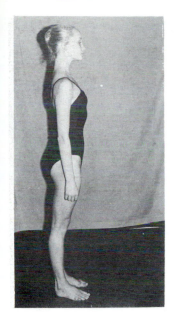

5.7   Three lordotic postures from the side.

5.8   **Kyphotic posture with correction of the compensatory lordosis (which was seen in Fig. 5.6A). As a result the head pokes forwards and the neck has to be hyperextended.**

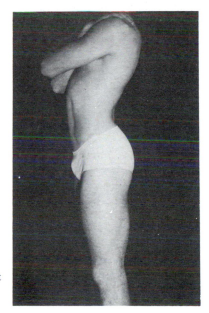

5.9   Pelvic tilt due to tightness at the fronts of the hips and a secondary lordosis.

becomes impractical (Fig. 5.8). Similarly, a fixed pelvic tilt due to very marked tightness in the fronts of the hips will produce a similar difficulty in correction (Fig. 5.9).

CAUSES OF A LORDOSIS

1.   Dorsal kyphosis (**Section 5.5**).
2.   A forward pelvic tilt due to tightness in the fronts of the hips (**Section 5.9**).
3.   Weakness of the abdominal muscles.

4.   Weakness of the gluteals. (3 and 4 usually go together, although not invariably so.) Weakness of the hamstrings is also commonly associated with weak gluteals.
5.   Working over turned out at the feet in relation to the hips will produce a forward tilt of the pelvis (Fig. 5.10). This may be due to a genuine limitation of turn-out at the hips or a failure to hold the available turn-out (**Section 5.7**).

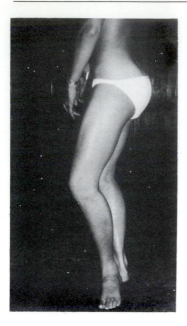  

5.10   Over turned feet producing
a forward tilt of the pelvis.

5.11   Swayback knees producing
a compensatory pelvic tilt and a
lordosis.

5.12   Lordosis because the arms are
too far back. This also produces a
forward poking chin.

6.   Weakness of the adductors produces a failure to hold the turn-out and results in the same problem as 5 (**Section 5.10**).

7.   Swayback knees produce a compensatory pelvic tilt and a lordosis (Fig. 5.11) in order to bring the line of weight-bearing through the feet. Having been displaced backwards by the swayback knees being pushed back, the line of weight-bearing must be brought forward in order to maintain balance (**Section 5.13**).

8.   A tibial bow (**Section 5.15**) produces weight-bearing more laterally and this makes it difficult to get a hold on the inner sides of the thighs. This results in a situation similar to that associated with adductors which are weak (**Section 5.10**).

9.   Weakness of the forefeet (**Section 5.18**) causes the weight to be pushed back with similar consequences to those associated with other causes for the weight being back (**Section 5.20**).

10.   Any other technical fault which causes the weight to be taken too far back will produce a compensatory lordosis.

11.   Working with the arms too far back causes the upper trunk to tilt backwards and this will produce a compensatory lordosis in order to bring the weight forward. It is often accompanied by a forward poking chin, which is also part of an attempt to maintain balance (Fig. 5.12).

12.   Tight shoes produce curling of the toes with the consequence that the weight will be pushed back, producing a lordosis.

13.   In some dancers there appears to be a naturally occurring lordosis which, although initially postural and theoretically therefore correctable, can in practice prove almost impossible to improve or fully correct. In some of these people the lordosis, which has been present since they started to walk, can become at least partly fixed as they approach maturity. It is then uncorrectable, even when they lie flat on their backs and pull their knees up to their chests. Normally this manoeuvre rotates the pelvis and flattens the lumbar spine. If this does not occur, then it can be accepted that there is at least a degree of lordosis which is uncorrectable as the necessary mobility is lacking. It must be emphasised that the aim is to achieve the *normal lumbar curve* and not to flatten this curve out when working. This is as undesirable as an exaggerated curve or lordosis. However, unless the spine is supple enought to be able to attain this flattening, it is not possible for the dancer to work satisfactorily, as forward flexion of the trunk in the lumbar region cannot take place and forward bending can only occur at the hips.

14.   Tight hamstrings may also contribute to a lordosis (**Section 5.12**).

Consequences of a Lordosis

These are the same as the Consequences of the
Weight Back Situation (**Section 5.20**).

TREATMENT

This must be by elimination of the cause of the
lordosis whether this be weakness of muscle groups,
faulty technique producing lordosis secondarily, or
an incorrect weight-bearing line.

The rehabilitation programme will certainly be
based on a programme of trunk strengthening
exercises, as well as strengthening and balancing the
various muscle groups in the lower limbs.

The rehabilitation programme should start by
strengthening the feet and leg muscles and ensuring
that the position is correct. If the legs and feet are
not correct, all attempts to strengthen and align the
pelvis and trunk and eliminate the lordosis will be
unavailing.

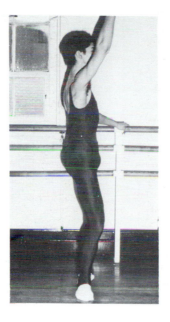

5.13. Over turned
feet in relation to the
hips.

5.7 Over Turning

By this is meant that the foot and lower leg are
being turned out (externally rotated) beyond the
degree of turn-out available at the hip joint (Fig.
5.13). The over turned foot may reflect either an
anatomical limitation of the degree of turn-out
required by ballet technique, or it may be due to a
lack of correct muscular control of the turn-out,
therefore producing an apparent restriction in
turn-out at the hips, with over turned feet.   Only
too frequently the degree of turn-out being
demanded may be too great to be realistic. Very
few dancers have flat turn-out (180°) and even if
they do, they cannot work like this because of the
difficulty in achieving correct balance. Therefore
they tend to drop into the lordotic position, thus
weakening the trunk muscles.

Much more disastrous than any of the above is
the method of teaching which demands a flat 180°
turn-out at the feet, despite the fact that the hips
may not approach anything like this degree of
external rotation. The results of this method of
teaching may be

1. A marked pelvic tilt forward with the
    development of a lordosis.
2. Severe weakening of the trunk muscles,
    particularly the abdominals.
3. A greatly increased rate of injury in the lumbar
    spine, including stress fractures. On average it
    takes a bad teacher eight months to so weaken
    a previously adequately strong dancer that the
    risk of a serious back injury is imminent.

4. General sequential weakening of the various
    muscle groups from above downwards – the
    abdominals, the back extensors, the latissimus
    dorsi (as the shoulders are back), the glutei, the
    hamstrings (especially the lateral hamstrings),
    the adductors and the vastus medialis, the
    lateral part of the calf muscle and the lateral
    intrinsic muscles of the feet. This in total
    produces complete imbalance of the legs. Most
    of these muscle groups are required in order to
    hold the turn-out so their gradually increasing
    weakness brought about by being made to work
    grossly over turned, causes increasing difficulty
    in holding the available turn-out. This becomes
    especially noticeable when they leave the barre
    to start centre work. During barre work the
    dancer will grip the barre tightly to give
    support in the unattainable (at the hips) flat,
    turned out position. Teachers who demand this
    flat turn-out demonstrate their total ignorance
    of the mechanics of the body and by this
    culpable attitude must accept complete
    responsibility for injuries they cause to their
    students. The situation is not only a cause of
    injuries but it is also greatly detrimental to the
    development of a good technique.

Unfortunately, many teachers who insist on a flat
turn-out at the feet believe that they are following
the Russian method of teaching. This is a double
misunderstanding of the situation. Firstly, and
importantly, the body types that are reaching this
stage of training are different. Secondly, the ground
work leading up to this method of teaching is quite

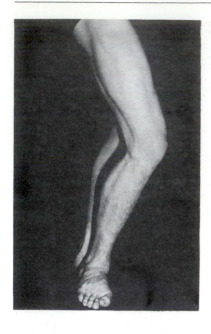

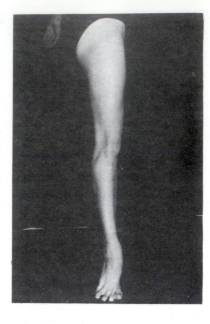

5.14 (far left)   Over turned feet with rolling and a valgus strain on the big toe.

5.15 (left)   Over turned foot on demi-pointe with valgus pressure on the great toe.

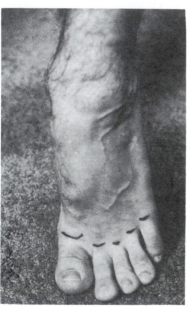

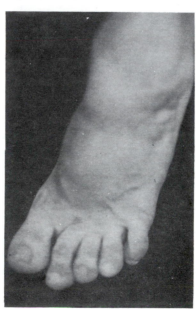

5.16A (far left)   Sickling on demi-pointe with the weight being transmitted down the medial side of the foot. Doctors and physiotherapists would refer to this as sickling *out* but dancers would usually call it sickling *in* (because of the direction that the ankle goes as opposed to the direction the foot takes).

5.16B (left)   Sickling on demi-pointe with the weight being transmitted down the lateral side of the foot. This is a precursor to sickling in the opposite direction when on full pointe (see Fig. 5.17).

different and far more thorough. As a result the child will be far more mobile and much stronger before a nearly flat turn-out is required of him or her.

In the Western world where the selection of correct body types is far less rigorous and demanding than in the Russian schools, it is quite wrong to try to follow the Russian method with the students. Only a small proportion will be able to cope satisfactorily with this method.

The schools have two choices: either a very much more rigorous selection of the correct body type, plus adequate preparatory groundwork in the training, or else accepting less satisfactory bodies with the accompanying knowledge that a flat turn-out cannot be achieved without a high injury rate. The schools cannot have it both ways and a little more insight into the whole of the Russian methods instead of a superficial and partial knowledge would greatly help matters. For example, a tendu will fail to be effective behind the hindfoot as the unstable supporting leg inhibits the correct muscle action in the working (tendu) foot. Another example is that over turning will cause the dancer to sit in the supporting hip, thus effectively producing a leg length discrepancy as well as inhibiting proper muscle contraction and control of the supporting hip. As a result, there will be insufficient space to move the leg in all directions because it will tend to strike the floor. To avoid this, the dancer will hitch at the waist on the working side. Once he does this the weight comes off the supporting leg even further and the pelvis and trunk will wave around in an unsupported fashion even more than before.

Although a student or dancer will usually over turn on both sides, the over turning may sometimes be confined to one side only. Even if both sides are over turned, frequently or even usually the over turning will not be symmetrical but one side will be forced out to a greater extent than the other. The ability to over turn lies in the use of friction between the foot and the floor. This friction can be increased by the use of rosin. It is impossible to over turn if the foot is not on the floor.

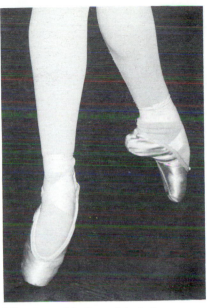

5.17 Sickling on full pointe with the weight being transmitted down the medial side of the foot.

Consequences of Over Turning

1. *Rolling*. This puts a strain on the great toe tending to push it into a valgus position (Fig. 5.14). This can cause damage to the capsule and ligament of the medial side of the joint, aggravated by actual local pressure there, which will occur as the rolled foot is pressed on the floor. Any underlying valgus deformity will be increased by the rolling, especially during work on demi-pointe, during relevés and during pointe work (Fig. 5.15). In the latter, the rolling will change during the relevé into a sickle position with the weight medially through the foot. The situation can be complicated by the presence of lower tibial bows or swayback knees. In both these instances, the natural weight-bearing line is back and at demi-pointe the foot will tend to be sickled (Fig. 5.16), i.e. the foot has the weight on the outer side. As the relevé continues the direction of sickling changes to the opposite situation so that the weight is medially when they reach full pointe (Fig. 5.17). Therefore, the observer may be misled if the dancer is only seen on demi-pointe. For further complications of rolling see **Section 5.17**.

2. *Injuries of the 1st Metatarso-phalangeal Joint*. These come about mainly as a result of the rolling but may occur even if the rolling is corrected or absent. The weight will still be back due to over turning, the use of the wrong muscles and the friction of the floor. The injury may be due to valgus strain or to rotation of the great toe (**Section 3.19**).

3. *Clawing of the Toes and Intrinsic Muscle Weakness*. This is caused by the weight being back and the failure of the muscles in the thigh to hold the turn-out. The toes claw in an attempt to hold on at floor level and this increases intrinsic weakness due to their lack of proper use and function (**Section 5.18**).

4. *Stress Fractures* in the tibia and fibula can occur, in part due to the lack of shock absorption by the weak feet and in part by the rotational twist transmitted down the over turned leg (**Sections 3.26** and **3.27**).

5. *Anterior Compartment Syndrome* can be induced for similar reasons (**Section 3.28**).

6. *Tibialis Posterior Tenosynovitis* occurs because of an attempt to correct the rolled feet at the foot and ankle level instead of at the hips (**Section 3.13**).

7. *Injuries of the Medial Side of the Knee*. These may be tears of the medial meniscus or sprains of the medial ligament, both of which will occur as a result of the twist at the knee (Fig. 5.18) (**Sections 3.31, 3.32** and **3.35**).

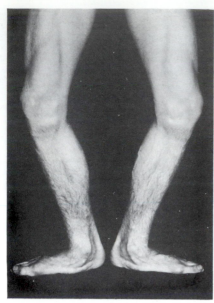

5.18   Over turning showing tension on the inner side of the knee.

8. *Chondromalacia Patellae and Patellar Tendonitis.* These are both induced or aggravated because the rotation at the knee brings about lateral tracking of the patella (**Section 3.30**).
9. *Weakness of the Lateral Hamstrings.* This is induced by rotation at the knee. The unequal pull then exerted by the lateral and medial hamstrings leaves the lateral meniscus more likely to sustain an injury. The weakened hamstrings are also more likely to be injured (**Section 3.41**).
10. *The Adductors* weaken because they do not function fully in the over turned position. The adductors become more prone to injury due to the lack of stability of the pelvis by their own weakness, especially during grands battements when either adductor may be injured, i.e. that on the suppporting side or that on the working side. (**Sections 5.10** and **3.30**).
11. *Lordosis.* This will occur in over turning as the pelvis rotates forward in an attempt to increase the available turn-out at the hips. In most people, any flexion at the hip joints will increase the apparent degree of external rotation available (**Section 5.6**). Associated with this will be a tightening at the fronts of the hips which may be real or apparent. This is aggravated by over action of the quadriceps (but not the medialis) which are used to grip in a weight back situation. As the rectus femoris crosses the front of the hip, it will also

add to the forces causing the pelvis to rotate forward.

12. *Groin strains.* These are not infrequent as a direct result of the over turning coupled with the associated muscle weakness (**Section 3.40**).

TREATMENT

Basically the dancer should avoid turning the feet out further than the available turn-out at the hips.

In a student who has been over turning, any of the above complications may need individual treatment and the various weak muscle groups will certainly need a considerable programme of strengthening exercises. A great amount of technical correction will be required to undo the harm caused by the previous bad teaching.

5.8 Restriction of Turn-out at the Hips

Everybody has an anatomical limit to their range of external rotation of the hips (i.e. turn-out). This range cannot be exceeded. In the young student, limitation due to ligament tightness can be gradually improved by correct working and gentle judicious stretching. This is most likely to be achieved before puberty.

Apparent limitation may be due to tightness at the fronts of the hips (**Section 5.9**) or frequently by weakness of the muscles controlling the turn-out, especially the adductors (**Section 5.10**).

For classical dance the lower limit of external rotation at the hip is about 45°. Anything less will tend to produce greater or lesser problems. The method of measurement of turn-out is particularly important. Only too frequently, particularly in auditions, one sees children being put into the frog position (Fig. 5.19) under the misapprehension that the degree of turn-out is being assessed. In most people, the frog position will appear to have a very much greater range of turn-out than actually exists when the hips are fully extended. The following series of photographs show how misleading the frog position can be when assessing turn-out (Fig. 5.20). It is when the hips are extended, i.e. when the person is standing up straight with the legs in line with the trunk, that they are in their normal working position for dancing. The method for assessing the degree of turn-out at each hip is shown in the accompanying photographs (Fig. 5.21). The hip which is not being measured is flexed up. Care must be taken to make certain that the hip which is being assessed is held in the fully

5.19   Frog position in an audition.

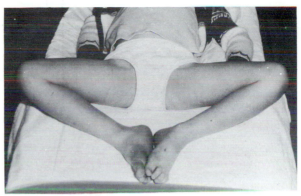

5.20A   Frog position – very good.

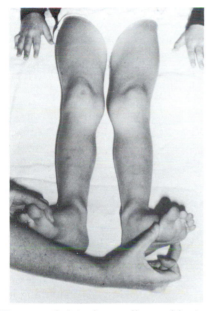

5.20B   Hips extended (as in standing position) and fully turned out (externally rotated). This demonstrates very well the great discrepancy which frequently occurs between an assessment of turn-out in the frog position and the true turn-out when the dancer is standing.

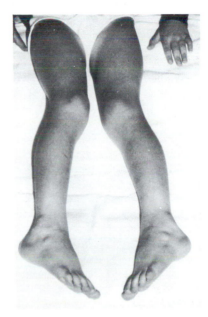

5.20C   Hips extended and internally rotated, showing that the total joint range in rotation is full but that most of it is in internal rotation.

extended position as, if it is allowed to flex even a small amount, the apparent degree of turn-out can be increased markedly.

It is possible to measure turn-out with the dancer lying on his face but the results can be misleading. In this position it is very much easier for the dancer to drop the lumbar spine into the lordotic posture, thus producing flexion of the hip and an apparent increase in the turn-out.

The problems associated with a restriction of turn-out are those dealt with under over turning (**Section 5.7**).

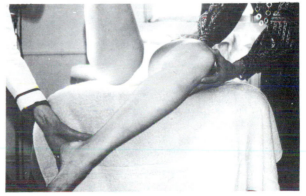

5.21   Assessing turn-out accurately with the leg over the end of the couch, keeping the hip being examined fully extended. The other leg is flexed out of the way.

TREATMENT

The muscles controlling turn-out, mainly the adductors, must be strengthened in order to control and hold the best available amount of turn-out. Additionally, many other groups may also require strengthening, notably the trunk, the glutei and the feet. Posture, weight position and weight transference must be corrected. Gentle and progressive stretching can be carried out under controlled conditions once the strengthening programme is under way. Stretching must not take place in the presence of weak muscles. In the stretching, attention must be given to any tightness in the fronts of the hips.

Muscles must be stretched in the line in which they work and function. This is not necessarily in the longitudinal line of the limb. Cross stretching is unproductive and achieves nothing.

The common method used, in the vain hope that turn-out is being stretched, is sitting or lying in the frog position. In this situation the hips are flexed, nearly always giving an apparent increase in turn-out range. More important, this is not the position in which the hips are working when the dancer is standing or moving when turned out. He does this with the hips extended, i.e. standing up straight, apart from the relatively infrequent occasions when going down into a plié or fondu at which time the hip is indeed flexing. Lying in frogs is not stretching the actual structures which are tight. *The end results of various structures being tight can be restriction of turn-out.* It is necessary to assess and define which of the various structures associated with the turn-out are tight and then to stretch these individually. *Frequently, this means that the stretch is not in the actual direction of turn-out.* For instance, if there is tightness at the front of the hip, it is a cross pull on these structures which causes a limitation of turn-out but the actual stretch of these tissues must be longitudinal to their fibres and not, in this instance, in the actual direction of turn-out. This would be unproductive.

It is noteworthy that although the adductors are the main muscles which turn the hip out and hold it turned out, tightness in portions of the adductors as a whole may actually limit external rotation. These portions have to relax while the bulk of the muscle concerned is contracting. Therefore the adductors themselves may need some gentle stretching in order to improve turn-out.

Additionally, it is of great importance to note that a well stretched muscle (not over-stretched) will contract much more efficiently and strongly.

5.9 Tightness at the Fronts of the Hips

As this implies, there is restriction of full extension of the hip joint, extension meaning carrying the leg backwards in relation to the trunk.

It is assessed by the following method (Fig. 5.22).

The tightness may lie in any of the anterior structures. The most superficial is the rectus femoris portion of the quadriceps. The rectus femoris crosses the front of the hip joint. It and the other three components of the quadriceps can be part of a generalised tightness. Also superficially placed is the tensor faciae latae which may be tight. Deeper, the restriction may be caused by the ilio-psoas which is an internal rotator as well as a flexor of the hip. In addition to limiting extension it can also restrict external rotation. Restriction of external rotation or turn-out is an overall complication of tightness of the front of the hip. Additionally, pectineus and adductor brevis as well as the anterior capsule of the hip can all play a part in the tightness at the front of the joint.

CAUSES

Although the tightness frequently exists in its own right it may be precipitated or aggravated by any one of the following.
1. Lordosis, when the forward tilt of the pelvis will gradually lead to tightening of the anterior structures (**Section 5.6**).
2. Any technical or anatomical fault which causes a forward rotation of the pelvis resulting in a secondary shortening of the structures in the front of the hips. If long-standing it can progress to an actual tightness or contracture.
3. Tightness of the hamstrings will lead to a tendency to work with the knees very slightly flexed thus preventing the hip from fully straightening (**Section 5.12**).

EFFECTS

1. The production of a lordotic posture and all its associated problems (**Section 5.6**).
2. Restriction of turn-out. This may be brought about by two factors:
   (a) *actual limitation* as occurs when the ilio-psoas or other strictures which limit external rotation are tight, or
   (b) apparent limitation by prevention of the external rotators from acting effectively in turning out and in holding the turn-out.

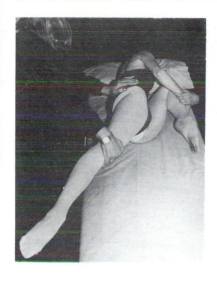 

5.22A (far left) Assessing tightness at the front of the hip, this photograph showing the normal range required for a dancer.

5.22B (left) A tight hip with limited extension.

TREATMENT

Initially this is by exercise of all the weakened muscle groups where applicable (trunk, hamstrings, adductors and gluteals, etc.). Then when all these groups are becoming stronger and alongside the continuing strengthening programme any tight groups or areas, e.g. tensor fascia lata, hamstrings, quadriceps or adductors are stretched out gently.

In general, these stretching techniques of the different groups and structures should be well understood by a competent physiotherapist so detailed descriptions have been omitted. However, it cannot be repeated often enough that stretching should be gentle and gradual and never forcible, great care being taken not to tear any tissues otherwise scarring and contracture will occur.

5.10 Weakness of Adductors

These are the muscles which produce and hold the turn-out position. In dance they need to be very strong to produce the turn-out and then to *hold* it. They are naturally, in the average person, rather a weak group and they can be weakened further by overstretching. The weakness can also have the opposite effect and lead to the adductors becoming tight.

CAUSES

The most important cause of weakness of the adductors is the execution of an *incorrect technique.*
1. Sitting in the hip.
2. Rolling (**Section 5.17**).
3. Weight too far back (**Section 5.20**).
4. Over turning (**Section 5.7**).
5. Swayback knees (**Section 5.13**).
6. Weak forefeet preventing correct weight placement (**Section 5.18**).
7. Lordosis (frequently a postural fault in children which becomes a technical fault if the teacher fails to correct it) (**Section 5.6**).

TREATMENT

This is by exercising in order to strengthen the adductors. They should be stretched gently if tight, and technique should be corrected – all else is pointless if a fault in technique remains.

5.11 Quadriceps Insufficiency

This means weakness of the quadriceps complex (vastus medialis, vastus intermedius, vastus lateralis and rectus femoris). This weakness may be total weakness where all muscle groups in the body are weak; a relative weakness compared with other muscle groups; a differential weakness with one leg compared to the other; a weakness within the complex where one part is weak compared to the others. This latter occurs mainly and commonly where the vastus medialis is differentially weak compared with the other three components.

CAUSES

1. Swayback knees are a potent cause of quadriceps insufficiency in dancers because of a failure to pull up, which results in the weight being allowed to remain too far back. The dancer will then relax into the posterior capsule

and the muscles do nothing to support the knee (**Section 5.13**).

2. Tight hamstrings which cause the dancer to work with slightly flexed knees will weaken the quadriceps by making them work inadequately. It is also frequently seen that some people walk and stand without ever fully extending the knees and this is particularly noticeable in women who wear very high heels (**Section 5.12**).

3. After even a minor knee injury the quadriceps will waste and weaken within two to three days so a special effort will be required to strengthen them again, together with other associated or affected muscle groups. In this context special care should be taken to ensure that the vastus medialis is built up and that the quadriceps strength is balanced out between the two legs (**Section 5.11**).

RESULTS

1. Anterior knee pain (**Section 3.30**). Note particularly that lack of balance between various muscles which make up the whole quadriceps (especially vastus medialis weakness) leads to lateral tracking of the patella.

2. An increased risk of knee injury, notably meniscal damage (**Section 3.35**). Also it can lead to rupture of the quadriceps tendon or the patellar tendon (**Section 3.37**). A teacher who suddenly demonstrates a step requiring an explosive contraction of the quadriceps, e.g. a big jump, is particularly at risk.

3. Weakness of the vastus medialis prevents full locking of the knee in extension (**Section 5.11**). This can lead to a decrease in use of and a tightening of the lateral hamstrings (**Section 5.12**).

4. Calf over-development will occur because the calf muscles are taking more of the load in landing and expending more force in jumping. This in turn can lead to an Achilles tendonitis (**Section 3.9**) and an anterior compartment syndrome (**Section 3.28**) as well as anterior foot strains.

TREATMENT

This is by strengthening exercises. Balancing out within the quadriceps is essential. This usually calls for extra work on strengthening the vastus medialis. This part of the quadriceps complex only contracts effectively in the last 15° of extension (straightening) of the knee. Balancing out between the two legs is required. There should be correction of any technical fault which may have lead to the original weakness.

5.12 Tightness of the Hamstrings

CAUSES

1. The hamstrings can be naturally tight to the extent that many people cannot lift their legs with the knees straight to a 90° angle. As the hamstrings cross behind the knee flexion of the knee will allow full hip flexion to take place even in the presence of tight hamstrings. The flexion of the knee relaxes the hamstring muscles. As will be recalled from **Section 1** on Anatomy, the hamstrings act as hip extensors and knee flexors.

2. The hamstrings tend to tighten as a normal course of affairs during any growth spurt, as do all other muscle groups. This is because the bones grow during growth spurts more rapidly than the soft tissues. This tightening will ease up and the student will regain the previous flexibility once the growth spurt has stopped.

3. Working with the weight back from any of its many causes will tend to cause a forward rotation of the pelvis (**Section 5.20**). The knees tend to flex slightly and the hamstrings then weaken and tighten. In particular, the lateral hamstrings tighten and weaken in this situation. Associated with the weakening and tightening of the hamstrings there are frequently weak quadriceps due to a failure to lock the knee. In over turning, the hamstrings cannot be utilised to their full extent because the pelvis becomes tipped forwards. Also the twist at the knee will cause an imbalance between the medial and lateral hamstrings with differential weakening and tightening.

RESULTS

1. Any tightness will aggravate the weight back situation which may in itself have been the precipitating factor, so there can be a vicious circle of deterioration (**Section 5.20**).

2. Tightness, of course, predisposes to hamstring injuries, both pulls and tears (**Section 3.41**).

3. Unequal tightness (medial versus lateral) can aggravate rotational pulls on the knee when it is partly flexed and therefore predisposed to meniscal damage (**Section 3.35**).

4. Like quadriceps insufficiency and weakness, tightness of the hamstrings will put an overload on the calf muscles with resulting muscle injuries and Achilles tendon problems. (**Sections 3.9**, **3.10** and **3.11**).

5. Hamstrings which are not being pulled up and used correctly will lead to tightening of the tensor fasciae latae as this muscle tries to stabilise the pelvis. This overwork laterally will spread to the lateral quadriceps, and as a direct result of this, lateral tracking of the patella will occur and then anterior knee pain (**Section 3.30**). This lateral tracking cannot be fully corrected by merely quadriceps medialis exercises and build-up without first dealing with hamstring tightness and weakness and stretching the tensor fasciae latae.

TREATMENT

Correct the underlying causes, e.g. weight placement and technique; strengthen all weak groups and gently stretch out the tight areas. As in other situations treatment will be ineffective if the technical faults remain uncorrected.

5.13 Swayback Knees

This name is given to knees which hyperextend beyond neutral (neutral is when the line between the thigh and the shin is 180°). Hyperextension from that point can be as much as 20° or even more (Fig. 5.23).

CAUSES

This hyperextension or swayback is a naturally occurring situation in anyone who is fairly loose-jointed and is within the range of normal variation from one individual to the next. It can however be aggravated by incorrect working.

The question is often raised as to whether ballet training causes swaybacks. This is almost certainly not the case. As such knees give a very pleasing line aesthetically in the working leg, students with swaybacks (among other attributes) will tend to be preferentially selected, as evidenced by the large number of dancers with swayback knees. However, having said that, there is no doubt that bad teachers may aggravate and increase the amount of swayback by allowing the dancer to push the knee back on the supporting leg instead of teaching him to pull up with the thighs and then keep the knee in neutral.

RESULTS

The most important feature of swayback knees is the creation of the weight back situation, together with all its problems which have been mentioned so repeatedly. Swayback knees are, together with weak forefeet, the most important and potent cause of the weight back situation (**Section 5.20**).

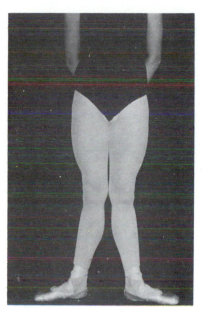

5.23A   Swayback knees, from the front.

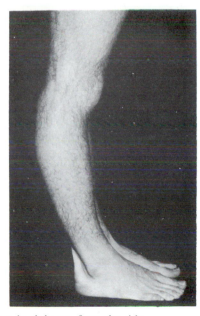

5.23B   Swayback knees, from the side.

Weight back and swayback knees will lead to the adoption of a lordotic posture and working with the arm line too far back. Associated with these is a marked tendency for these dancers to be poor breathers, this weakness being related to the faulty trunk posture. They will be upper chest breathers and this will cause upper trunk tension.

TREATMENT

Exercises are given to strengthen all the weak groups which will be in particular the adductors, vastus medialis, hamstrings and gluteals. In the lower leg the deep calf muscles will not be used and will need strengthening. Swaybacks are always associated with weak feet, so much attention needs to be paid to strengthening the intrinsic muscles.

Alongside this the trunk muscles, particularly the abdominals (cross fibres and longitudinal fibres), the trunk extensors and latissimus dorsi need to be strengthened and the lordotic posture corrected. Breathing exercises using lateral expansion are necessary.

Only too often treatment and technical correction is confined to the knee region with total neglect of the feet and even more often of the trunk. In these cases the weight back will persist with a continuation of the dancer's problems often leading him to the wrong assumption that the treatment received was incorrect, whereas the true situation is that the treatment was not extensive or widespread enough to encompass the whole situation. Unfortunately, any condition that is only partially corrected due to insufficient or too localised treatment tends to lead the dancer to assume that any treatment received was wrong rather than inadequate.

5.14 Tight Achilles Tendons

Although this expression is in common usage what is, in fact, meant is tightness of the calf muscle and Achilles tendon complex and not just the tendon alone. Very frequently the tightness is confined to the gastrocnemius muscle so that when the knee is flexed, allowing the gastrocnemius to relax, the ankle can be dorsi-flexed very freely, showing that the soleus is not tight. (Remember that the gastrocnemius takes its origin from the lower end of the femur and therefore crosses behind the knee, whereas the soleus muscle which lies deep to the gastrocnemius takes its origin below the knee joint.)

CAUSES

As with tight hamstrings the tightness can merely be part of a general tightness, although occasionally it may appear to be confined to the calf and Achilles tendon area. This type of tightness tends to be permanent, although it can be helped to a very limited extent.

Far more often the tightness which seems to be present when working is only apparent and is not real, so that when the foot and ankle are dorsi-flexed passively a full range is obtained.

Therefore this type of 'tightness' is due to faulty technique, usually associated with weakness of various muscle groups. It often accompanies swayback knees and weight back. When the weight is pushed onto the back of the heel instead of being distributed between the heel and the forefoot the calf muscles cannot work properly or be stretched out fully when weight-bearing. Weight back also tends to weaken the calf muscles and this can be accompanied by tension and tightening in them because of their lack of strength in a controlled relaxation situation.

If the weight is back the dancer cannot utilise the full depth of the plié. When trying to do so, visible tension is present in the dorsi-flexors of the ankle and this can be seen to be obviously prominent at the front of the ankle in this case.

Shoes that are too short can lead to this happening because the toes are curled up, pushing the weight back. This happens to boys more than girls and may be the only cause of the weight back, without any other underlying anatomical or technical problem.

Anterior knee pain (**Section 3.30**) can be associated with a tightening of the calf and the Achilles tendon complex. This is primarily brought about by the weight being back, in which case the quadriceps are used as a brake when jumping rather than using the calf muscles and quadriceps equally. It is more common in boys because they are used to much bigger jumps. As the calf is under-used it will tend to tighten and this may then lead to an Achilles tendonitis (**Section 3.9**) as well as all the various problems described in the section on anterior knee pain (**Section 3.30**).

Achilles tendonitis (**Section 3.9**) and Achilles bursitis (**Section 3.11**) are both very frequently associated with tightness and/or weakness of the calf muscles (not only when there is anterior knee pain). Following on from this there can then develop anterior compartment syndrome (**Section 3.28**) and stress fractures of the tibia (**Section 3.27**). All these problems being greatly aggravated by solid floors.

TREATMENT

Strengthening first and then gentle stretching of the calf muscles must be carried out (the actual Achilles tendon cannot be stretched). The condition requires technical faults to be identified and corrected as much as or more than almost any other technical or anatomical problem. Together with its associated Achilles tendonitis and bursitis it is probably the commonest source of apparent treatment failures.

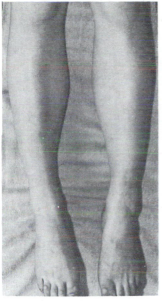
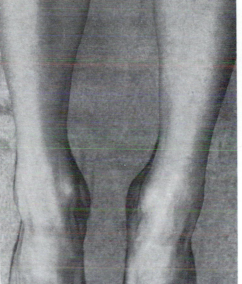
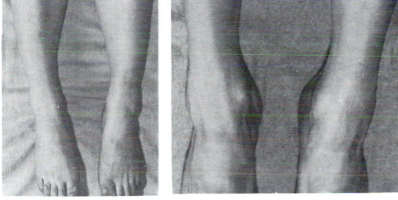
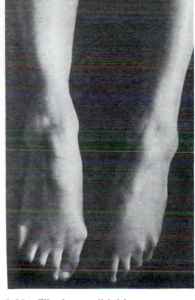

5.24A   The whole tibial bow.   5.24B   The lower tibial bow.

5.25   The lower tibial bow. The foot on the left of the photograph is aligned with the leg as a whole. The foot on the right is aligned with the lower end of the tibia and the ankle. In the presence of lower tibial bows the dancer has of necessity to work with the foot aligned with the leg.

5.15 Tibial Bow

Although the tibia has a natural mild curve, which is convex laterally, this can commonly be exaggerated when it is known as a tibial bow. The bow can affect the whole length of the tibia or, more usually, the lower third (Fig. 5.24).

CAUSES

This is an anatomical variation of normal growth. Other causes ,such as Vitamin D deficiency are extremely rare nowadays in affluent societies.

RESULTS

Most of the problems are brought about because the ankle joint is slightly angled in relation to the centre line of the leg (Fig. 5.25). As a natural result of this the foot is rolled when standing flat. Dancers have to work very much harder to hold the turn-out and not to over turn, otherwise this rolling becomes greatly exaggerated. They need to work conscientiously on the inner side of thigh exercises (**Section 5.17**).

Stress injuries of the lower tibia and fibula (**Sections 3.26** and **3.27**) are more common as a result of the abnormal foot posture produced by the bow. In addition, soft tissue problems around the lower fibula occur.

When the foot is pointed it is sickled in naturally and this needs correction. Similarly, when on demi-pointe the foot will tend to assume the same sickle position until corrected. On pointe the dancer finds it very hard to get up into the right position and may sickle in either direction, much depending upon toe length variations and foot strength or weakness. These latter factors contribute towards the greater tendency for stress fractures of the 2nd metatarsal to occur (**Section 3.16**) with tibial bows.

TREATMENT

A great deal of exercise is required to strengthen the adductors, the gluteals and the hamstrings to give stability in the upper leg. Work is required to strengthen the calf muscle equally. Frequently there is, as a consequence of the faulty foot position, weakness of the lateral part of the calf which tends to be present because of the overwork of the medial portion. Exercise to strengthen the intrinsic muscles of the feet are essential. Accompanying this, technical help is required to gain the hold of the turn-out and adjust the weight-bearing line through the leg. Once that is achieved it will have to be followed with correction of the foot position to the optimum. The foot position correction cannot be carried out before the upper part of the leg is correct. Any attempts to do so merely compounds the problem.

5.16 Posterior Block of the Ankle Joint

By this is meant an interference with full plantar-flexion at the joint due to a bony prominence impinging between the dorsum of the os calcis and the posterior articular margin of the tibia (Fig. 5.26). The causes for this are an os trigonum or a large posterior tubercle of the talus or, more rarely, a bony prominence or exostosis on the dorsum of the posterior part of the os calcis or finally an osteophyte on the posterior angle of the talus. This latter is an acquired prominence which comes as a result of repeated minor injuries and early degenerative change. The first three are situations with which the dancer is born and occur normally in a certain percentage of the population.

Although the os trigonum has been described by anatomists and given its own name as a separate little bone occurring at the back of the ankle in some 14–15% of the population, studies of sections of the os trigonum, in cases where this has necessitated removal in dancers, suggest that at least some are in fact stress fractures which have occurred in the large posterior tubercle of the talus. It may well be that in every case the os trigonum is a stress fracture of the posterior tubercle and was not at birth a separate bone. However, as far as the dancer is concerned, whether or not this is the case is purely academic.

CAUSES

The symptoms are produced by the presence of a piece of bone interfering with the full rotation of the talus in the ankle mortice during plantar-flexion. As the talus rotates towards the plantar-flexed position (or full pointe) the heel bone or os calcis rises towards the posterior articular margin of the tibia. The bony prominence projecting beyond the posterior angle of the talus comes between the dorsum of the os calcis and the posterior articular margin of the tibia. When this happens the capsule

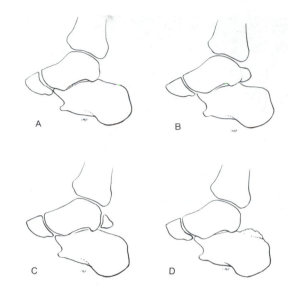

5.26   A. Lateral of a normal ankle.

   B. Lateral of an ankle with a large posterior tubercle of the talus.

   C. Lateral of an ankle with an os trigonum.

   D. Lateral of an ankle with an exostosis on the dorsum of the os calcis.

and the underlying synovium will be squeezed between the two bony surfaces and these soft tissues are the source of the pain. When this local pressure is repeated local swelling develops and this is followed by thickening of the soft tissues. The symptoms will steadily increase and pointing of the foot becomes more difficult and painful.

Symptoms are unusual before the mid-teens. It is not until this time that the student has achieved the maximum natural point and therefore any further plantar-flexion of the ankle is prevented by the bony block. Also about this time in a professional dance school the amount and pressure of work is increasing greatly. As a result the soft tissues do not have time to settle between one class and the next as would happen in students who were only doing one or two classes a week. The condition tends to be far more common in girls who are working for a far better pointed foot and who are dancing a lot of the time on pointe. However, in boys who are putting in efforts at big jumps or having to rise onto three-quarter pointe there may be a precipitation of symptoms. Before this stage in their career the amount and pressure of work has usually been insufficient for a full pointe to have been

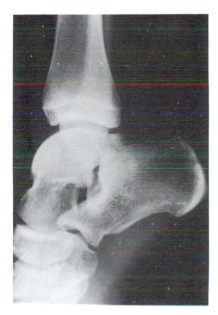
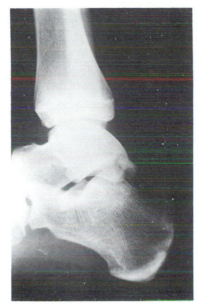
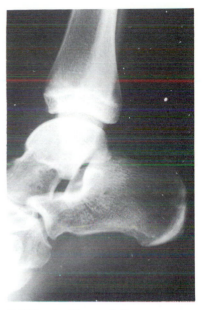

5.27A   An X-ray showing an os trigonum just about to impinge on the posterior articular margin of the lower end of the tibia. Remember that soft tissues (synovium and capsule in this case) are being trapped and squeezed between the two bones. These soft tissues cannot be seen on an X-ray.

5.27B   Os trigonum with the ankle in neutral dorsi-flexion/plantar-flexion showing the large distance between the os trigonum and the posterior articular margins of the lower end of the tibia. Comparison with Fig. 5.27A gives an excellent impression of the actual range of movement which occurs at the ankle joint (a hinge joint).

5.27C   An X-ray of the same patient following removal of the os trigonum.

developed. It is only gradually that stretching of the soft tissues has occurred and has allowed maximum rotation of the talus into plantar-flexion. Even when there is an os trigonum or similar bony prominence, in many instances, despite the mild limitation of full plantar-flexion at the ankle joint, the mid-tarsal region will have been mobile enough to have produced compensation and a satisfactory pointing of the foot. In these instances symptoms do not usually develop.

SYMPTOMATOLOGY

1. Usually the dancer complains of a painful Achilles tendon and general discomfort behind the ankle and around the Achilles tendon area. This tends to increase with work and settles with rest.

2. Pain over the anterior and antero-lateral aspect of the ankle is not at all uncommon and this may be accompanied by swelling. The attempts at improving the pointe throws a strain on the antero-lateral aspect of the ankle and the anterior capsule. Hence the pain.

3. Recurrent calf muscle strains, usually around the region of the musculo-tendinous junction, are not uncommon and they may be accompanied by more or less pain around the Achilles tendon and the posterior part of the ankle (**Section 3.9**).

4. Sometimes the student will present with pain under the plantar aspect of the foot brought about by straining to pointe the foot. Very frequently the dancer will curl the toes in an effort to improve the pointe (**Section 3.18**).

5. Only rarely do the dancers complain of very well localised pain at the back of the ankle joint itself.

    Clinical examination will reveal very well localised tenderness at the back of the ankle joint and frequently the lump of the bony prominence can actually be felt. X-rays will show the presence of either a large posterior tubercle of the talus or an os trigonum or, far less commonly, a prominence on the dorsum of the posterior part of the os calcis. Occasionally a degenerative-type osteophyte will be seen. However, it is important to emphasise that the presence of any of these does not mean they are the cause of the patient's symptoms. Only too frequently the symptoms are precipitated by weakness of the intrinsics, by lack of proper control of the ankle and foot and by general weakness of the muscles around the lower leg and foot.

TREATMENT

Initially, every effort should be made to relieve the symptoms by conservative measures. Strengthening up the muscle groups and the intrinsic muscles together with local treatment such as interferential therapy may be sufficient. Only if this fails should operation be considered in order to remove the prominent piece of bone (Fig. 5.27).

If operation is undertaken it is essential that the aftercare is treated seriously. The leg should be elevated until the swelling has settled. Early exercises are instituted both in order to retain the increased plantar-flexion or pointing that has been gained by the operation and also to prevent the scar tissue contracting at the back of the ankle which has been the site of the operation. Walking can be allowed as soon as the foot can be dorsi-flexed to the neutral position but the walking should be limited and the foot kept well elevated in order to decrease any tendency for swelling. Once the stitches have been removed treatment should be directed at reduction of any swelling, general strengthening of the intrinsic muscles of the foot and of all the muscle groups controlling the foot and ankle. The ankle joint should be actively mobilised during the whole phase of treatment but passive mobilisation should in general be avoided.

If the treatment has been efficiently carried out the dancer should be fit by the end of four weeks to start a gentle barre and work from there for a gradual return to class. During this period he will also need some technical help and correction. Even after the dancer has returned to full work a careful follow-up should be continued for a minimum of six months as during this period there is usually a tendency for some contraction to occur in the tissues at the back of the ankle and this will result in a gradual decrease in the depth of the plié. The follow-up is required in order to treat any suggestion of contracture by vigorous and active exercises and probably also some passive stretching. When stretching the foot in the plié it is extremely important that the posterior stretch is evenly applied and that one or other side is not allowed to become tight.

5.17 Rolling

The nature of rolling is best seen in the accompanying photograph (Fig. 5.28).

CAUSES

1. Weak intrinsic muscles in the feet (**Section 5.18**) and weak lower leg muscles which can occur normally during a period of rapid growth make the occurrence of rolling almost inevitable. In this instance the rolling normally ceases after the growth spurt has ended.
2. Over turning (**Section 5.7**). There is a very fine division between the adequately turned out and over turning. Once the dancer has gone past the former and starts to over turn then rolling at the foot is inevitable, producing many faults.
3. Incorrect teaching of placement and the resulting over turning can lead to rolling. Certainly rolling is a natural consequence of the weight back situation and it becomes a compensatory mechanism in trying to maintain balance (**Section 5.20**).
4. Failure to adjust to a raked stage may also lead to rolling.

RESULTS

1. The turn-out is not under correct control because when the foot is rolled the weight is back and as a result the muscles around the hip cannot be correctly held. There will also be a tendency for the dancer to adopt a lordotic posture (**Section 5.6**).
2. A strain is exerted on the inner (medial) side of the knee (**Sections 3.32** and **3.35**).
3. There is a lack of adequate function of the calf muscles and of the peronei. The tibialis anterior and tibialis posterior become more liable to strain. Tendonitis can be the end result, particularly in the tibialis posterior (**Section 3.13**).
4. Damage to the lateral ligament of the ankle can occur because it becomes crushed on the flat foot and stretched on the rise because on rising the foot would go in the opposite direction to the rolling in order to maintain balance (**Section 3.1**).
5. Strain of the structures along the medial border of the foot, strain of the longitudinal arch and of the plantar fascia in its medial part are all associated with rolling (**Section 3.18**).

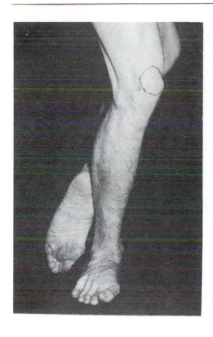

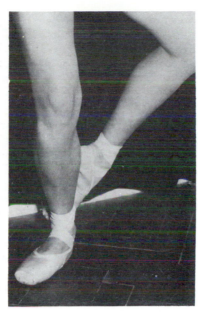

5.28A (far left)   Rolling, shown without a shoe.

5.28B (left)   The effect on the foot is less obvious in a shoe although it still occurs to the same extent.

6. Because the majority of the weight is taken on the medial part of the foot the great toe takes most of the strain. This causes sprains of the capsule of the 1st metatarso-phalangeal joint (**Section 3.19**), sesamoiditis (**Section 3.20**) (these two little bones lie under the 1st metatarsal head) and frequently a twist in the great toe which can finally end with a permanent rotation at the metatarso-phalangeal joint, and severe valgus strains occur, thus aggravating any tendency towards a hallux valgus deformity (**Section 3.21**). In the longer term this valgus pressure (i.e. pressure from the medial side directed laterally) can cause some valgus deformities of all the toes and of the distal part of the forefoot.

7. Continued incorrect weight transference leads to stress fractures of the metatarsals – mainly the 2nd (**Section 3.16**).

8. The rolling will cause not only a valgus posture in the great toe but will also cause a flexion at the interphalangeal joint of the toe with a hyperextension at the metatarso-phalangeal joint and, following that, an increased tension in the extensor hallucis longus tendon and an extensor hallucis longus tendonitis (**Section 3.15**).

TREATMENT

Identification and correction of all the underlying technical faults and strengthening exercises for all the weakened muscle groups is essential. This can commonly require exercise regimes from the trunk downwards. Although the treatment is relatively easy it can be very time-consuming for the dancer but in the long term is a protective measure and will save a great deal of injury time in the future.

5.18 Weak Intrinsic Muscles of the Feet

These are the small muscles which maintain the transverse arch and allow the toes to be extended at the interphalangeal joints while they are being flexed at the metatarso-phalangeal joints. They also spread the toes and pull the toes together (adduction and abduction). When correctly used they prevent clawing of the toes.

RESULTS

1. Weak intrinsic muscles interefere with the correct transmission of weight through the foot, the result of which is that the weight is almost entirely taken on the heel instead of being distributed between the forefoot and the heel (**Section 5.20**).

2. On pointe the toes cannot be held extended (straight) in the absence of strong intrinsic muscles and they will claw up in the shoes. At the extreme the dancer will be on pointe on the knuckles of the toes. This is known in the United States of America as 'knuckling'. Also on pointe the weight will be pushed back (**Section 5.20**) and as a result there is a greatly

increased tension in the structures at the back of the ankle, notably producing an Achilles tendonitis (**Section 3.9**) and bursitis (**Section 3.11**) and/or a tibialis posterior tendonitis (**Section 3.13**), depending on the individual build-up of the dancer. A small os trigonum which would otherwise have been symptomless can start to cause pain and symptoms.

3. On jumps or landing or during relevés there is an incorrect weight transference through the foot because of the weakness of the forefoot. The landing will be heavy and the dancer will crash down with the weight back (**Section 5.20**). If a jump is started with the weight incorrect the landing will also have an incorrect weight placement, frequently leading to shin (**Section 3.27**) and knee injuries (**Sections 3.30, 3.31, 3.32, and 3.35**).

TREATMENT

Faradic foot baths and intrinsic muscle exercises and correction of technique, together with correction of weight placement, are the essentials of treatment. Inspect shoes in order to make sure that they are fitting well and giving adequate support. They must not be too wide or too short. The steel in the sole of some shoes, used by some dancers who have weak intrinsics, prevents correct use of the feet in relevés as the dancer cannot go through the foot correctly in order to achieve the optimum position for pointe work. Therefore this type of shoe only aggravates the situation and makes the muscles and feet even weaker.

5.19 Variations in the Length of the Toes and of the Metatarsals

The ideal forefoot is one where the toes and metatarsals are all about the same length across the foot from the first toe. Inevitably the lateral side of the foot, i.e. the 4th and 5th toes and metatarsals, tend to be a little shorter but when this slope is not very marked the dancer has a foot that is stable on both demi-pointe and on full pointe. Considering the metatarsals first, there can be considerable variations in length. It is quite common to have a 2nd metatarsal which is markedly longer than either the 1st or the 3rd (Fig. 5.29). Another fairly common variation is a very short 1st metatarsal (Fig. 5.30) with the lesser metatarsals much of a length. Another variation is where the lesser metatarsals shorten quite markedly progressively

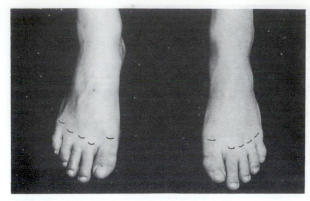

5.29   Long 2nd metatarsal and 2nd toe. Here the situation is aggravated by the presence also of a short 1st metatarsal.

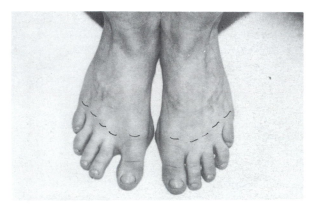

5.31A   Sloping (oblique) line of metatarsal heads. This is a difficult foot on demi-pointe.

towards the 5th metatarsal, giving a sloping line of metatarsal heads (Fig. 5.31). In all these instances the dancer will have greater or lesser difficulty when on demi-pointe, the degree of difficulty depending upon the particular anatomical variation which is present.

As far as the toes themselves are concerned, the length of the toes may mirror what is happening at the metatarsals. However, one also sees variations in actual length of the toes even if the metatarsals themselves are of a fairly even length (Fig. 5.32).

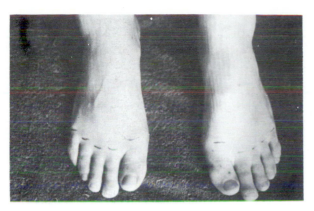

5.30A (above)   Short 1st metatarsal.

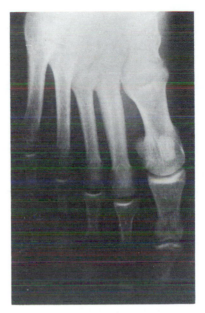

5.30B (right)   An X-ray showing the short 1st metatarsal.

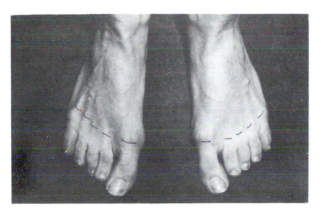

5.31B   Here the situation is made much worse by also having very short lesser toes. This foot is extremely difficult for both demi-pointe and pointe work.

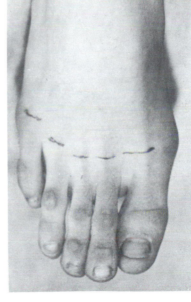

5.32   Long 2nd and 3rd toes. In this particular foot the first three metatarsals are much the same length, giving a very stable foot for demi-pointe despite the short 5th toe and metatarsals. On pointe work the larger 2nd and 3rd toes make it more difficult even though here the discrepancy in length between 1st and 2nd is not as great as frequently occurs.

The commonest situation is where there is a long 2nd toe either with or without an accompanying long 2nd metatarsal. This gives the so-called 'classical foot' as is seen in most of the Greek statues and also, very frequently, in fifteenth-, sixteenth- and seventeenth-century paintings. This is, however, no comfort to the dancer as discrepancies in toe lengths cause considerable problems when doing pointe work. A long 2nd toe is inevitably going to become flexed up during pointe work.

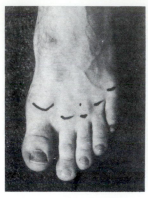

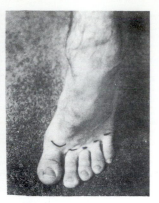

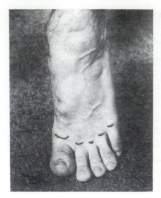

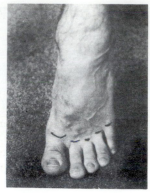

5.33A   Unequal metatarsal lengths—short 1st metatarsal; 2nd and 3rd metatarsals equal length; and 4th and 5th metatarsals very much shorter.

5.33B   Sickling, with weight being transmitted laterally.

5.33C   Sickling, with weight being transmitted medially.

5.33D   In best position achievable.

When on demi-pointe, the weight is taken only on the 2nd and 3rd metatarsal heads with some support from the 1st and 4th toes and the 5th toe only just touching the floor.   .

RESULTS

Discrepancies in metatarsal lengths cause marked unsteadiness and instability on demi-pointe. This can cause strains of either the medial or lateral sides of the foot and ankle (**Sections 3.1, 3.3 and 3.4**) depending upon the nature of the metatarsal length discrepancy and the way in which the foot will tend to fall. On half-pointe the foot may be either sickled inwards or outwards in an attempt to gain stability (Fig. 5.33).

In toe length discrepancy on full pointe the problems tend to be associated more locally with the toes themselves and the difficulty in satisfactorily fitting the shoe into the blocks. Local damage to the toes can occur in the form of blistering and marked callosity formation (**Section 3.24**). Additionally, the foot itself can be somewhat unstable on pointe.

In both situations, but particularly in metatarsal length discrepancies, stress fractures of the longer metatarsal or metatarsals are very common (Fig. 5.34) (**Section 3.16**).

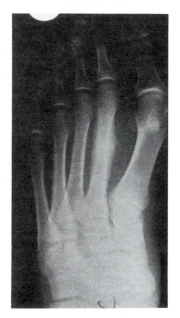

5.34   Stress fracture of the 2nd metatarsal. Healed with plentiful callus (new bone) formation.

TREATMENT

A great deal of attention must be paid to strengthening the intrinsic muscles of the foot and to strengthening all the muscle groups controlling the foot and the ankle. A lot of technical help may be required in order to get the dancer adjusted to the optimum position on both demi-pointe and pointe. It is important to try and correct any tendency to sickling one way or the other.

5.20 Incorrect Weight Placement

This usually means that the weight is too far back. When weight transmission is correct the line runs down vertically from the mastoid processes just behind the ears through the centres of the shoulder, hip, knee and ankle joints to join the sole at the anterior edge of the heel pad. Occasionally a dancer will overcorrect and take the weight too far forward so that it passes through the balls of the feet and, in these instances, the heels are frequently slightly lifted from the ground.

Causes of the Weight Back Situation

1. Lordosis (**Section 5.6**).
2. Kyphosis and a stiff thoracic spine produce a compensatory lordosis (**Section 5.6**) which tilts the pelvis and moves the weight back.
3. Scoliosis will frequently produce a pelvic tilt often accompanied by pelvic rotation (**Section 5.4**).
4. Tightness at the fronts of the hips (**Section 5.9**) produces a forward rotation of the pelvis and pushes the weight back on the legs.
5. Weak trunk muscles cause tension in the upper back muscles which on movement makes the upper trunk fall back as a result of the lack of control of the middle of the trunk. This is accompanied by prominence of the front of the rib cage and relaxation of the abdominal muscles. Frequently this is accompanied by upper chest breathing which aggravates the problem by producing even more tension in the upper back muscles, including the trapezius.
6. Weak abdominal muscles, gluteals, hamstrings and adductors (namely any muscle group which takes part in the stabilisation of the pelvis) can together or individually allow a pelvic tilt.
7. Over turning of the feet associated with either a genuine limitation of the external rotation available in the hip or lack of muscle control of an adequate turn-out produces a forward tilt (**Section 5.7**).
8. Inappropriate muscle development. This may be produced either by faulty teaching or by heavy weight resisted exercises or by *over*-indulgence in unsuitable recreational pursuits such as gymnastics, riding or skating. While these latter can be perfectly satisfactory for pleasure, if carried to excess they may lead to over-development of muscle groups unhelpful to dance.

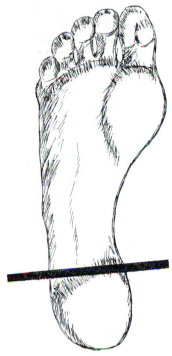

5.35 Although weight bearing is distributed throughout the sole of the foot, the line of weight transmission from the centre of gravity of the dancer should pass through the heavy black line shown above.

9. Lack of control of hyper-extended knees (**Section 5.13**) because pushing back the knees causes relaxation of the muscle groups controlling the pelvis.
10. Tibial bowing (**Section 5.15**) because of its tendency to produce rolling when flat, and sickling when rising. The bowing alters the line of weight transmission from the centre of gravity.
11. Tight pointe renders the dancer incapable of rising correctly through the foot to achieve correct half and three-quarter pointe. The weight is therefore taken back. When jumping the tight pointe prevents the dancer going up through the foot or coming down through the foot correctly. They start the jump with the weight back and land with the weight back. This is a potent cause of anterior leg problems and stress injuries of metatarsals (see also **Section 5.16**).
12. Stiff big toe joints (**Section 3.22**) push the weight on to the outer sides of the feet when rising instead of taking it through the centre of the foot. As a result the weight is pushed back.

13. Sloping line of metatarsal heads also pushes the weight on to the outer side of the foot in a similar fashion to stiff big toe joints.
14. Weak intrinsic muscles of the feet accompanied by clawing of the toes pushes the weight back too far on the heels.
15. Tight shoes will produce clawing of the toes with similar results to 14.
16. Growth spurts cause a generalised decrease in muscular control. As a result any of these affected areas can cause the weight to be taken too far back whether the weakness be at the feet, in the trunk or anywhere in between.

Consequences of the Weight Back Situation

1. Low back strains.
2. Stress fractures of the partes intra-articulares (**Section 3.51**).
3. Groin injuries (**Section 3.40**).
4. Buttock pain (**Section 3.44**).
5. Hamstring injuries at various levels (**Section 3.41**).
6. Adductor muscle injuries (**Section 3.39**).
7. Anterior knee pain (**Section 3.30**).
8. Strains of the back of the knee joint (**Section 3.31**)

9. Stress fractures of tibia and fibula (**Sections 3.27, 3.26**).
10. Anterior compartment syndrome (**Section 3.28**).
11. Calf injuries (**Section 3.29**).
12. Achilles tendonitis (**Section 3.9**).
13. Extensor hallucis longus tendonitis (**Section 3.15**).
14. Stress fractures of metatarsals (**Section 3.15**).
15. Weakening of the intrinsic muscles due to lack of proper use (**Section 5.18**).
16. Damage to big toe joints (**Section 3.19**).

TREATMENT

This is really a misnomer because the weight back situation is not an injury. It is, however, one of the most common and important faults in the dancer and its correction is essential. This can only be achieved by first determining which cause or causes (often multiple) are producing the weight back state. Considerable effort and attention must then be paid to correcting and eliminating all these causes. Treatment may in fact be necessary but this will be aimed at any injuries which have arisen secondarily to the weight back situation. *As in all other cases of injury simple treatment of the injury alone, without any correction of the underlying technical fault, will be useless.*

Index

Page references in **bold** denote illustrations